S0-AEG-547

GRAMMAR AND
SECOND LANGUAGE
TEACHING

GRAMMAR AND SECOND LANGUAGE TEACHING

A BOOK OF READINGS

Edited by

WILLIAM RUTHERFORD

University of Southern California

MICHAEL SHARWOOD SMITH

Rijksuniversiteit, Utrecht

NEWBURY HOUSE PUBLISHERS
A division of Harper & Row, Publishers, Inc.

New York, Philadelphia, San Francisco, Washington, D.C.
London, Mexico City, São Paulo, Singapore, Sydney

Sponsoring Editor: Leslie Berriman
Project Coordination: Total Concept Associates
Cover Design: 20/20 SERVICES INC.
Compositor: Alpha Graphics
Printer and Binder: McNaughton & Gunn

Grammar and Second Language Teaching: A Book of Readings

NEWBURY HOUSE PUBLISHERS
A division of Harper & Row, Publishers, Inc.

Language Science
Language Teaching
Language Training

Copyright © 1988 by Newbury House Publishers, a division of Harper & Row, Publishers, Inc. All rights reserved. No part of this book may be used or reproduced or transmitted in any form or by any means, electronic or mechanical, including photocopying, recording, or by any information storage and retrieval system without permission in writing from the publisher except in the case of brief quotations embodied in critical articles and reviews.

For information address Harper & Row, Publishers, Inc., 10 East 53rd Street, New York, NY 10022.

Library of Congress Cataloging in Publication Data

Grammar and second language teaching: a book of readings / William Rutherford and
 Michael Sharwood Smith, editors.
　　p. cm.
　Bibliography: p.
　Includes index.
　ISBN 0-06-632494-7
　1. Language and languages—Study and teaching.　I.Rutherford,
William E.　II. Sharwood Smith, Michael, 1942–
P53.P36　1988
418'.007—dc19　　　　　　　　　　　　　　　　　　　　　　87-22335
　　　　　　　　　　　　　　　　　　　　　　　　　　　　CIP

Printed in the U.S.A.　　　　　　　　　　　　　First Printing: August 1987
63-24941　　　　　　　　　　　　　　　　　　2 4 6 8 10 9 7 5 3

Contents

INTRODUCTION

This is a book of readings that explores the dimensions of what has often been called *pedagogical grammar* (PG), or the means by which acquisition of second or foreign language grammar may be expressly facilitated. As an area of academic interest, PG is not new; it has in a loose sense been with us for the entire two and a half millennia of attested foreign language teaching, although actual PGs written expressly for language learners probably date from no earlier than the eighteenth century.[1] If so much has already been done in and with PG, why do we need a book like this? One can begin to answer this question by noting that the long history of PG notwithstanding, only very recently have we begun to look at the discipline with any real seriousness—that is, to pose research questions having to do with the possible relationships among what formal properties may be "raised to consciousness," how this step may effectively be accomplished, and how the learning of such properties proceeds—thus, to work toward articulation of a coherent theory of PG. We intend that this collection of readings should contribute to the development of such a theory.

One point that has often been made by language professionals of whatever theoretical stance, ideological camp, or disciplinary calling is that language, whatever else it may be, is rule-governed behavior. It would no doubt be difficult to find anyone who could quarrel with this concept. The notion that verbal and written communication among humans is made possible through a network of systems that can be expressed in terms of rules is a presupposition that underlies every language research endeavor from phonological analysis to the study of discourse, from dialectology to the examination of historical change. And the concept of language as rule-governed behavior is no less presupposed by those engaged in research into how languages are acquired or learned and how they might best be taught.

Rules, then, figure prominently in any discussion of language. For many people the rules are the language—rules for how words are formed, rules for assembling words as syntactic constructs, and rules for how constructs serve the various purposes of language use. This way of thinking is perhaps most true of those professionally involved in some aspect of language pedagogy, theory as well as practice. And with the invocation of a rule, it is usually assumed that one knows what one is talking about. The assumption is that since a language has rules, they can be explicitly formulated. The rules therefore constitute a repertoire of target language facts to be communicated to the learner.

Is such an assumption justified? And is justification possible without (1) metalinguistic knowledge in a purely formal sense (i.e., a rule's formal properties); (2) metalinguistic knowledge in a psycholinguistic sense (i.e., a rule's potential for both teachability and learnability); and (3) knowledge of what kind of learner behavior one might expect as the result of having imparted such knowledge (e.g., Is the rule brought to bear in learner production?). And if there are different kinds of grammatical knowledge, are there also different senses of the concept "rule" that need to be agreed on? Asking such questions implies that much is often presumed in discussions of these matters that *is* open to challenge.

One convenient way of talking about rules in different senses would be to speak of three basic types—namely, *L-Rules*, *Psycho-Rules*, and *psycho-rules*. We define these terms as follows, using upper- and lowercase typography for partial differentiation:

1. *L-Rule*: A rule construct devised by the formulator-as-linguist (professional or amateur, general or applied) and set down on paper.
2. *Psycho-Rule*: The psychological correlate of a rule devised by the linguist as in (1) and deliberately learned. One example of a Psycho-Rule system would be represented by Krashen's "Monitor" (Dulay, Burt, & Krashen, 1982).
3. *psycho-rule*: The outcome of intuitive psycholinguistic processes (the nature of which is spelled by any particular psycholinguistic theory) whose existence we infer from the principled spontaneous linguistic behavior of those who seem to perform successfully (i.e., accurately and systematically). They do so without having consciously analyzed what they are doing and without having been given formulas—that is, Psycho-Rules. A good example of the development of psycho-rules is mother-tongue learning.

L-Rules can be found in books; Psycho-Rules and psycho-rules are mental representations. For example, an L-rule must at one time have been devised via some sort of conscious psychological process. We could therefore say that an L-Rule in a grammar is simply the outcome of a Psycho-Rule created in the mind of a particular linguist at a particular time. To the extent that a collection of rules hangs together as a system, we may in the same way talk of *L-Grammars*, *Psycho-Grammars*, and *psycho-grammars*. We draw attention to this three-way division merely as a practical means of underscoring major issues that pedagogical grammarians will have to come to grips with when they search for ways in which to enhance grammatical representation in the minds of learners. Thus, given this complexity of the notion of rule, for general purposes we employ the cover term *rule* to designate a wide assortment of formal rules, schemata, formulas, principles, conditions, constraints, postulates, hierarchies, maxims, and algorithms—in short, whatever means, formal or informal, by which an account of language system might be rendered.

The issues we have been discussing can be raised as well with respect to those approaches that deny the value of attempting to impart explicit knowledge of language form in the classroom as an aid to learning. Often implied in such discussion are a view of language and its complex organizing principles that is considerably impoverished, a view of language learnability that is seriously wanting, and thus a view of the possible contributions of pedagogical consciousness raising (CR) that is quite misconceived. Language, so the reasoning would have it, is a hierarchic assemblage of language constructs—phonological units at the bottom, discourse units at the top; language learning would be tantamount to the cumulative "mastery" of these entities; and pedagogy would serve to "teach" the constructs in question. Perhaps the most serious aspect of these kinds of misconceptions is the implied assumption that the L2 (second language) learner [and by logical extension, of course, the L1 (first language) learner] comes to the learning experience with an acquisitional mechanism whose linguistic component is a tabula rasa. It then logically follows that the only conceivable task of PG would be to pump as many of the target language rules into the learner as possible to fill this L2 grammar "void." Since the difference between what there is to know about the grammar and what the average language learner can possibly absorb is vast, however, the explicit rule-learning endeavor is futile, or so the reasoning would go. The seeming facetiousness of these remarks should not obscure the fact that the misapprehensions about PG already mentioned are quite widely held.

Since we have introduced the term consciousness raising (CR), we need to define it. CR is intended to embrace a continuum ranging from intensive promotion of conscious awareness through pedagogical role articulation on the one end, to the mere exposure of the learner to specific grammatical phenomena on the other. The matter of raising the grammatical consciousness of the learner in this broad sense is thus a highly complex one in which a number of nonlinguistic considerations are also involved. What is important, then, are possible answers to questions having to do with *what* we choose to bring to consciousness, what *motivates* the choice, *when* and *how* (i.e., by what means) we raise something to consciousness, *how often* we call attention to it, *how detailed* is the information revealed in the exemplars, and *what effect* on learner behavior the information is intended to have. More important, however, meaningful PG exploration of questions such as these carries the assumption that grammatical CR is not an end in itself. Herein lies the crux of the fallacy represented by belief in the futility of trying to impart complex grammatical information to the learner. To quote from the Corder paper in this book, "pedagogical descriptions of the target language must be devised to help the learner learn whatever it is he learns, but are not necessarily *what* he learns. Pedagogical descriptions are *aids* to learning, not the *object* of learning; so long as we keep that firmly in our minds we shall not get confused by the ambiguity of the expression 'teaching grammar'" (p. 130).

The appeal for PG as the means to an end rather than the end itself is consistent with what little we know so far about how grammatical competence is actually acquired, at least where formal instruction is absent. One thing we do know, however, is that grammatical information tends to be assimilated in decomposed form rather than in the form of tidy and comprehensive rules. McCawley (1983), in fact, has noted with regard to native language development that "acquisition of the factors that figure in rules of grammar [e.g., lexical categories and meanings of the various lexical items and the correspondence between particular surface configurations and semantic structure] can be far in advance of acquisition of the rules themselves" (p. 372).

At issue is the question of how L2 grammatical competence is achieved and, more specifically, whether L2 grammatical CR serves to facilitate its acquisition.[2] The question has been articulated more formally as the *pedagogical grammar hypothesis*, or PGH, formulated in its earliest version in Sharwood Smith (1980), stated fully in the Rutherford and Sharwood Smith paper in part one, and repeated here:

> Instructional strategies which draw the attention of the learner to specifically structural regularities of the language, as distinct from the message content, will under certain specified conditions significantly increase the rate of acquisition over and above the rate expected from learners acquiring that language under natural circumstances where attention to form may be minimal and sporadic. [p. 109]

The organization of this book—indeed, its very existence—is testimony to the nontriviality of the PGH. Most of the papers that appear here have adopted the hypothesis in principle, whether explicitly or implicitly. Another theme, however, is common to these papers, though not often stated as such. This is the assumption that hypothesis testing on the part of the learner is an integral part of the achievement of his or her L2 grammatical competence.[2] But the testing of hypotheses about the organization of the target language cannot, of course, take place without the learner's being exposed to the kinds of L2 data required for hypothesizing. The task for PG then becomes clear, as Corder points out in his paper (part two): "Teaching is a matter of providing the learner with the right data at the right time, and teaching him how to learn, that is, developing in him appropriate learning strategies and means of testing his hypotheses" (p. 133). And the role of the teacher in the activity of hypothesis testing becomes clear as well. Again Corder: "The minimal irreducible and indispensable function of the teacher is to tell the learner what is or is not an acceptable utterance" (p. 143). Mackenzie, in his paper in part three, refers to hypothesis testing as a form of "original research" on the part of the learner, one way in which the learner can manage part of his or her learning.[3] Rutherford's paper (part three) turns the learner's predilection for hypothesis testing into a proposal for a number of classroom activities designed to activate it. Finally, as revealed in a paper by Cook, there is a possible paradox in the previous claims for hypothesis testing and attempts to redefine the concept within the framework of Chomskyan Universal Grammar. As Cook points out:

> Hypothesis-testing by feedback has usually been claimed to be the "natural" informal way of learning a second language, the provision of correction and explanation an "unnatural" formal way. If this argument is right, hypothesis-testing only works in the "unnatural" situation and cannot be used in the informal real world situation. Hence L2 learning research has to be cautious in its support of hypothesis-testing; in the sense of testing by feedback this is only possible in artificial situations where non-primary forms of evidence are available. Only in the sense that the learner checks positive evidence against his internal language principles can hypothesis-testing be acceptable. [Cook 1985, p. 13]

In fact, in the Rutherford and Sharwood Smith paper (part one) we find a recognition of hypothesis testing in precisely this sense of the term.

What emerges from this set of papers is evidence of a number of aspects of second language learning, formal linguistics, and PG that are consistent with one another and whose interrelationships are worth continued exploration as the PGH is subjected to more critical scrutiny. We list these aspects now in the form of questions addressed by various contributors to this book:

1. What is required of PG so that it is consistent with the notion that language acquisition is the development of cognition as well as the development of communicative resources?
2. What special implication for PG derives from the notion that learning is more effective to the extent that it can establish a link with, and build on, prior knowledge?
3. In what sense is PG best seen as a means (aid) to learning rather than the end (i.e., what is actually learned)?
4. What are the implications for the organization of PG of current views on language learnability?
5. To what extent is the distinction between language-universal and language-specific aspects of the target language related to implicit/ intuitive knowledge and explicit/conscious knowledge, respectively?
6. How may PG be seen as consistent with the notion that a learner's increasing grammatical competence represents less an accumulation of knowledge than continued restructuring of prior knowledge?
7. Is it reasonable to suppose that one of the functions of PG is to provide the learner with appropriate and timely data for the testing of L2 hypotheses?

Discussion of PG is certainly not a new or even a recent phenomenon, as we mentioned at the outset. Attention to grammatical form has been perceived by at least some professionals as integral to pedagogy for as long as language instruction has been discussed. Through the years the large number of articles on this topic in the many journals devoted to matters of language teaching and learning has never really waned, the ebb and flow over time of novel methodologies notwithstanding. Does anything then distinguish this collection of papers from others that have preceded it, apart from the intrinsic interest and value of the papers themselves? We believe, as we earlier intimated, that there is such a distinction and that it is rooted in what constitutes the essence of modern scientific inquiry: the development of theoretical foundations upon which may be constructed testable hypotheses. For the first time, then, at least to our knowledge, we have the stringent proposal that research in PG subsumes a scientific framework within which the PGH can begin to undergo the crucial empirical testing that thus far has for all intents and purposes been missing. Only by proceeding in this fashion can pedagogical decisions concerning CR with respect to grammatical form be made on a principled basis, and we assume that all serious research on the subject will henceforth, explicitly or implicitly, constitute evidence bearing one way or the other on the PGH.

We find it no coincidence that the onset of serious work in PG should coincide with the emergence of second language acquisition research as a professional field. We will in fact go further and state that theoretical issues related to the PGH could not even be satisfactorily articulated, perhaps even conceived of, were it not for interesting research in second language acquisition bearing on these matters—for example, work reported on in collections such as Richards (1974), Hatch (1978), Gass and Selinker (1983), and Davies, Criper, and Howatt (1984), among others. From such research has come the formulation, among other things, of an important hypothesis that is subsumed in the PGH—namely, the *interface hypothesis* (IH). The IH is an essentially psycholinguistic claim about the accessibility of subconscious grammatical knowledge in the mind of the learner, and it suggests that the learner's metalinguistic perception of structural regularities in the language can affect the growth of such subconscious knowledge. This accessibility seems to have been assumed in some vague sense by generations of language teachers utilizing formal instruction within traditional methodologies. It has been seriously questioned by L2 acquisition researchers[4] who claim that there is an unbridgeable gap between (1) the learner's inaccessible subconscious mental grammar and (2) his or her conscious mental disposition to focus on form, such that (2) cannot affect (1). The IH denies this unbridgeable gap by allowing the conscious aspect of linguistic knowledge to contribute to the unconscious, and the papers in part one offer general support for this claim.

Following from the interface position is an additional hypothesis (in a sense, an application of the IH): since the learner's metalinguistic awareness of the outer form of the target language may partly shape the developing mental representation of the target language, pedagogical intervention that boosts this metalinguistic awareness may *ipso facto* affect the learner's subconscious grammar.

Again, one cannot overstress the fact that these are empirical questions. We pose them for the stimulation of rational inquiry and not for the purpose of pushing premature decisions about how to teach languages. It is in this spirit that we offer the readings that follow.

NOTES

1. See, for example, Kelly (1969).
2. Note that we are not referring here to L2 *communicative competence*. Our use of *grammatical competence* is more akin to the formal linguistic notion of *competence* (i.e., as distinct from *performance*) in the sense of what the speaker knows intuitively about his or her language. Grammatical competence serves functions other than (perhaps even more important than) communication (e.g., cognition), and communication can be accomplished by other than linguistic means.
3. In yet another approach, Landa (1980) views hypothesis testing as an algorithmic exercise wherein learners are led to think for themselves: "One of the shortcomings of conventional instruction consists in the fact that students are taught primarily *knowledge* about objects but are not taught (or taught inexplicitly, incompletely, unsystematically) cognitive *operations* that should be performed on knowledge in order to successfully solve certain classes of problems. In other words, they are taught knowledge but not how to think" (pp. 2–3).
4. For example, Krashen (1982).

REFERENCES

Cook, V. 1985. Chomsky's Universal Grammar and second language learning. *Applied Linguistics* 6:2–18.

Davies, A., C. Criper, and A. Howatt. 1984. *Interlanguage.* Edinburgh: Edinburgh University Press.

Dulay, H., M. Burt, and S. Krashen. 1982. *Language Two.* New York: Oxford University Press.

Gass, S., and L. Selinker. 1983. *Language Transfer in Language Learning.* Rowley, Mass.: Newbury House.

Hatch, E. 1978. *Second Language Acquisition: A Book of Readings.* Rowley, Mass.: Newbury House.

Kelly, R. 1969. *Twenty-five Centuries of Language Teaching.* Rowley, Mass.: Newbury House.

Krashen, S. 1982. *Principles and Practice in Second Language Acquisition.* Oxford: Pergamon Press.

Landa, L. 1980. The contrastive algo-heuristic theory and method of teaching foreign languages. In E. Hopkins and R. Grotjahn (eds.). *Studies in Language Teaching and Language Acquisition* (*Quantitative Analysis,* vol. 9). Bochum: Studienverlag Brockmeyer.

McArthur, T. 1983. *A Foundation Course for Language Teachers.* Cambridge: Cambridge University Press.

McCawley, J. 1983. Towards plausibility in theories of language acquisition. *Communication and Cognition* **16**:169 183.

Richards, J. 1974. *Error Analysis: Perspectives on Second Language Acquisition.* London: Longman.

Sharwood Smith, W. 1980. Strategies, language transfer, and the simulation of the second language learner's operations. *Language Learning* **29**:345–361.

Wilkins, D. 1984. Teaching without a language syllabus but with a linguistic focus. *TRANEL* (Numéro espécial) **6**:73–91.

one

THEORETICAL CONSIDERATIONS

It is interesting to note that, for all but the past century and a half of the 2,500 years of documented language teaching, it has been assumed that the teaching of grammar is a necessary component of any language-teaching program. Indeed, in language pedagogy before the nineteenth century, grammar teaching was considered not only necessary but also sufficient. Until that time, in other words, language teaching and the study of grammar were virtually synonymous. It thus would have been impossible in earlier times to question the value of grammar focus in language pedagogy without questioning the value of language pedagogy itself.

Issues concerning the historical development of pedagogical grammar are the substance of the paper by Rutherford that begins this section. As he points out, challenges to the importance of grammatical focus did not come about until the emergence in the early nineteenth century of methodologies deriving from the first consideration of language as another form of human behavior rather than from the need for manifestation of literary skills. This, then, was the pedagogical climate in which appeared a century and a half ago the Direct Method and the Natural Method, both arising somewhat in consequence of the formal excesses of nineteenth-century grammar-translation methodology, which toward the end of that century had finally lost all relationship to the realities of language use.

Controversy surrounding the status of grammatical consciousness raising (CR) in language pedagogy is now more than 150 years old. To our knowledge, however, it is only since the late 1970s or so that claims advanced for or against a role for grammar have been based on the findings of empirical research. To some extent, this rather late turning of attention to the scientific justification of grammatical CR could not really have come about until serious attention had also been turned to the question not just of how second languages should be taught but also of how they are learned. Thus, the comparatively new field of second language acquisition, infused with insights from an invigorated educational psychology and from a revolutionary linguistic theory, has made it possible to design the kind of research wherein the proper sorts of pedagogical questions can be asked and meaningful answers occasionally provided.

The question perhaps most fundamental for addressing these issues is whether or not language learning by a child is essentially different from language learning by an adult and, if it is, in what ways and to what extent. Some possible answers to these questions form the substance of the paper by Bley-Vroman early in this section. Bley-Vroman cites ten characteristics that serve to differentiate these two areas of language learning and concludes that adult language learning has more in common with other kinds of adult learning (i.e., where the task at hand can be represented as the solution to a problem) than it does with language learning by children. A conclusion of this kind has significant implications for what one does in the classroom.

Two of the characteristics tallied by Bley-Vroman are similar to two observations that have been made by a number of researchers: (1) that the provision of comprehensible input alone is not sufficient to ensure L2 grammatical accuracy and (2) that at appropriate times some form of grammatical CR is effective in improving such accuracy. The papers in Part II provide support, for the most part and to varying extents, for one or the other (or both) of these observations.

Before briefly discussing the theoretical support for CR in the other papers of Part II, we call attention to some research bearing on this issue that comes from another discipline—psychology. The paper by Reber et al., which does not appear in this book, is concerned with the learning of complex rule structures. Reber et al. (1980) report the results of several experiments designed to study the interaction between two learning modes termed *implicit* (in which organizational patterns and their underlying rules are to be discovered by the learner) and *explicit* (where the patterns to be observed are made salient). They found that the learning of patterned strings of symbols was enhanced to the extent that the symbols were arrayed to render salient the patterns in question, that the learner is made aware of the existence of such patterns, and that the learner is told to seek them out. These authors conclude that optimum learning occurs where the two modes are synthesized such that the imparting of (explicit) information precedes the display of (implicit) patterns represented in the exemplars. What makes this paper of some interest for discussion of the issues surrounding CR is that the structural information given to the learner is by definition correct (since the structures were created by the experimenters) and that the very nature of the experiment precludes any fuzziness in distinctions between *formal* and *informal* instruction of the kind that must inevitably characterize all classroom language learning. The authors' emphasis on the importance of an exploitation of the relationship between the learner's code-breaking strategies and the underlying formal grammatical structure has echoes in two papers in this section, those of Bialystok and of Pienemann.

Bialystok effectively reveals the inadequacy of one-dimensional models of developing L2 proficiency and their failure to account for learner variability. Proficiency, in her view, can best be described ultimately by attempting to identify the underlying factors whose intersection results in performance variability. Bialystok's empirical findings lead her to conclude that, for a plausible accounting of second language learning, one needs to delineate two kinds of coordinates or dimensions along which language development may be plotted. One of these dimensions, termed *analyzed*, reflects the capacity of the learner at a given time to impose an unconscious structural analysis on received language data and thereby to render those data potentially usable in a commensurately wider grammatical context. The other dimension, termed *automatic*, reflects the extent to which the learner at that given time may have access to such analyzed data and thereby register gains in the attainment of fluency. Bialystok's view of learner development in terms of these two dimensions and in combination with other kinds of knowledge—linguistic, conceptual, and contextual—is thus a "componential" one, wherein the subtle interplay of the various components is what determines learner variability. One of the particular strategies of learning and communication that Bialystok's learner would ostensibly benefit from—the one that principally concerns us here—is Reber et al.'s (1980) code-breaking strategy, where CR might seem at first glance to have its broadest employment.

The thesis of the Pienemann paper, however, is that the effective utilization of CR is highly constrained, at least to the extent that it may be brought into play within a learning context characterized by the sequential deployment of interrelated syntactic movement operations. In examining the possible effect of formal instruction on the L2 learning of German subject-AUX inversion following fronted adverbials, Pienemann concludes first that the processing demands inherent in the learning of such inversion must have been prepared for through the prior learning of the less demanding "particle shift" and, second, that the effect that teaching may have on this natural learning progression is to be found rather in the speed of acquisition, in the frequency with which the rule in question is invoked, and in the variety of contexts in which it must be applied. The importance of Pienemann's contribution is thus to have shown that there may be a tight relationship between learning and teaching (his so-called teachability hypothesis) that is rooted in principles of cognition and that consequently we may have to re-examine all varieties of current language-teaching methodology in terms of their psychological validity.[1] One may make an additional point about the more specific claims in Pienemann's paper—namely, that not only are his claims theory-dependent (What theory or which principles of cognition are at issue?) but also that they are true of perhaps only a small subset of the grammar in question.

Pienemann's Teachability Hypothesis (TH) would seem to bear a systematic relationship to Sharwood Smith's Pedagogical Grammar Hypothesis

(PGH), as it is reformulated in the Rutherford and Sharwood Smith paper; that is, the more precisely conceived TH would serve as a constraint on the more broadly defined PGH, or the general claim of validity for the crucially important enterprise of CR in adult language learning. Rutherford and Sharwood Smith go on to suggest that for the necessarily principled decision making entailed in CR one might reasonably be informed by, among other things, relevant principles of Chomskyan Universal Grammar, though here again subject, as always, to pedagogical validation. Their approach focuses on the problem of deciding what evidence for the L2 grammar is available in the input in principle and what ways teachers and syllabus designers might have of making the relevant existing evidence salient and also of supplying that evidence that is in fact *not* normally present. The approach adopted here, in contradistinction to that advanced by others in this book such as Bley-Vroman and Pienemann, assumes that general principles of cognition are quite enough for the second language adult learner to make sense of the data and that he or she, like the child, may well have access in some useful sense to a specifically code-cracking device. The paper then considers what kind of instructional strategy might be adopted for investigation if this claim turns out to be valid.

The Sharwood Smith paper effectively describes the kind of variety that CR may manifest in terms of explicitness and elaboration. In a sense, this paper serves to relate more closely to CR the issues involving cognitive knowledge that are raised by Bialystok.

To the extent that the papers in Part II approach the question of CR, they do so in principled fashion. This is also true even of the one paper that comes out in favor of a functional approach to language teaching—namely, that by Canale and Swain. These authors probe the relationships between what have been termed *communicative approaches* to second language pedagogy and their theoretical underpinning or lack thereof. They argue that misconceptions about the nature of language have often resulted in an overemphasis on communicative function at the expense of grammatical accuracy, especially in the early part of the learning experience. Canale and Swain formulate a tripartite theory of communicative competence that incorporates three distinct competences: grammatical, sociolinguistic, and strategic, where the second is related to language appropriateness and the third to language utility. The kind of pedagogy that their theoretical framework leads them to favor (though cautiously) is one in which different kinds of knowledge figure prominently— knowledge of language in general, knowledge of the target language, knowledge of the target culture—but in which overall organization is articulated in terms of language function. Apart from the value of their insights, the Canale and Swain paper stands as a model of the kinds of questions one needs to ask for any serious consideration of the relationship of theory to practice.

NOTES

1. Other authors have said similar things. See, for example, McLaughlin et al. (1983).

REFERENCES

McLaughlin, B., T. Rossman, and B. McLeod. 1983. Second-language learning: an informal processing perspective. *Language Learning* **33**:135–158.

Reber, A., S. Kassin, S. Lewis, and G. Cantor. 1980. On the relationship between implicit and explicit modes in the learning of a complex rule structure. *Journal of Experimental Psychology: Human Learning and Memory* **6**:492–502.

1
Grammatical Consciousness Raising in Brief Historical Perspective

William Rutherford
University of Southern California

The notion that language teaching should have as one of its components (whatever else it may include) the need to raise in some way the learner's consciousness of aspects of the grammatical structure of the language he is learning goes back perhaps several millennia.[1] By contrast, the advancement of language-teaching methods that accord little or no importance to grammatical consciousness raising are about a hundred years old and thus, in terms of this more sweeping time scale, relatively recent. It must be realized, moreover, that not only has grammatical focus long been considered a *necessary* part of language instruction; it has also even to this day often been considered a *sufficient* condition for successful language learning. In the words of one researcher, D. Wilkins, "this is the tradition that we have inherited" (Wilkins, 1984, p. 73).

The importance attributed to a knowledge of language form throughout the history of language pedagogy derives in part from a number of other historical circumstances. One of the most important of these is the early relationship of language study to scholarship in general. In the Middle Ages, for example, our modern concept of a multidisciplined academia simply did not exist. Academic learning in medieval Europe embraced the three branches of law, theology, and medicine, but even among these the disciplinary bound-

Second Language Grammar: Learning and Teaching. London: Longman, 1987, pages 27–30. Reprinted by permission.

Note: Much of the material in this section is based on Kelly (1969).

aries so familiar to us today were considerably blurred. Within the medieval academic world the study of grammar was accorded a prominent place in philosophy, which was in turn a branch of theology. The inclusion within philosophy of grammar, logic, and rhetoric was an inheritance from classical antiquity and serves to underscore the fact that at the time they "were all thought of as facets of the same reality of language use" (Kelly, 1969, p. 301). Since one of these uses—or one of the purposes of language teaching in the Middle Ages—was the development of rhetorical skill, it is not very difficult to understand the close relationship of grammar study to the other medieval disciplines. Parenthetically, the modern notion of hyphenated disciplines and the "application" of the findings of one discipline to another—as in, for example, "psycholinguistics" and "applied psycholinguistics"—can have come about only in an academic world wherein an original holistic universe of knowledge and belief has first been fragmented, the continually subdividing parts eventually entering into our smaller-scale specialized recombinations. Early grammar study was thus not "applied-" anything, or not "grafted on to" any of its sister disciplines, but rather fused with them in a general embodiment of prevailing knowledge, which itself was believed in the Middle Ages to be the property of the soul (see Kelly, 1969, p. 302). In fact, the very word *grammar* traces back ultimately to the ancient Greek *grammatikos*, pertaining to letters or learning.

Grammatical consciousness raising in pedagogy carries one indispensable prerequisite, and that is that something be known abut the grammatical structure in question. Now during the milennium preceding the sixteenth century the only language whose structure was thought to be known—indeed, the only language in the Western world (other than Greek) whose structure was deemed worth knowing—was Latin. Thus, when we talk about language study a thousand years ago it must be realized that we are referring essentially to the study of Latin, which was the language of theology, of medicine, and of law— in short, the language of the Western world in which most knowledge of the time was encoded and through which it was transmitted. To study Latin was to study its grammar, and until the invention of printing and the first appearance of books in the fifteenth century the actual teaching of Latin was entirely oral, its grammar rules even being presented in verse form.

With the Renaissance came increased interest in the European vernaculars as cultural vehicles and as languages worth studying in their own right. Language learning of the time drew a distinction between the study of grammar and of literature, strived for accuracy over fluency, used Latin (until the eighteenth century) as the language of grammatical explanation, and relied upon an inductive methodology. The induction principle was carried into the seventeenth century, when we find the first promulgation of "the idea later to become the keystone of nineteenth-century methodology: that languages are to be learned in the same way as one's mother tongue" (Kelly, 1969, p. 39).

The rising importance of the vernaculars led to other developments that were to influence significantly the course of future language teaching—the growing belief that the study of another language was best accomplished via knowledge of one's own, and the recognition of Latin grammar as the model for studying the grammar of any language. It was in this climate that emerged the early development at Port-Royal in the seventeenth century of *general grammar*, not unlike, in its assumptions, what the twentieth-century generativists now call *universal grammar*. And, as "the only possible analytical scheme to follow was that which had been developed for Latin, so the illusion that all languages shared a basic grammar was complete" (Kelly, 1969, p. 55).

From belief in the essential oneness of basic structure across languages it was but a short pedagogical step to propound the teaching of languages by translation between the known language (the mother tongue) and the one being learned, that is, *grammar-translation methodology*. And with the ascendancy of grammar-translation in the eighteenth century came the first language descriptions expressly for language learners, or the first "pedagogical grammars." The continued entrenchment of grammar-translation throughout the nineteenth century saw a gradual loosening of the relationship between literary models and grammar study, to the point that by the early twentieth century the study of formal language systems per se bore little relation either to literature or to the purposes for which language learning was undertaken. In Kelly's words, "language skill was equated with ability to conjugate and decline" (p. 53).[2]

The formal excesses of grammar-translation methodology had early on provided the impetus for alternative approaches to language teaching based upon how children were believed to learn their mother tongue. Language learning was thus starting to be regarded as a form of behavior, rather than just the internalization of sets of abstractions, and the most important exponents of this movement in the nineteeth century were the "Natural Method" and the "Direct Method." Although the two differed sharply in that the Natural Method, unlike the Direct Method, recognized no distinction between the way in which first and second languages are learned, both methods, at least in principle, accorded little or no instructional role to grammatical attention. In a sense, the differential regard for grammatical CR, as embodied in early twentieth-century grammar-translation vis-à-vis direct methodism, has continued to this day, though the names of the methodologies in question keep changing. As for consciousness raising itself, however, all its proponents throughout history seem always to have assumed that the matter to be raised to consciousness comprised the *combinatorial units* of whatever model of language analysis happened to prevail at the time.

Just as virtually every contemporary "innovation" in language teaching seems to have an antecedent somewhere back in the 2,500-year history of language pedagogy, so it is perhaps also with grammatical consciousness raising conceived as a tool of language learning rather than the object of such learning. An apt example of this would be the variety of inductive methodology in vogue during the Renaissance and traceable to St Augustine, wherein the learner was made to play an active role in the discovery of principles of language organization whose subsequent articulation in formal terms could only complete a learning process that had already begun. We have ample reminders, it seems, that the profession of language teaching, like so many other professions, is far more preoccupied with where it imagines it is going than with where it actually has been.

NOTES

1. This is not to say by any means that the purpose or the manner of consciousness raising has always been a consistent one. Quite the contrary. Kelly (1969, p. 34) notes that

   since the beginning of language teaching the manner of learning the syntax and flexions of language has been disputed. Accepted methods have ranged from the inductive, by which the pupil himself arrives at rules from examples, to the deductive whereby one proceeds from rules to a knowledge of the language. At all periods of language teaching both have existed, but never on an equal footing. Inductive methods were most fashionable during the late Renaissance and early twentieth century, while deductive approaches reached their greatest development during the late Middle Ages and the eighteenth century.

2. It is well to note, in the words of McArthur (1983, p. 59), that "those who used and developed classical grammar . . . were . . . basically concerned with reading and writing; speech was a secondary consideration for people who wanted to train scribes, clerks, and scholars or readers of a revered foreign literature. Those were the primary goals, and for such goals the grammar-translation method worked adequately for centuries."

REFERENCES

Kelly, L. 1969. *Twenty-Five Centuries of Language Teaching*. Rowley, Mass.: Newbury House.
McArthur, T. 1983. *A Foundation Course for Language Teachers*. Cambridge: Cambridge University Press.
Wilkins, D. 1984. Teaching without a language syllabus but with a linguistic focus. TRANEL (Numero Speciale) 6: 73–91.

2
The Fundamental Character of Foreign Language Learning

Robert Bley-Vroman
University of Hawaii

In this paper I briefly discuss ten fundamental characteristics of adult foreign language learning. These are relatively apparent, large-scale characteristics, and few are controversial. Scholarly research has in general confirmed common-sense observation. It will be useful to compare in each case foreign language learning with child language development on the one hand and with general adult skill acquisition and problem solving on the other. The picture that emerges is that, at least in its gross features, adult foreign language learning is much more like general adult learning than it is like child language development.

LACK OF SUCCESS

The lack of general guaranteed success is the most striking characteristic of adult foreign language learning. Normal children inevitably achieve perfect mastery of the language; adult foreign language learners do not. Any model which entails uniform success—as child first language acquisition models must—is a failure as a model of adult language learning. Lack of inevitable perfect mastery is of course a characteristic of general adult learning in fields for which no domain-specific cognitive facility is thought to exist, especially in areas of substantial complexity. Not everyone with an opportunity to learn chess will become a world-class chess player; not everyone who is exposed to geometry becomes skilled at geometry proofs; careful schooling and years of

"The Logical Problem of Foreign Language Learning" by Robert Bley-Vroman, 1986. Printed with permission of the author.

experience do not guarantee that one will be a competent auto mechanic. Lack of guaranteed success in adult foreign language learning of course would follow from a theory which holds that it is controlled by general human cognitive learning capacities, rather than by the same domain-specific module which guarantees child success in first language acquisition. Frequent lack of success in adults, against uniform success in children, is a serious obstacle to the view that the same process underlies child and adult language acquisition.

GENERAL FAILURE

Not only is success in adult foreign language learning not guaranteed; complete success is extremely rare, or perhaps even nonexistent, especially as regards "accent" and the ability to make subtle grammaticality judgments. Indeed, in his influential "Interlanguage" paper, Selinker (1972) even suggested that the rare cases of apparent complete success could perhaps be regarded as peripheral to the enterprise of second language acquisition theory. The rare successes may have the same "pathological" status for adult acquisition as the rare failures in first language acquisition are considered to have.[1] One has the impression of ineluctable success on the one hand and ineluctable failure on the other. For a theory which holds that adult foreign language acquisition and child first language development are fundamentally different, this follows naturally. Language is not merely difficult to learn with only general cognitive strategies, it is virtually impossible. This is one important reason for attributing an innate domain-specific language faculty to children. Later, I will consider how the fundamental difference hypothesis can accommodate the fact that adults do even as well as they do.

VARIATION IN SUCCESS, COURSE, AND STRATEGY

Among adults, there is substantial variation in degree of success, even when age, exposure, instruction, and so forth are held constant. Adults not only generally do not succeed, they also fail to different degrees. This fact is so evident that it has never been thought necessary to demonstrate it by formal academic study. Rather, the assumption of variation in attainment has formed the basis of a whole tradition in second language acquisition scholarship: the attempt to correlate something else with this wide variation in success. It also forms the basis of the Test of English as a Foreign Language (TOEFL) and Michigan Test industries. Again, the similarity to general adult skill acquisition is striking, as is the difference from child language development, where there is no such variation. The lack of variation among first language learners requires that the child language acquisition theory "must be embedded in a theory of Universal Grammar that allows only one grammar . . . to be compatible with the sorts of sentences children hear" (Pinker, 1984, p. 5). Clearly, a formal model of adult foreign language learning must allow many different "grammars" to be arrived at.

In foreign language acquisition, different learners also "follow different paths" (as Meisel, Clahsen, and Pienemann, 1981, put it, in their study of stages of learning of German syntax in adult *Gastarbeiter*). There is a good deal of intersubject variation in second language "acquisition order" studies (see especially Rosansky, 1976). There is also variation in what one might call "learning strategies": from large-scale differences like the distinction between *avoiding* and *guessing* suggested by Madden, Bailey, and Eisenstein (1978) to something as specific as the use of poetry memorization or of a particular mnemonic trick in vocabulary learning. The same is true among adults learning to play bridge or to do phonology problems.[2]

Again, substantial variation among learners—variation in degree of attainment, in course of learning, and in strategies of learning—is exactly what one expects to find in general adult skill acquisition.

VARIATION IN GOALS

There is not only variation in degree of attainment; there also is variation in what one might call "type" of attainment. For example, some adult learners seem to develop "pidginized" systems which have rudimentary grammatical devices but which seem nonetheless to be quite successful in fulfilling the communicative needs of the speaker (see Schumann, 1976, 1978; Meisel, Clahsen, and Pienemann, 1981, esp. p. 121). Others seem concerned for grammatical correctness, even though fluency may be seen to suffer. Some develop just the subpart of foreign language competence necessary to wait on table or to lecture in philosophy; others may become skilled at cocktail party story telling. Some have good pronunciation but primitive grammar. Some lay great importance on vocabulary size. Some work at passing for a native speaker; others seem proud of their foreignness (the "Charles Boyer phenomenon"). Instruction which is consonant with student goals is more successful.[3]

This sort of variation follows naturally from the hypothesis that adult foreign language acquisition is general problem solving. Cognitive models of general problem solving involve setting "goals." It is to be expected that different people will view the problem to be solved in different ways and will set different goals in a given domain. A keyboard student may want to be able to play popular songs by ear at parties, or to play harpsichord continuo with friends in the math department; a friend of mine once had as primary goal to be able eventually to play the promenade from Moussorsky's "Pictures at an Exhibition"—and that was all. Differing goals will require setting differing subgoals, involving perhaps different learning strategies. All of this is commonplace in general human problem solving. Children, on the other hand, driven by the inexorable operation of the domain-specific language faculty, do not have the luxury of setting their own individual goals. For children, the "goal"—if one can even speak of it as such—is predetermined by the language faculty and not under learner control.

CORRELATION OF AGE AND PROFICIENCY

Studies which attempt to correlate age acquisition with degree of ultimate proficiency show that "younger is better." In studies of immigrants, for example, learners who immigrate as young children learn the language of the country well; adults do not. In population studies of immigrants who arrived over a range of ages, the correlation of age of arrival with measures of ultimate attainment is usually in the range of about $r = -.7$ (see Krashen, Long, and Scarcella, 1979, and the references cited there, especially Seliger, Krashen, and Ladefoged, 1975).

Teenagers, interestingly, often seem to achieve native-speaker competence. Indeed, some studies show that in the age range of about 10 to 15, they not only reach native-speaker competence, but they also progress more rapidly and perform with greater accuracy in the early stages of learning than do their younger counterparts. Snow (1983) makes this point especially well. The phenomenon of the highly successful teens suggests that Lenneberg's (1967) conjecture that puberty is a cut-off point cannot be correct.

FOSSILIZATION

It has long been noted that foreign language learners reach a certain stage of learning—a stage short of success—and that learners then permanently stabilize at this stage. Development ceases, and even serious conscious efforts to change are often fruitless. Brief changes are sometimes observed, but they do not "take": the learner "backslides" to the stable state. Selinker (1972) called this phenomenon "fossilization." Fossilization seems often to be observed in learners who have achieved a level of competence which easily ensures communicative success, even though the grammar may be very unlike that of a native. Fossilized learners are the despair of language teachers: nothing seems to have an effect. Sometimes in a classroom drill with abundant opportunity for conscious monitoring, a change is observed. But minutes later during the break, all the old forms reappear—completely unaffected. In children, of course, there is no fossilization (short of success). Stages are inevitably passed through: the system remains plastic until success is achieved.

It is not entirely clear exactly what to make of this difference. What triggers fossilization in foreign language learners is not understood (for some thoughts see Selinker and Lamendella, 1979, and the references cited there). The reason why "defossilization" seems so difficult is also mysterious. The phenomenon of fossilization is at least anecdotally known in other areas of human learning.[4] There seems to be little systematic psychological study of fossilization (but the concept of brain rigidity/plasticity of Penfield and Roberts, 1959, may possibly be relevant). Nonetheless, since the phenomenon is so frequent in foreign language learning, and unknown in child language development, it constitutes a serious obstacle to the assertion that adult and child language acquisition are fundamentally the same.

INDETERMINATE INTUITIONS

In a substantial number of cases, even very advanced nonnative speakers seem to lack clear grammaticality judgments. The unclear character of nonnative intuitions has even prompted some scholars to suggest that a third class of grammaticality judgments–"indeterminate"—is needed in the description of learner language (Schachter, Tyson, and Diffley, 1976). This suggests that the knowledge which underlies nonnative-speaker performance may be incomplete (in the technical sense) and thus may be a different sort of formal object from the systems thought to underly native-speaker performance. A nonnative system may, for example, be in part a relatively heterogeneous collection of strategies for achieving communicative goals: a system of rules generating all and only the sentences of a language may even be absent. Despite the early conjecture that "an 'interlanguage' may be linguistically described using as data the observable output resulting from speaker's attempt to produce a foreign norm" (Selinker, 1969, p. 71), no systematic grammar has yet been produced for any substantial portion of any learner's language (see Bley-Vroman, 1983, for discussion). Such fundamental differences in kind between the knowledge systems produced in first and foreign language acquisition suggest that the same cognitive learning system does not give rise to them both.

IMPORTANCE OF INSTRUCTION

Children clearly do not require organized formal lessons. "While it is debatable exactly how much deliberate shaping the average child receives, no one would claim that deliberate feedback and control over the child's linguistic experience is necessary" (Moulton and Robinson, 1981, p. 245). On the other hand, a whole industry is built on the consensus that instruction matters to foreign language learning.

One must, to be fair, use caution in this argument. Does formal instruction really make a difference in foreign language learning? Might not mere exposure to native-speaker input be equally effective? (Clearly, instruction can help the learner who needs to pass a test of ability to cite explicit grammar rules, but this is learning about the language, not language learning.) Experimental tests of the general efficacy of the instruction are difficult to carry out. Uncontrolled variables abound; individual variation will often swamp the data; the Hawthorne effect may interfere; not all instruction is expected to be equally successful: some may actually impede success. In spite of the difficulties, such studies as exist seem to show that instruction does aid foreign language learning (Long, 1983; Krashen and Seliger, 1975). Also, the survival of the industry amid selective economic pressures suggests that it has some utility.

Much the same may be said of the importance of practice. Systematic, organized, controlled drill is believed to be important by many teachers and learners (though certainly not by all). It plays no obvious role in child language acquisition. Of course practice of this sort is well known to have an important function in adult skill acquisition, where it is held to be the mechanism whereby controlled processing becomes automatized. Again, foreign language learning more closely resembles general adult learning. To be fair, it must be said that this evidence, especially as it depends on the evaluation of belief data, must be interpreted cautiously.

Despite these difficulties, it does seem prudent to take such evidence seriously to the extent that it does not conflict with such experimental evidence as exists and does not contradict common sense.

NEGATIVE EVIDENCE

Child language acquisition seems not to use and surely does not rely upon any consistent source of negative evidence. Indeed, all serious attempts to construct formal first language learning theories assume that negative evidence is not used and that success is possible nonetheless (Wexler and Culicover, 1980; Pinker, 1984). Even attempts made outside the tradition of generative gammar make this assumption (e.g., Moulton and Robinson, 1981, Chapter 6).

Among teachers and learners of foreign languages there is general agreement that negative evidence is at least sometimes useful, and sometimes, though not always, necessary. Experimental evidence is inconclusive, but suggests that correction, in particular, may be helpful (Cohen and Robbins, 1976). As shown by theoretical work, some of the errors made by foreign language learners suggest that they hold hypotheses requiring negative evidence for disconfirmation (Bley-Vroman, 1986). Despite the lack of very convincing empirical evidence, even scholars who argue for essential similarity of first and foreign language acquisition are forced cautiously to conclude that the unclear findings of empirical studies on the efficacy of correction "do not mean that correction plays no role in language learning," and that one may expect that research will "uncover specific situations in which error correction may be effective" (Dulay, Burt, and Krashen, 1982, p. 36).

ROLE OF AFFECTIVE FACTORS

Success in child language development seems unaffected by personality, socialization, motivation, attitude, or the like. This is consistent with the view that the process is controlled by the development of an innate domain-specific faculty, and it contrasts strongly with the case of general adult skill acquisition, which is highly susceptible to such "affective factors."[5]

There is a universal consensus among second language acquisition researchers, as well as language teachers and students, that such factors are essential in foreign language learning. Since the early seventies, beginning with the work of Gardner and Lambert (1972), numerous empirical studies have shown significant correlations between affective factors and proficiency. The situation is, to be sure, very complicated: affect itself is complex and hard to measure; different groups and different situations show different sorts of correlations; explanations are in short supply. Still, the central role of affect in foreign language learning is absolutely indisputable.

These general characteristics of foreign language learning tend to the conclusions that the domain-specific language acquisition system of children ceases to operate in adults, and in addition, that adult foreign language acquisition resembles general adult learning in fields for which no domain-specific learning system is believed to exist. Let us tentatively assume, therefore, that the same language acquisition system which guides children is not available to adults. The assumption that the acquisition system no longer functions easily predicts failure. Nevertheless, although few adults, if any, are completely successful, and many fail miserably, there are many who achieve very high levels of proficiency, given enough time, input, and effort, and given the right attitude, motivation, and learning environment. The *logical problem of foreign language acquisition*, then, becomes to explain the quite high level of competence that is clearly possible in some cases, while permitting the wide range of variation that is observed.

Language remains an abstract formal system of great complexity—one which is, furthermore, underdetermined by the data of experience. On the face of it, the contention that the language acquisition faculty effectively does not exist in adults could be understood to suggest that the adult learner should abandon all hope of any degree of success. This would be the correct conclusion were it not for the fact that the adult possesses other knowledge and faculties which are absent in the infant. And these may, in part, take some of the explanatory burden usually assumed by the language acquisition device. Most obvious is that the adult already has knowledge of at least one language. My proposal here is that the function of the innate domain-specific acquisition system is in adults filled (though indirectly and imperfectly) by this native language knowledge and by a general abstract problem solving system.

In order to be more precise, let us say that the child learner possesses a language acquisition system which contains the following two subcomponents:

A. A definition of possible grammar: a *Universal Grammar*
B. A way of arriving at a grammar based on available data: a *Learning Procedure* (or set of procedures)

Workers in the formal theory of language acquisition have generally assumed such a framework with these components, at least since Chomsky (1965). There have been differences in terminology, emphasis, and specific proposal. Chomsky, in *Aspects*, proposed that a formal evaluation metric would fill function B: would allow the learner to "select from the store of potential grammars a specific one that is appropriate to the data available to him" (Chomsky, 1965, p. 36). A different approach to B is, for example, that of Pinker (1984), who suggests a system of many highly specific learning procedures which construct and revise a grammar (within the constraints provided by Universal Grammar) bit by bit, as data become available. Also, there is clearly a potential trading relationship between A and B: tight constraints on possible grammars (A) may carry some of the burden of choosing a grammar which would otherwise fall on B. Despite the numerous possible variations, something like a distinction between A and B seems justified. For terminological clarity, let us say that function A is filled by a system which we shall call "Universal Grammar" and that function B is filled by what we shall call a system of "Learning Procedures."[6]

The picture of the difference between child language development and foreign language learning which is advocated here is thus the following:

Child Development	Adult Foreign Language Learning
A. Universal Grammar	Native language knowledge
B. Domain-specific	General problem-
Learning Procedures	solving systems

There are two ways in which the native language knowledge can provide partial information about Universal Grammar. First, the learner's general problem-solving systems may directly observe the native *language* itself, considering both its general character and specific facts about its individual sentences. Second (and more speculatively), the general cognitive system may be able to access the internal representation of the particular native language *grammar*, though of course not consciously. Here I will discuss the contribution of the language. The discussion is at a very general level and is intended to be theory-independent.

By the adult's knowledge of a language, I do not mean simply the set of well-formed sentences but also the full range of subtle intuitions which native speakers possess. A great deal of information about the general character of language—about language universals—is implicit in a single language, precisely because universals are universal. This is most evidently true in the broad architectural features of language. The learner will have reason to expect that the language to be learned will be capable of generating an infinite number of sentences: a language of finite cardinality will not be expected. The learner will expect that the foreign language will have a syntax, a semantics, a lexicon which recognizes "parts of speech," a morphology which provides systematic ways of modifying the shapes of words, a phonology which provides a finite set of phonemes, and syllables, feet, phonological phrases, etc. Universals of this sort are available to the foreign language learner merely by observing the most obvious large-scale characteristics of the native language—no deep analyses are necessary—and by making the very conservative assumption that the foreign language is not an utterly different sort of thing from the native language.

In syntax, the learner might also expect to find principles of constituent structure, and of recursive embedding with no intrinsic limit. There will be grammatical functions, and these will not always correspond to thematic roles. There also may be assumed to be something like relative clauses, sentential complements to verbs, and the like. There will be Boolean-like connectors, quantifiers, pronouns, anaphors, "understood" elements of various kinds.

There will be devices for giving orders, making requests, asking yes-no and wh-questions. There will be devices for focus, for backgrounding.

Thus, even supposing that the original scheme of Universal Grammar is no longer available, the foreign language learner can, in a sense, "reconstruct" much of it by observing the native language. The foreign language does not therefore come to language as "an organism initially uninformed as to its general character" (Chomsky, 1965, p. 58).

In some regards, the foreign language learners may even know more than children equipped with a general Universal Grammar. They will know that there will likely be words for the sun, the moon, for mother, father, for body parts, colors, directions; that there will probably be styles, registers, and regional and social dialects.

This information which the foreign language learner has is of course not complete. The speaker of a language with little inflectional morphology and heavily dependent on word order to convey grammatical function may initially be surprised by many of the characteristics of a language less dependent on rigid configuration. The phonemic use of tone will not be expected by speakers of a non-tone language. The speakers of a language with obligatory overt subjects may initially be baffled by a null-subject language.

On the other hand, foreign language learners also may be said to know too much. They may presume that features of the native language are universal, may not only expect that the language to be learned will have some relatively small set of phonemes, but that it will have exactly the same set as the native language; that the language to be learned will have an analogous politeness system; that noun phrases with numerals may omit plural marking; and so forth.

The adult foreign language learner constructs, therefore, a kind of surrogate for Universal Grammar from knowledge of the native language. The native language must be sifted: that which is likely to be universal must be separated from that which is an accidental property of the native language. Different learners may be expected to approach this task differently, and not all can be expected to come up with the same surrogate, and not all will be equally successful. The process of learning a foreign language may have itself an effect, as the learner gradually realizes what of the native language seems to transfer well. And learners of third and fourth languages may be presumed to have a richer source of information and to stand a better chance of building an adequate surrogate Universal Grammar. In an interesting and ingenious series of studies, Kellerman (1977) showed that adult learners had ideas of what, in their native languages, was "universal" (and hence transferable to the language to be learned) and what was specific to the native language (and hence probably would not transfer well). These ideas were sometimes, but not always, right. He also showed that notions of universality differed from learner to learner and changed over the course of foreign language learning. He pointed out also that learners can develop a "psychotypology" of languages, so that the Finnish learners of English who already know Swedish correctly expect English to be more like Swedish than like Finnish.

In summary, for what success is achieved in foreign language learning, the knowledge of the native language can assume much of the burden taken in child first language development by the assumption of access to an innate Universal Grammar. The foreign language learner is not a Martian or a hypothetical blank-slate infant. But because the indirect knowledge of Universal Grammar possible through the native language is incomplete and accidental, and since it also depends on the individual learner's ability to construct a Universal Grammar surrogate, one can expect some partial success, little chance of perfect success, and some considerable individual variation. This, of course, is exactly what is found.[7]

NOTES

1. There is some debate among workers in second language acquisition about the frequency of perfect success. Selinker hazarded 5%. See Seliger (1978) for a more generous estimate. The scholarly literature is complicated by the question of who one counts, and what one means by success, or potential success. I believe that virtually no normal adult learner achieves perfect success, if what one means thereby is development of native-speaker competence, even though some may have performance difficult to distinguish from that of native speakers. This is the strongest possible form of the fundamental difference hypothesis.

2. "Different paths" have also been claimed to exist among children in first language performance. The variation appears, on the face of it, to be much less dramatic than among adult learners. The situation is complicated by the fact that it is always difficult to know, especially in the case of young children, whether we are faced with actual differences in the course or "methods" of language development, or merely with different responses to the exigencies of communication using an incompletely developed grammar or with differing enjoyment of certain sorts of verbal play— which may or may not actually "feed" language development.

3. The fact of such variation, and its central importance to second language acquisition, is not only universally accepted by all scholars of adult language learning, it is even the basis of a whole pedagogical theory of curriculum design: so-called needs-based, specific purpose, and communicative syllabi. See especially Van Ek (1975) and Munby (1978). The journal *English for Special Purposes* (the *ESP Journal*) is dedicated to this tradition.

4. One sometimes hears music teachers despair of undoing the damage caused by a previous teacher, especially when the student has particular facility. Athletic coaches, too, seem to find it difficult to "defossilize" their trainees. I sometimes feel that my substantial early success in the high jump prevented the radical changes in technique which would have been required in order to achieve greater heights.

5. Here and throughout, I use "affect" loosely to refer to a whole range of loosely associated factors. This is not to deny the correctness of the distinctions among them; it is just that the distinctions are not relevant to the argument.

6. The term *Universal Grammar* is sometimes also used to comprise both A and B: this is especially appropriate within evaluation metric theories, where the procedure for selecting a grammar is so closely related to the formal properties of rules. I shall use the term in the more restricted sense.

7. Although it seems to me that the view is quite plausible that both components of the domain-specific acquisition have ceased to function in adults, there are other reasonable possibilities. One potentially interesting one is that the principles which define

"possible language" may still be around, but that the means of constructing a particular grammar given the data of experience may not be. Thus A is still functioning, but B is not. Clahsen (personal communication) and Schmerling (personal communication) have suggested this. Shuldberg (1986) has developed a model of L2 acquisition which makes this assumption. Though this alternative view is conceptually coherent, I do not pursue it here. The empirical issue is essentially whether there are characteristics of learner language which prove a knowledge of "possible language" above that which can be obtained as a by-product of the native language. As of now, there is no clear evidence of such characteristics. If such evidence should turn up, a somewhat less radical view of the fundamental difference hypothesis than that proposed here may be justified.

QUESTIONS FOR DISCUSSION

1. Bley-Vroman advances the claim that adult language learning bears a closer resemblance to general skill development than it does to language learning with children. If we believe and/or assume for the sake of discussion that this is so, then how would you rate language-teaching methodologies (past and present) in terms of degree of consistency with this claim?

2. To what extent does the rating you came up with in answer to Question 1 align with your assessment of the methodologies in terms of overall effectiveness?

3. Can you think of any personal skill development experiences, other than language learning, in which attainment of the skill beyond a particular point seemed to have stopped—where no amount of additional practice, instruction, and so forth seemed any longer to make a difference? Is an extension of fossilization to cover this sort of phenomenon an appropriate use of the term?

4. Is it possible to interpret fossilization in language learning as tantamount to solution of the problem from the learner's standpoint? That is, has the learner acquired enough of the language-learning skill to satisfy his communication needs, such that the problem as far as he is concerned is perhaps now solved?

5. Can you think of any other differences between adult and child language learning that have *not* been developed in the Bley-Vroman paper? What about language transfer? What about the fact that obviously not everyone undertakes to learn a language in adulthood, whereas one can hardly help doing it in childhood? What about possible orders in which the so-called four skills (listening, speaking, reading, writing) are learned? In which learning experience, child or adult, is the order a flexible one? Are any of these skills typically acquired through instruction for both adults and children?

REFERENCES

Bley-Vroman, R. 1983. The comparative fallacy in interlanguage studies: the case of systematicity. *Language Learning* 33:1–17.

Bley-Vroman, R. 1986. Hypothesis testing in second language acquisition theory. *Language Learning* 36:353–376.

Chomsky, N. 1965. *Aspects of the Theory of Syntax*. Cambridge, Mass.: MIT Press.

Cohen, A., and M. Robbins. 1976. Toward assessing interlanguage performance: the relationship between selected errors, learners' characteristics, and learners' explanations. *Language Learning* 26:45–66.

Dulay, H., M. Burt, and S. Krashen. 1982. *Language Two*. New York: Oxford University Press.

Gardner, R., and W. Lambert. 1972. *Attitudes and Motivation in Second Language Learning.* Rowley, Mass.: Newbury House.

Kellerman, E. 1977. Toward a characterisation of the strategy of transfer. *Interlanguage Studies Bulletin* 2:59–92.

Krashen, S., M. Long, and R. Scarcella. 1979. Age, rate, and eventual attainment in second language acquisition. *TESOL Quarterly* 13:573–582.

Krashen, S., and H. Seliger. 1975. The essential contributions of formal instruction in adult second language learning. *TESOL Quarterly* 13:173–183.

Lenneberg, E. 1967. *Biological Foundations of Language.* New York: John Wiley.

Long, M. 1983. Does second language instruction make a difference? A review of the research. *TESOL Quarterly* 17:359–382.

Madden, C., N. Baily, and M. Eisenstein. 1978. Beyond statistics in second language acquisition research. In W. Ritchie (ed.), *Second Language Acquisition Research: Issues and Implications.* New York: Academic Press.

Meisel, J., H. Clahsen, and M. Pienemann. 1981. On determining developmental stages in natural second language acquisition. *Studies in Second Language Acquisition* 3:109–135.

Moulton, J., and G. Robinson. 1981. *The Organization of Language.* Cambridge: Cambridge University Press.

Munby, J. 1978. *Communicative Syllabus Design.* Cambridge: Cambridge University Press.

Penfield, W., and L. Roberts. 1959. *Speech and Brain Mechanisms.* Princeton, N.J.: Princeton University Press.

Pinker, S. 1984. *Language Learnability and Language Development.* Cambridge: Harvard University Press.

Rosansky, E. 1976. Methods and morphemes in second language acquisition. *Language Learning* 26:409–425.

Schachter, J., A. Tyson, and F. Diffley. 1976. Learner intuitions of grammaticality. *Language Learning* 26:67–76.

Schuldberg, K. 1986. Syntactic and semantic issues in second language acquisition. Ph.D. dissertation, University of Texas, Austin.

Schumann, J. 1976. Social distance as a factor in second language acquisition. *Language Learning* 26:135–143.

Schumann, J. 1978. *The Pidginization Process.* Rowley, Mass.: Newbury House.

Seliger, H. 1978. Implications of a multiple critical periods hypothesis for second language learning. In W. Ritchie (ed.), *Second Language Acquisition Research: Issues and Implications.* New York: Academic Press.

Seliger, H., S. Krashen, and P. Ladefoged. 1975. Maturational constraints in the acquisition of second language accent. *Language Sciences* 36:20–22.

Selinker, L. 1969. Language transfer. *General Linguistics* 9:67–92.

Selinker, L. 1972. Interlanguage. *IRAL* 10:209–231.

Selinker, L., and J. Lamendella. 1979. The role of extrinsic feedback in interlanguage fossilization. *Language Learning* 29:363–375.

Snow, C. 1983. Age differences in second language acquisition: research findings and folk psychology. In N. Bailey, M. Long, and S. Peck (eds.), *Second Language Acquisition Studies.* Rowley, Mass.: Newbury House.

Van Ek, J. 1975. *The Threshold Level.* Cambridge: Cambridge University Press.

Wexler, K., and P. Culicover. 1980. *Formal Principles of Language Acquisition.* Cambridge, Mass.: MIT Press.

3
Psycholinguistic Dimensions of Second Language Proficiency

Ellen Bialystok
York University, Ontario

As our methods of describing second language performance become more sophisticated, so too does the underlying complexity of second language learning become more apparent. The descriptions of learner performance and their implications for the language-learning process have needed to accommodate an increasing number of factors—from the contrastive hypothesis which considered only native language factors (e.g., Lado, 1957), to error analysis which accepted a role for other influences on learner performance (e.g., Richards, 1973), to recent discourse analysis which includes as well social and interactive aspects of language use (e.g., Larsen-Freeman, 1980). Throughout these developments it has become apparent that quantitative notions of language proficiency which assess a single dimension of the learner's performance have limited power in reflecting the learner's actual ability with the language. It appears rather that learners may be differentially equipped to perform in different types of linguistic situations and that assessment of performance in one may not be reflective of performance in another, if the two situations differ in critical ways (see, e.g., Savignon, 1972; Tarone, Frauenfelder, and Selinker, 1976; Cathcart, Strong, and Fillmore, 1979; Swain, 1981). In this case, the underlying features of language use that result in such critical differences need to be discovered so that appropriate qualitative descriptions of proficiency may be generated.

Thischapter was originally a paper presented at the BAAL Conference on Interpretive Strategies in Language Learning, Lancaster, 1981. Printed with permission of the author.

In response to this need for qualitative descriptions of language proficiency, a framework based on psycholinguistic principles of language learning and use is proposed. Following the description of the framework, some empirical evidence is presented in support of aspects of the framework. Finally, the implications of the framework for some current issues in second language learning are discussed.

The proposed framework is designed to meet four criteria. First, it must be consistent with current conceptions of language. While no theoretical position is taken with respect to the most appropriate linguistic description, the minimum assumptions are that language is a structured, generative system. This minimal commitment to a theoretical description of language appears essential if the endeavor is ultimately to describe the learner's use of that system. Chomsky (1977), in fact, has made the same point:

> No discipline can concern itself in a productive way with the acquisition or utilization of a form of knowledge without being concerned with the *nature* of that system of knowledge. [p. 43]

Hence, the first constraint on the framework consists of these minimal assumptions about the nature of language.

Second, the framework must similarly be based on a conception of cognitive functioning. The assumption here is that the mind does not process information about language in fundamentally different ways than it processes any information. Thus, what we know about cognitive operations in general should be applicable to the description of the learning and use of linguistic material.

Third, the framework must be capable of accounting for the variability in language performance referred to previously. The system must contain a means for determining what constitutes a significant difference in a language situation and therefore predicting occasions when learner performance may be expected to fluctuate.

Finally, the framework must be able to account for the development of that proficiency in its various aspects. The description of development must, of course, be compatible with the various aspects of proficiency identified in response to the preceding criterion.

The principle upon which the framework is based is that proficiency can be described by extracting the underlying dimensions that are responsible for variation in language performance. If such dimensions can be identified, then language performance becomes predictable and systematic. These dimensions are considered to be continua along which change in the learner's control over the relevant information about the language can be described.

DIMENSIONS IN THE CONTROL OF LINGUISTIC INFORMATION

Language proficiency in the present framework comprises development along two dimensions. First, the *Analyzed* dimension is the type of mental representation assigned to the information which differentiates degrees of control over that information. The second, the *Automatic* dimension, is the procedures for using that information which differentiates relative access to it in terms of fluent or nonfluent performance.

In the discussion of these dimensions, two epistemological assumptions will be made. First, following philosophers such as Polanyi (1958), the assumption is that we can know more than we can tell. Second, in line with cognitive theorists such as Miller and Johnson-Laird (1976), it is also assumed that concepts are not encoded as words. For these two reasons, words, or verbal descriptions, can neither exhaustively nor exactly represent what we know. And since verbal description serves a critical role in language instruction, the nature of that relationship must be examined.

Analyzed Knowledge

If we assume that all knowledge is structured, then a difference emerges in terms of whether or not the learner is aware of that structure. It is this awareness of structure that underlies the dimension Analyzed.[1] At any point along the dimension, the information itself may be the same, but as control over that information moves toward the Analyzed, then the learner becomes increasingly aware as well of the structure of that information. It is this control of the structure of knowledge which is responsible for the differential applicability of knowledge to various situations.

The psychological basis of the distinction is in the form of mental representation assigned to information or knowledge. Following theorists such as Pylyshyn (1973), Miller and Johnson-Laird (1976), and Clark and Clark (1977), analyzed knowledge is represented as a proposition in which the formal structure and the relationship to meaning are apparent.[2] Nonanalyzed knowledge is assigned a mental representation in which the underlying formal constituents are not necessarily identifiable. Nonanalyzed knowledge is nonetheless organized, possibly in terms of propositions, but the structure of those propositions is not apparent. In these terms, analyzed knowledge can be described as access to the propositional structure of nonanalyzed knowledge. Note that the information represented as analyzed knowledge is not different from that represented as nonanalyzed knowledge; rather for analyzed knowledge, the learner is in addition in control of the structural properties and relations governing the knowledge already known in an unanalyzed form.

The application of the dimension of analyzed knowledge to descriptions of language proficiency is functional. The assumption is that if knowledge is assigned a representation for which the propositional structure is known, then certain *uses* may be made of that knowledge which cannot be made of knowledge which is represented in a nonanalyzed form. For example, if a structural regularity of a language is known as analyzed knowledge, then the learner may use that structure in new contexts, decipher language, especially written forms which make use of that structure, and modify or transform that structure for other literary or rhetorical purposes. If an aspect of the language is nonanalyzed, then it is understood more as a routine or pattern (cf. Hakuta, 1974) and has limited application to new contexts or new purposes. Only a very minimal degree of analysis is necessary to use language creatively in the generation of novel grammatical utterances.

This functional differentiation of knowledge in terms of the extent of analysis will be illustrated by examples from three different areas—epistemology, cognitive development, and psycholinguistics.

In epistemology, a distinction is often made between forms of knowing. Polanyi (1958), for example, distinguishes *personal knowledge* from *objective knowledge* in terms of the person's awareness of the structure of that knowledge. In "tacit knowing" (personal knowledge), he claims *we attend from something of which we are largely unaware, to* something which is directly known (Polanyi, 1966). A blind man, for example, attends *from* the tactual information provided by his cane (the first event), *to* the meaning of that information in terms of obstructions in his path (the second event). Similarly, in language we may attend from certain forms or structures to the meanings of those structures without necessarily being aware of the formal features which gave rise to those meanings. In objective knowing, however, the first event and its relationship to the second event are also known, thus providing both the meaning and the structure of that meaning through its relationship to the first event—for example, the particular sound and feel of the cane.

The important aspect of Polanyi's distinction is that it provides a description, not of the substance of knowledge but of its structure. The difference between tacit and objective knowledge can be seen only if knowledge is considered as a structured system or schema, characterized by connections among events. Polanyi argues that in tacit knowing, only the second event is known; in the above example, the blind man knows only the obstructions on the path. In objective knowing, the relationship between the second event meaning and structures which generate them are both known.

A more compelling example of Polanyi's distinction is given by his description of the recognition of human faces. While each of us is capable of discriminating a large number of faces, we are largely unaware of the features employed to make those discriminations. Consequently, our knowledge of an individual's face is adequate for tasks such as recognizing the person, but inadequate for tasks such as describing the relevant differences between two people or producing a representation—for example, through drawing—of an individual's face. Certain specialists, however, such as police artists, have an objective (or analyzed) representation of human faces and can recreate an individual face because the underlying critical features which give rise to certain appearances are known.

This description of knowledge in terms of relationships between events Polanyi applies to both practical and theoretical knowledge—for example, to both the "know how" and "know that" of Ryle (1949). If the structure of the connection is known, then the knowledge is accepted as a logical necessity and therefore has a different status for the learner than do more impressionistic or intuitive forms of knowing. Similar, too, is the distinction proposed by Scheffler (1965) between *knowledge* (known structure) and *belief* (intuitive).

The second example, from cognitive development, is taken from Piaget (1954). He proposes a distinction between figurative knowledge and operative knowledge. *Figurative* knowledge provides a nonanalyzed impression of the world and is inadequate for the solution to most tasks. The same information stored as operative knowledge, however, may be applied to various situations as abstract knowledge with its own internal structure. In this case, transformations in structures and relationships between events are clear because the structure of the system is transparent. In Piaget's theory, cognitive development involves the growth of operative knowledge.

To illustrate, in Piaget's classic conversion of liquids task, a child is shown two identical beakers containing equal amounts of fluid. In the first step, the child is required to confirm that the two quantities are indeed identical. (Adjustments in amount are made if the child so requests.) In the second step, the child watches while the experimenter pours the contents of one beaker into a third beaker of a different shape. Finally, the child is asked again to make a judgment of the equality of the fluid in the two beakers which no longer appears the same. Until about six or seven years of age, the child will insist that the two quantities are no longer equal and usually argue that it is the taller beaker which now contains more liquid. Piaget's explanation is that children in the pre-operational stage, before about six years old, have only figurative knowledge of the situation. In the concrete operational stage, however, the child has access to operative knowledge of the situation. Rather than attending, in Polanyi's terms, simply *from* the transformation *to* the appearance of the new beaker, the child can also attend to and understand the relationship or transformation that binds the two beakers. At this point, the child knows the two beakers *must* contain the same quantity. In the first stage the knowledge is nonanalyzed and is based only on the appearance of the beakers at one point in time; in the second stage the knowledge is analyzed since it includes an understanding of its structure. With such analyzed knowledge, the child is not seduced by the appearance of inequality and can respond in terms of the structure of the problem.

Finally, the third example is taken from the work of Reber and his associates (Reber, 1976; Reber and Lewis, 1977; Reber and Allen, 1978). In a series of studies concerning the learning of an artificial language, Reber and his colleagues have proposed that there are both an *explicit* and *implicit* system available and have demonstrated the learner's use of each by means of a grammaticality judgment task. By presenting the task under various conditions which bias toward learning by means of either the explicit or implicit system, they have shown that the learners have different control over the system as a function of this factor, and the difference is reflected in their ability to make grammaticality judgments and generate the rules of the system.

Similar arguments have been proposed both empirically in terms of grammaticality judgments (Bialystok, 1979a) and theoretically in terms of descriptions of metalinguistic awareness (Pylyshyn, 1981; Mattingly, 1972, 1979; Gleitman and Gleitman, 1979). Such differences in control as determined partly by the use of an implicit or explicit representational system might well contribute to an explanation of the variability in performance. Success on a particular task would depend not only on the learner's having been exposed to the relevant aspect of the language but also on the learner's having appropriate control over that information. If, for example, a task requires the manipulation or transformation of information, not only must the learner know the information but also the learner's control of the information must permit the necessary transformation.

Automatic Access

The second dimension, *Automatic*, refers to the case with which information may be accessed by the learner, irrespective of its extent of analysis. Clearly, learners vary in their ability to retrieve information, and different situations place different demands on that retrieval. Fluent conversation, for example, requires better access to the relevant linguistic information than does the preparation of written text. In the latter case, the learner may consult various sources to assist where memory fails. Even in various oral situations, the relative automaticity of information comprises an important part of what we mean by fluency. In general, however, an individual's retrieval procedures vary according to the demands of the situation, the information required, and the fluency or automaticity of the individual's control over the information. This conceptualization is similar to Chomsky's (1980) notion of "pragmatic competence," which refers to procedures for the appropriate use of linguistic information.

The problem of fluent access to knowledge has also been addressed in the context of descriptions of metalinguistic awareness. Mattingly (1979) and Chomsky (1979) both include access to knowledge as part of the definition of metalinguistic awareness, while Cazden (1974) argues that accessibility to knowledge is the first condition of awareness, the second and more demanding being consciousness. Thus it appears reasonable to separate the learner's representation of knowledge from access to that knowledge and that each of these variables contributes to the learner's control over that knowledge.

Combining the Dimensions

The multiplication of these two dimensions yields the framework illustrated in Figure 1. While the figure is divided into four major sections, the lines of the dimensions do not define categories but continua. Nonetheless, it is possible to generalize across a range of values on each dimension and group together various language tasks which are somewhat equivalent in their demands in these two ways. Some examples of learner groups who illustrate each of the competencies indicated by the four major sections in the framework are listed in Figure 3-1.

The relationship between the endpoints of the two dimensions can be described in terms of the linguistic concept of markedness. Analyzed is marked with respect to nonanalyzed, and Automatic is marked with respect to non-

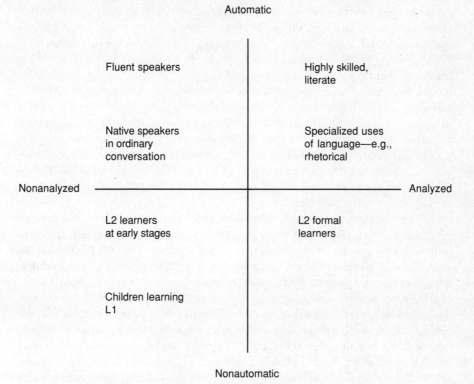

Figure 3-1 Two dimensions of language proficiency

automatic. The *analyzed* and *automatic* endpoints contain all the information and features of the nonanalyzed and nonautomatic plus the features for specialization. Thus higher values on either of those dimensions imply cumulative control up to that point; information that is analyzed is thereby necessarily known in the less specialized (nonanalyzed) form as well.

By placing various language tasks in this framework as a function of their hypothesized demands on each of these dimensions and by examining the learner's success with the tasks, we may infer the learner's control of the language in terms of these dimensions. The prediction concerning the development of proficiency is that the unmarked forms of control precede the marked forms. Thus development involves achieving an analyzed understanding of and automatic access to information which was already known in less specialized forms.

The two dimensions are considered to be independent; nonanalyzed, for example, does not imply automatic. The development of more automatic access to information must be achieved for every point along the analyzed dimension. While such a separation proliferates categories of proficiency, it nonetheless provides the means for more subtle descriptions of proficiency. The conflation of nonanalyzed and automatic yields binary concepts of language as, for example, in Krashen's (1981) theoretical model, which distinguishes learning from acquisition. In these terms, learning would be characterized as *analyzed, nonautomatic* and acquisition as *nonanalyzed, automatic.*[3] Thus, two parts of the present framework are excluded. First, there is no means of handling the earliest stages of language learning for either first or second language acquisition, in which the knowledge is nonanalyzed but the access to it so difficult that it is barely adequate as utterance initiator, one of the primary responsibilities of acquisition. Second, there is no means of handling highly sophisticated uses of language characterized by the combination of analyzed and automatic control. Accomplishments such as simultaneous translation and the exceptionally high levels of rhetorical and literal ability achieved by some native speakers (e.g., skilled writers) would be difficult to explain in a binary paradigm.

This framework has three implications for the development of language proficiency. First, all learners enter the system in the region for which information is unmarked on both factors. Second, control over that information specializes in terms of these two factors in a relatively independent manner, always progressing toward the more marked forms of control. Finally, the combination of both forms of marking is substantially more difficult than is the use of information marked in one way only; that is, information may be specialized for both analyzed and automatic, but the simultaneous combination of these in a situation is difficult. Many studies in cognitive development have shown that children may be in control of all the components of a problem yet be unable to combine them when they are required to solve a particular problem (a review of this limitation with respect to the development of spatial cognition is given in Bialystok, 1976).

THE DEVELOPMENT OF LANGUAGE PROFICIENCY

In a series of studies investigating the development of proficiency for adults learning English as a second language, we have found evidence both for the existence of the two proposed dimensions of linguistic control and for their developmental progression as outlined earlier (Bialystok, 1982). The learners were tested for their control of selected English structures under task conditions which varied in their demands for automatic and analyzed control of those structures. There were learners at two proficiency levels and a group of native English speakers. For nonanalyzed nonautomatic control, learners were required to use the target forms in informal conversations where the context supplied support to the learner and fluency pressures were minimized. For analyzed nonautomatic control, learners were required to supply a correct form for the structure in a written grammar test. For nonanalyzed automatic control, learners were asked to engage in an abstract discussion with a group of other learners where fluency was important. The spontaneous use of the target forms by the learners was later analyzed from the transcripts of those discussions. Finally, for analyzed automatic control, learners were placed in a formal interview situation and required both to provide immediate information about a selected topic and to place the information in the correct grammatical form while conversing with a native speaker. In addition, transcripts of free discussion were examined for the rhetorical applications of the target forms. In all cases, scoring proceeded on the basis of the same target structures, so tasks were not more difficult because more difficult structures were required to solve them.

All the learners had been taught all the forms in their language classes. To the extent that their understanding of these forms was successful, the learners would then have at least nonanalyzed and nonautomatic control over these structures. If, in addition, the various language tasks used in the study made different demands on the control over those forms, then that control may be inadequate to solve some of the other tasks; that is, the learners may appear to know the forms only in certain contexts. Other contexts which require the same forms may exceed the ability of these learners. Further, the advantage of the advanced learners should be in the additional types of control which may be demonstrated over exactly the same forms which are understood in a more limited way by the intermediate learners.

The results showed both a general performance advantage for the more advanced group of learners on tasks requiring marked control and an increasing independence in performance on these different tasks for the advanced group. The intermediate group could solve only those tasks requiring information unmarked on both factors. The advanced group, however, could solve tasks based on information unmarked on both factors, or marked on one and unmarked on the other, where either factor was marked. It was only the native-speaker group whose control of the target forms was sufficient for solving the tasks marked on both factors. For example, while the advanced learners demonstrated both automatic access to and analyzed control of wh-questions in contexts where only one form of specialization was required, it was only the native speakers who could use wh-questions for rhetorical purposes such as expressing indirect speech acts. Thus, the description of tasks in terms of the number of marked features presupposed for their solution provides a means of describing task difficulty, even when the linguistic structures examined across tasks are identical.

This ability of the advanced learners to handle situations requiring some marked control accounts for the second finding—namely, that performance across tasks was unrelated for the advanced learners. These learners performed quite differently in the various situations, sometimes achieving almost native-like accuracy. Moreover, that advantage appears when marked control was required on one factor only.

The indication is that proficiency is progressing in terms of gaining control of the forms according to the two factors, one factor at a time. Their performance, then, is more like native speakers and less like the intermediate learners for those tasks which demand marking in the ways they have already achieved. Thus, they do better in some tasks than in others, resulting in apparently variable control of the system. Stated another way, once knowledge is specialized for either analyzed or automatic aspects, all language situations are no longer alike.

ISSUES IN SECOND LANGUAGE LEARNING

The paradigm outlined here is proposed as a description of some qualitative aspects of language proficiency. It attempts to set out some major distinctions between the types of skills learners can achieve with a second language, irrespective to some extent of their quantitative level of proficiency as measured on standardized tests. The assumption is that a single test demonstrates only one aspect of language proficiency and so gives little indication of the learner's ability to use the language in other ways and for other purposes. Consequently, what remains to be done is to examine the implications of this paradigm for some traditional problems of language learning and use.

Knowledge of Language Rules

Analyzed knowledge, as was described, is characterized by the learner's access to the structure of the knowledge. It was also indicated, however, that knowledge itself is not verbal but propositional. Thus it is erroneous to equate analyzed knowledge with articulated knowledge, or knowledge of rules, although that assumption has often (and understandably) been made. Thus in the study by Seliger (1979) in which learners were shown to be able to perform in fairly sophisticated tasks without being able to provide rules, it remains to be demonstrated whether or not those learners were operating from analyzed knowledge.

In second language learning, there is clearly a role for rule learning, although theorists differ vastly in their proposals for what that role might be (cf., e.g., Krashen, 1981; Jakobovits, 1970). How, then, does the ability to provide specific rules fit into the present paradigm?

The suggestion is that articulated knowledge is one of the forms of specialized knowledge made possible by analyzed knowledge; that is, if knowledge is analyzed, then rules *may* be generated, although they need not be to demonstrate that the knowledge is analyzed. In Seliger's study, for example, the failure to articulate the rules is ambiguous with respect to the extent of analysis of those rules for the learner. An expression of the rules, however, would provide some evidence for analyzed knowledge. Similarly, analyzed knowledge is seen to provide the basis of metalinguistic knowledge, although these two also are not equivalent. Metalinguistic knowledge, like articulated knowledge, is viewed as one specialized use of language made possible by analyzed knowledge.

It is important to note that demonstrations of analyzed knowledge through the articulation of verbal rules provide evidence of such knowledge only when the rule has been generated by the learner on the basis of analyzed knowledge. Rules memorized as routines and recited verbatim may indicate nothing about the learner's knowledge if that rule has no meaning for the learner. This seems to be an obvious point, but nonetheless places an important qualification on the statement that rule articulation may be taken as evidence of analyzed knowledge. Classroom instruction often provides learners with rules but does not always guarantee that the learners have analyzed knowledge of those rules.

Language Mastery and Instruction

The most general claim about language instruction, even of the most informal kind (i.e., natural language learning, natural methods, etc.), is that it aims primarily to develop one of these two dimensions of language proficiency, either the Analyzed or Automatic functions of language control. In formal language classrooms, for example, the intention is usually to provide the learners with an understanding of the structure of the language and competence with the literary uses of that language. Consequently, success in these situations would depend on the development of analyzed knowledge of the target language. Similarly, languages learned for specialized or technical purposes would require analyzed, although not necessarily automatic, control. Reading technical texts may be too demanding a task for a nonanalyzed knowledge of the language. The degree of grammatical awareness expected by most formal language programs would likewise demand some analyzed understanding of the language.

To achieve these goals, formal language programs then aim to increase the learner's analyzed knowledge of the language. This is manifested in the many activities and routines that occur in the classroom and is epitomized by the nature of testing that usually accompanies such programs. Language tests typically focus on specific points of structure, and solutions to the problems generally involve some linguistic manipulation, such as providing correct forms.

In the proposed framework, however, analyzed knowledge does not exist as an independent epistemological entity. Rather, it is conceived only as a specialized or marked form of nonanalyzed knowledge. Thus it is logically impossible to develop analyzed knowledge exclusively; it can only evolve from nonanalyzed knowledge. In language instruction aimed at the development of analyzed knowledge, then, the highest form of success would be the simultaneous acquisition of analyzed and nonanalyzed knowledge; that is, the learner immediately receives and encodes new information in complete cognizance of its structural composition. While this may be possible for some learners at some stages of language learning—notably, the more advanced stages—it is surely an idealistic aspiration for most learners under most circumstances. Thus, the expectation is that new information enters the system as nonanalyzed knowledge and, depending on instructional and other factors, may at some point emerge into the analyzed regions of the continuum. This temporal gap between nonanalyzed and analyzed control over specific aspects of the language may contribute in some way to the common observation that comprehension precedes production. Comprehension, being cognitively less demanding (Huttenlocher, 1974), may adequately proceed from a nonanalyzed representation of the system while aspects of production await analyzed knowledge.

The same analysis may be applied to other instructional approaches. Methods such as natural language learning (Terrell, 1981) are more concerned with the learner's progress along the Automatic dimension. Similarly, nontraditional language programs, such as The Silent Way, differ in their selection of one of these two factors of language control as the goal of the program. The division of language control into these two factors suggests that language programs must be diversified in order to achieve complete mastery for all purposes. The appropriate instructional program for a particular learner who has specific needs in the target language depends on an analysis of those needs and the skills promoted by a given approach. The benefits of different instructional programs are specific to designated types of mastery.

Role of Other Knowledge

The discussion thus far has proceeded on the facile assumption that performance in a language may be explained by reference only to knowledge of that language. Clearly that is not the case. An individual performing in any cognitive task, including linguistic tasks, exploits a wealth of cognitive and other resources which critically affect performance. These other factors have been deliberately set aside in the description of this paradigm so that a more detailed examination of simply the linguistic aspects of performance may be achieved. What, then, is the role of the learner's other knowledge?

All the knowledge of the learner which is not specifically relevant to the target language is encompassed by the general term *other knowledge*. Included in this category are knowledge of other languages, or *language knowledge*; knowledge of the world, or *conceptual knowledge*; and knowledge of the specific situation or topic, or *contextual knowledge*. The extent to which this other knowledge is implicated in language performance varies as a function of the type of language task. Specifically, tasks which are more communicative and occur in a known context permit the learner to rely more heavily on other knowledge than do tasks which are more abstracted from a concrete situation. Donaldson (1978), in fact, has proposed that it is this removal of language from its context and its resultant effect of precluding the use of other knowledge that makes many aspects of schooling so difficult for children. Cummins (1981), too, has argued that language use increases in difficulty along a dimension of context-embedded to context-reduced tasks. Cole and Scribner (1974) have made a similar point from an anthropological perspective.

The relationship between other knowledge and linguistic knowledge may be simply expressed in terms of the contextual aspects of the language situation. Consider a continuum of language situations which range from highly contextualized to highly abstract. This continuum is represented by the abscissa in Figure 3-2.

In general terms, the far right includes the types of conversations which characterize "motherese" (see, e.g., Snow and Ferguson, 1977) while the far left

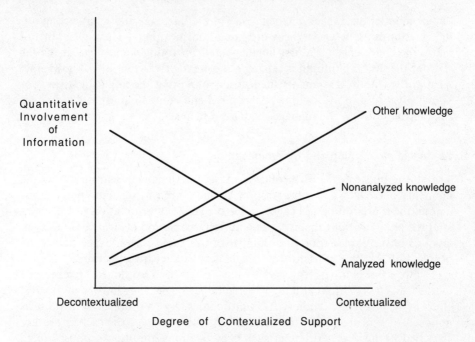

Figure 3-2   Role of three types of information in language tasks as a function of contextual support

includes technical texts, abstract discussion. Clearly there is a context for those tasks on the left, but it is of a different nature than those on the right. A physics text, for example, however decontextualized, can be understood only if the reader possesses some knowledge of physics, irrespective of the degree of analysis of the language in which the text is written. The lines on the graph indicate the relative involvement of the three kinds of knowledge in performing in situations which move gradually along this continuum. To summarize the trend, the possibility of using other knowledge for more contextualized situations reduces the burden placed on linguistic knowledge in general and analyzed linguistic knowledge in particular. Thus, the role of analyzed knowledge becomes even more specialized; not only does it provide the learner with access to certain kinds of language use not possible with nonanalyzed knowledge but also does it provide the learner with a means of performing in situations for which even other knowledge—in particular, contextual knowledge—would be inadequate.

The relationship proposed between other knowledge, linguistic knowledge, and various other tasks is not unlike some early proposals for child first language acquisition. Brown (1956) was the first to argue that the child's conceptual understanding was the most important factor in language acquisition in that early language use depended on the child's hypotheses about the world and what the heard words referred to. Macnamara (1972) made a stronger claim and argued that the child learns language by first figuring out the meaning of utterances *independently* of the language and later sorting out the relationships between the words and the meanings. Thus, for Macnamara, the child learning a first language and operating somewhere at the far right of the task continuum is relying almost exclusively on other knowledge. Again, it is with developments such as schooling that the linguistic aspects of knowledge begin to overtake the conceptual and contextual aspects of knowledge in the solution to language-related problems.

Strategies of Learning and Communication

The status of strategies in problems of second language learning is at the moment controversial. Various proposals have been made, but comparisons among them are difficult because of the disparate interpretation of strategies adopted by the various theorists. In addition, the notion of strategies has been invoked in the explanation of a number of unrelated issues, exacerbating the problem of reaching consensus on the concept under investigation.

Two aspects of strategies which have often been examined are excluded in this framework. First, although particular strategies may have their greatest effect in dealing with certain types of difficulties (e.g., a problem of learning as opposed to a problem of communication), the strategies themselves are not classified in this way. Although such classifications are often proposed (e.g., Tarone, 1980), it seems that these descriptions best apply not to the strategies but to the problems they attempt to solve. Strategies deployed for one purpose—for example, communication—may well have a long-term effect on learning. The total effect of using a particular strategy, it seems, cannot be so restricted as to exclude a more diffuse and perhaps more subtle benefit. Second, the intentionality, or consciousness, with which the strategy is used seems also to be of little significance in the assessment of the strategy's effect. Consequently, both the learner's purpose in using a strategy and the consciousness with which the decision is made are probably impervious to accurate measurement and likely to be of limited importance in any case. What, then, is significant about strategies?

The conceptualization of strategies in the present paradigm is that they are the various activities or techniques used by learners when coping with a second language. Their effect is analogous to that of a catalyst in a chemical reaction; namely, the impact is on the rate rather than on the form of the process. Thus for language learning, the process of development is expected to honor the general principles laid out by the two-factor framework, but the ease or rapidity with which a learner may proceed through that process can be modified by effective use of strategies. In addition, strategies may actually appear to supplant formal proficiency by providing the learner with a means of dealing with situations for which the relevant language forms are lacking. However, since the learner has not actually progressed in the language, that ability to cope with a demanding situation does not really change the learner's status with respect to proficiency in the language per se. It is simply that the learner is more efficient at using whatever resources are available. The learner will progress in language mastery only through the gradual specialization of analyzed and automatic control.

In spite of this disclaimer about the effect of strategies on the process of language learning, there is a relationship between strategy use or ability and language proficiency. First, Bachman and Palmer (1981) have suggested that learners themselves differ along a measurable dimension of what might be called strategic ability. In addition, however, some evidence indicates that strategy use is effectively different for more advanced learners than for those who are less advanced. More advanced learners have been shown to derive more specific benefit from the use of particular strategies as opposed to less advanced learners who enjoy a lesser generalized effect (Bialystok, 1979b); more advanced learners show more sensitivity to the variety of strategies that are available, possibly because some strategies are simply more difficult to use, and so advanced learners benefit more by the availability of a greater and more flexible resource of strategies (Bialystok and Fröhlich, 1980); and finally, more advanced learners perform better in situations in which the solution to problems depends heavily on language strategies—that is, both formal and strategic ability improve concomitantly (Bialystok, 1980). Thus the use and impact of strategies is not unrelated to more formal aspects of proficiency and should therefore be examined in the context of the framework for language proficiency.

The interpretation of the role of strategies is related again to the two dimensions of language proficiency, Analyzed and Automatic. As various instructional experiences promote development along one of these dimensions, so too does the use of strategies advance the learner in one of these two ways. Strategies which assist in the automatization function might consist primarily of those strategies associated with practice (activities such as memorization and use of routines and prefabricated patterns). Strategies which primarily promote the analyzed control of the language would be those in which the learner uses knowledge of the language to arrive at deductions and inferences about the language. Many communication strategies are of this kind. Learners can only engage in strategies such as word coinage if their knowledge of the language is fairly advanced. Furthermore, the act of attempting to create a new word to fill a gap in proficiency may well make the learner's knowledge of some portion of the lexicon more analyzed. The learner may, for example, notice a regularity in that portion of the lexicon which was exploited in the construction of the coined word. Notice, however, that it is not necessarily possible to distinguish between the learning and communicative effects of the strategy, although deployed to solve a local communication problem, the strategy of word coinage may well result in learning.

To summarize, the various strategies assist the learner in the movement toward more automatic and more analyzed control over the target language. In addition, they help the learner to deal with local problems that arise in the use of the language. Since the strategies often rely on information that is not specific to the target language, their greatest effect of this kind will be in those situations that permit the introduction of other knowledge; that is, strategies may be invoked in much the same way as other knowledge to expedite communication in an imperfectly mastered language.

Individual Differences in Language Learning

Although models aim to provide a representation of what is essential and similar about all learners, clearly no model can capture the vast differences that characterize individuals. The general claim for individual learner differences in the present framework is much the same as that for various instructional approaches to language learning: some are probably better than others, and some aim to develop one of the two dimensions of proficiency rather than the other. In the first case, learners who are judged better according to any criteria (aptitude, attitude, motivation, intelligence, etc.) may proceed to the marked forms of knowledge more quickly than those who are less able in those ways. (Note, however, that no such evidence has ever been provided with respect to any of the factors mentioned above.) More important, however, their language-learning experience will not be any different from that of a less able learner; it may simply be easier. In the second case, different learners for reasons of either ability or need may develop more in terms of one of the two dimensions of control. This claim is potentially more significant if we are to consider the possibility of language for specific purposes.

There is some evidence of individual learner differences in the ability to analyze knowledge. It is probably the same difference which determines an individual's ability to analyze a body of information in math or the sciences for the purpose of deducing structural rules that distinguish as well the individual's ability to extrapolate regularity from a body of linguistic knowledge. Some evidence of this individual difference in the discovery of linguistic structure is offered by Kassin and Reber (1979) who attribute at least part of the variability to the learner being judged as an "internal" or "external" personality.

Other evidence for the role of individual differences is reported by Snow and Hoefnagel-Höhle (1979) who propose that grammatical and phonological ability are independent components of second language skill and that individuals vary with respect to their skill in each. Once the language skills have been separated, it is not a far step to extrapolate such divisions to the kinds of language controls proposed in the present framework. The same difference which underlies phonological as opposed to grammatical ability might also underlie the development of automatic access as opposed to analyzed knowledge of a target language.

On this view of the development of language proficiency, the learner's mastery of the target language is assessed in terms of development along two dimensions. These dimensions describe qualitative aspects of the learner's knowledge of the language in much the same way that similar analyses distinguish the depth or degree to which people understand principles in any field. Learners can demonstrate mastery of aspects of the language only when the task demands match the qualitative aspects of control the learner has over those portions of the language. And since develoment along the two dimensions may well be independent, so may be the learner's ability to function in different linguistic situations at various points in the development of proficiency, yielding apparently variable performance.

This paradigm is offered as one hypothesis to an explanation of variable linguistic control. It is theoretically consistent with other componential views of proficiency but differs in the localization of the components, specifically by proposing a more psycholinguistic origin for those components. The continued attempt will be to integrate this view with the other componential models of proficiency to generate a more comprehensive description of the intricate process involved in mastering a second language.

NOTES

1. The term *awareness* is used throughout but is not to be interpreted as *consciousness*. If consciousness is to be considered at all, then it is as a third dimension which is orthogonal to the two described in this framework; that is, any degree of consciousness is theoretically possible at any point along the analyzed dimension. Because of this free range of values, the concept has no explanatory power. *Awareness*, as it is used in the present context, is closer in meaning to *know* than it is to *conscious*.
2. In previous work I have called this end of the analyzed dimension "Explicit knowledge" and the nonanalyzed end, "Implicit knowledge." Because of the tendency to interpret *explicit* as implying conscious knowledge of rules, which is not intended by the concept in this case, I have selected the more neutral *analyzed* and *nonanalyzed*. These, I believe, represent the endpoints of the dimension.
3. Michael Sharwood Smith (personal communication) has suggested that both the nonanalyzed and Analyzed knowledge of the present framework are included in acquisition. It is only the articulated knowledge (described later) of the present framework that constitutes learning in Krashen's terms. In terms of the functions that Krashen assigns to learning and acquisition, this suggested mapping seems reasonable.

QUESTIONS FOR DISCUSSION

1. Bialystok draws a useful distinction between (unconscious) *knowledge* about the target language on the part of the second language learner and *access* to that knowledge. What thoughts do you have about the possible relationship between this intricate balance (knowledge vs. access) and consciousness raising (CR)? For example, is it reasonable to think of CR as a more valid endeavor for enhancing the learner's ability to call up what he already knows, or is it more valid as a means for imparting linguistic knowledge? Is it perhaps both but to varying degrees?
2. Researchers have noted that attainment of L2 grammatical accuracy for a given construction will not necessarily be uniform where the construction serves different discourse functions. For example, although the learner may appear to use inversion correctly for the asking of yes/no questions, he or she will not necessarily use it correctly if yes/no question form is being used as a "queclarative" (i.e., a negative statement phrased as an interrogative, as in *Would I lie to you*?), sometimes mistak-

enly called a rhetorical question. How would this kind of L2 performance be plotted on Bialystok's $+/-$ analytic/$+/-$ automatic grid, and how does the concept of "markedness" figure in?

3. Bialystok's model of language learning may be described as "componential" in that variability in learner proficiency is to be attributed to different points of intersection of the dimensions termed *Analyzed* and *Automatic*. Such variable proficiency may be related to the employment of methodologies whose performance objectives can be described by recourse to similar points of intersection of these same two dimensions—for example, grammar/translation: (exclusively) Analyzed; Natural Approach: (exclusively) Automatic; and so forth. How many other different methodologies are you familiar with, and to what extent are their objectives amenable to plotting in terms of the Bialystok schema?

4. Footnote 1 of Bialystok's paper discusses the difference between *awareness* and *consciousness*, as she is using these terms. What would you say is the relationship between these concepts and grammatical CR in pedagogy?

5. Bialystok proposes that there is basically one type of knowledge—in our case, linguistic knowledge—manifesting degrees of scope and degrees of analysis; that is, the greater the degree of analysis the more flexible and sophisticated is the learner's use of that knowledge. Compare this conception of linguistic knowledge with other perspectives—for example, perspectives in which learners are said to gain entirely different types of knowledge of a target language.

6. Discuss the following distinctions in terms of Bialystok's model:

   • proficiency versus knowledge
   • Analyzed knowledge versus articulated knowledge
   • articulated knowledge versus metalinguistic knowledge
   • comprehension and production

   Do you think these distinctions (as presented in this paper) are clear, comprehensible, and useful to the general field of pedagogical grammar?

7. Discuss the idea that being able to cite a grammatical rule (an L-Rule in the terminology proposed in our general introduction) does not necessarily imply Analyzed knowledge of the relevant area of the language.

8. Discuss the role of strategies as a facilitator or inhibitor of learning. Does a skillful user of strategies reduce to some degree the need for further progress in gaining Analyzed knowledge in contrast to a bad strategist who depends on further advances in Analyzed knowledge to achieve the same communicative success? That is, does the acquisition and use of successful strategies induce fossilization?

REFERENCES

Bachman, L., and A. Palmer. 1981. The construct validation of tests of communicative competence. Paper presented at the Colloquium on the Validation of Oral Proficiency Tests, University of Michigan, Ann Arbor.

Bialystok, E. 1976. The development of spatial concepts in language and thought. Ph.D. dissertation, University of Toronto.

Bialystok, E. 1979a. Explicit and implicit judgments of L2 grammaticality. *Language Learning* 29:81–103.

Bialystok, E. 1979b. The role of conscious strategies in second language proficiency. *Canadian Modern Language Review* 35:372–394.

Bialystok, E. 1980. On the relationship between formal proficiency and strategic ability. Paper presented at the Fourteenth Annual Meeting, TESOL, San Francisco, March 4–9.

Bialystok, E. 1982. On the relationship between knowing and using linguistic forms. *Applied Linguistics* 3:181–206.

Bialystok, E., and M. Frölich. 1980. Oral communication strategies for lexical difficulties. *Interlanguage Studies Bulletin* 5:3–30.

Brown, R. 1956. The original word game. In J. Bruner, J. Goodnow, and G. Austin (eds.), *A Study in Thinking*. New York: John Wiley & Sons, appendix.

Cathcart, R., M. Strong, and L. W. Fillmore. 1979. The social and linguistic behavior of good language learners. In C. Yorio, K. Perkins, and J. Schachter (eds.), *On TESOL '79: The Learner in Focus*. Washington, D.C.: TESOL.

Cazden, C. 1974. Play with language and metalinguistic awareness: one dimension of language experience. *The Urban Review* 7:28–29.

Chomsky, C. 1979. Consciousness *is* relevant to linguistic awareness. Paper presented at the International Seminar on Linguistic Awareness and Learning to Read, University of Victoria, Canada.

Chomsky, N. 1977. *Language and Responsibility*. New York: Pantheon Books.

Chomsky, N. 1980. *Rules and Representations*. New York: Harcourt Brace Jovanovich.

Clark, H., and E. Clark. 1977. *Psychology and Language*. New York: Harcourt Brace Jovanovich.

Cole, M., and S. Scribner. 1974. *Culture and Thought*. New York: John Wiley & Sons.

Cummins, J. 1981. The role of primary language development in promoting educational success for language minority students. Paper prepared for the Compendium on Bilingual-Bicultural Education. Sacramento: California State Department of Education.

Donaldson, M. 1978. *Children's Minds*. Glasgow: Collins Sons & Co.

Gleitman, H., and L. Gleitman. 1979. Language use and language judgment. In C. Fillmore, D. Kempler, and W. Wang (eds.), *Individual Differences in Language Ability and Language Behavior*. New York: Academic Press.

Hakuta, K. 1974. Prefabricated patterns and the emergence of structure in second language learning. *Language Learning* 24:287–297.

Huttenlocher, J. 1974. The origins of language comprehension. In R. Solso (ed.), *Theories of Cognitive Psychology: The Loyola Symposium*. Potomac, Md.: Lawrence Erlbaum Associates.

Jakobovits, L. 1970. *Foreign Language Learning: A Psycholinguistic Analysis of the Issues*. Rowley, Mass.: Newbury House.

Kassin, S., and A. Reber. 1979. Locus of control and the learning of an artificial language. *Journal of Research in Personality* 13:112–118.

Krashen, S. 1981. *Second Language Acquisition and Second Language Learning*. Oxford: Pergamon Press.

Lado, R. 1957. *Linguistics Across Cultures*. Ann Arbor: University of Michigan Press.

Larsen-Freeman, D., ed. 1980. *Discourse Analysis in Second Language Learning*. Rowley, Mass.: Newbury House.

Macnamara, J. 1972. The cognitive basis of language learning in infants. *Psychological Review* 79:1–13.

Mattingly, I. 1972. Reading, the linguistic process and linguistic awareness. In J. Kavanagh and I. Mattingly (eds.), *Language by Ear and by Eye*. Cambridge, Mass.: MIT Press.

Mattingly, I. 1979. Reading, linguistic awareness, and language acquisition. Paper presented at the International Seminar on Linguistic Awareness and Learning to Read. University of Victoria, British Columbia.

Miller, G., and P. Johnson-Laird. 1976. *Language and Perception*. Cambridge: Cambridge University Press.

Piaget, J. 1954. *The Construction of Reality in the Child*. New York: Ballantine Books.

Polanyi, M. 1958. *Personal Knowledge*. Chicago: University of Chicago Press.

Polanyi, M. 1966. *The Tacit Dimension*. Garden City, N.Y.: Doubleday.

Pylyshyn, Z. 1973. What the mind's eye tells the mind's brain: a critique of mental imagery. *Psychological Bulletin* 80:1–24.

Pylyshyn, Z. 1981. The imagery debate: analogue media versus tacit knowledge. *Psychological Review*.

Reber, A. 1976. Implicit learning of synthetic languages: the role of instruction set. *Journal of Experimental Psychology: Human Learning and Memory* 2:88–94.

Reber, A., and R. Allen. 1978. Analogic and abstraction strategies in synthetic grammar learning: a functionalist interpretation. *Cognition* 6:189–221.

Reber, A., and S. Lewis. 1977. Implicit learning: an analysis of the form and structure of a body of tacit knowledge. *Cognition* 5:333–361.

Richards, J. 1973. Error analysis and second language strategies. In J. Oller and J. Richards (eds.), *Focus on the Learner*. Rowley, Mass.: Newbury House.

Ryle, G. 1949. *The Concept of Mind*. London: Hutchinson House.

Savignon, S. 1972. *Communicative Competence: An Experiment in Foreign Language Teaching*. Philadelphia: Center for Curriculum Development.

Scheffler, I. 1965. *Conditions of Knowledge*. Glenview, Ill.: Scott, Forsman, and Co.

Seliger, H. 1979. On the nature and function of language rules in language teaching. *TESOL Quarterly* 13:359–369.

Snow, C., and C. Ferguson, eds. 1977. *Talking to Children: Language Input and Acquisition*. Cambridge: Cambridge University Press.

Snow, C., and M. Hofnagel-Höhle. 1979. Individual differences in second-language ability: a factor-analysis study. *Language and Speech* 22:151–162.

Swain, M. 1981. Linguistic expectations: core, extended, and immersion programs. *Canadian Modern Language Review: Festschrift for H. H. Stern* 37:486–497.

Tarone, E. 1980. Communication strategies, foreigner talk, and repair in interlanguage. Paper presented at the Fourteenth Annual Meeting of TESOL, San Francisco, March 4–9.

Tarone, E., U. Frauenfelder, and L. Selinker. 1976. Systematicity/variability and stability/instability in interlanguage systems. In H. Brown (ed.), *Papers in Second Language Acquisition*. Ann Arbor: Language Learning.

Terrell, T. 1981. The natural approach in bilingual education. Unpublished manuscript.

4

Consciousness Raising and the Second Language Learner

Michael Sharwood Smith
Rijksuniversiteit, Utrecht

The notions "explicit knowledge" and "implicit knowledge" have occurred in various forms both in the literature on language instruction and within a more strictly learning-oriented context.[1] Explicit knowledge, broadly speaking, denotes a conscious analytic awareness of the formal properties of the target language whereas implicit knowledge means an intuitive feeling for what is correct and acceptable (Bialystok, 1978). Although, as will become clear in the course of this paper, this binary distinction needs a great deal of qualification, it does serve to highlight generally different kinds of outcome resulting from the process of learning a new language. The ultimate, most highly prized goal of learning—that is, spontaneous, unreflecting language use—is uncontroversial. How this is achieved is, of course, a matter of considerable debate. Certain trends in language-learning research suggest that promoting conscious awareness of language structure is at best a luxury and does not lead in any meaningful way to the attainment of this ultimate goal. On the face of it, this lends support to the Direct Method and more recent attempts to focus on getting the learner to perform in lifelike communicative ways rather than in a strictly formal classroom context of the traditional type. A closer look at the issues, however, reveals how simplistic such pedagogical inferences are and how dubious the distinction is between two theoretically distinct types of knowledge where no allowance is made for different degrees of explicitness and the possibility of interaction between different types of competences.

"Consciousness Raising and the Second Language Learner" by Michael Sharwood Smith, 1981, *Applied Linguistics*, vol. 2, no. 2, pp. 159–168. Reprinted with permission of Oxford University Press.

It is a basic problem in teaching to know how much one has to tell a learner about the language and what to do with the language, and to what extent mere practice will invoke the appropriate learning mechanisms to cope with the task in hand. It takes a committed audiolingualist or believer in the Direct Method in its extreme and most consistent form to deny all learners even occasional explanations of linguistic structures. People who attempt such hard-line implicit methods will swiftly come to appreciate the fact that they require an inordinate amount of time and energy: in other words, full-scale intensive teaching programs are necessary for any success to be guaranteed. This also goes for a methodologically inspired refusal to use the native language in the classroom: where one translation equivalent would resolve the problem, long complicated paraphrases are needed to show the learner, in the target language, what a given word or expression means and how it is used. It is difficult to assess exactly how many people stick to such methodological principles in practice: one suspects that many deviations and compromises occur. For example, it is notoriously difficult to deny adult learners explicit information about the target language (TL) since their intellectual maturity as well as their previous teaching/learning experience makes them cry out for explanations. Teachers, one suspects, often resort to explanations (and the native language, for that matter). If explanations about the structural properties of the TL directed towards younger learners are rather less common, this is probably more due to the lack of intellectual maturity in the learners involved than to the particular methodological leanings of the teacher. Teachers, and doubtless many learners as well, view explanations as shortcuts. It may be "naturalistic" to learn languages in a purely intuitive manner, but how long will it take to amass a sufficient amount of implicit knowledge and the appropriate skills for using it? It may even be rewarding to discover formal regularities in a more or less conscious manner on one's own, without the aid of the teacher or textbook, but, again, what time is needed to accomplish this in more than just a piecemeal manner? The short cut, a ready-made *a priori* explanation (partial or otherwise), is attractive: at the very least, it provides an insight into the task and means of labelling and specifying the problem. By revealing some pattern or system in the target language, the teacher holds out the promise of a short cut as far as learning is concerned, in other words a shorter and more effective way of mastering a structure (via practice, of course). The fact that the young child may not have this (hypothetical) possibility to the same degree, that is, learning via explicit knowledge, puts him/her at a disadvantage when compared with the mature learner. This is presumably the motivation for the cognitive-code approach to language teaching. Armed with explicit information about particular linguistic tasks, the learner can use conscious applications of rules to practice in and out of class and to communicate in the target language at a higher level of proficiency, albeit without the speed and spontaneity associated with the notion of "fluency." Fluency is assumed to come later and as a result of practicing TL structures in formal and informal, naturalistic ways. It is therefore quite reasonable to state that the more mature the learner, the greater the variety of resources that he or she can exploit in learning (see

Faerch and Kasper, 1980, pp. 106–108). The onus is surely on those who wish to deny the value of explicit teaching techniques to show that explicit teaching is a waste of time and energy: the evidence will have to be very convincing.

What might be called *language consciousness raising* in the classroom is sometimes assumed to consist of the pedantic giving and testing of rules and lists of vocabulary items, that is, a complete and unrelenting focus on the formal structure of the TL. This impression is probably the result of what people associate with the grammar-translation method where learners were required to learn by rote and produce rules and lists of words almost as much for intellectual exercise as for learning to express meaning in the target language. The conveying of a rule or any other kind of information about the language can, however, be more or it can be less reduced to the familiar metalinguistic prescriptions of traditional grammars. And it may or may not be required of the learner to actually produce those prescriptions himself. The relevant information can vary in the degree of elaboration or conciseness with which it is presented, as well as the degree of explicitness or intensity in the way attention is drawn to the relevant regularities. Strictly speaking, the discovery of regularities in the target language, whether blindly intuitive or conscious, or coming in between these two extremes, will always be *self*-discovery. The question is to what extent that discovery is guided by the teacher. The guidance, where consciousness raising is involved, can take more or less time or space and it can be more or less direct and explicit. It is one thing, for example, to set up an illustrative pair of examples and draw the learner's attention to the relevant distinctions using verbal or nonverbal (visual) "hints" and quite another thing to give a formal rule couched in traditional metalinguistic terms and thereby appeal also to the learner's cognitive analytic capacities.[2] In both cases the learner is being made conscious of some aspect of the language itself but the manner varies. We may usefully speak of four basic types of manifestations as far as language consciousness raising is concerned. These are represented in Figure 4–1: a hypothetical ten-point scale is used; the types are represented within the four cells:

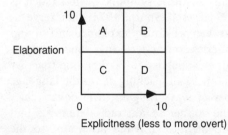

Figure 4–1 Consciousness raising in language learning

To begin with Type D, the most familiar and traditional type, this form of highly overt consciousness raising may be found in the standard school grammar and is characterized by fairly concise prescriptions couched in a metalanguage that is supposedly within the grasp of the teacher and learner alike. This

assumption is safer where mother tongue teaching has involved relevant terminology like "adjectives," "nouns," "clauses," and so on, less safe where mother
tongue grammar instruction has been accomplished in less formalistic ways.
The accuracy and effectiveness of such prescriptions is often limited. There
may be strictly linguistic reasons for this or the reasons may be of a psychologi-
cal/didactic character. An accurate, technically sophisticated formulation may
help a linguist to appreciate a theoretical point or an insight into a given
language but may be lost on the learner and the teacher as well. A technically
simple formation which somehow manages to retain the insight may nevertheless fail because it becomes clumsy, vague, and ambiguous: the conveying of
the insight is not guaranteed. Also, even if the statement of the information is
clear, comprehensible, and applicable, its effectiveness has to be assured via
practice in TL.

Type C—brief, indirect "clues"—if done well, may give the learner a
greater feeling of self-discovery in that the regularity is only hinted at, using
some linguistic or nonlinguistic perceptual clue. Also it is easily incorporated
into some naturalistic exercise. It may, however, be necessary to confine this
type of consciousness raising to relatively simple regularities in the language or
to combine it with other techniques. One might imagine some perceptually
attractive way of emphasizing the third person singular endings, say, but it is
difficult to see how this could be done effectively in an unelaborated manner
for semantically complex phenomena such as English aspect. A safer way of
ensuring that the appropriate insight was gained in such cases would be to opt
for Type B, namely, elaborated *and* explicit guidance. One obvious way of
doing this would be along the lines developed by Lev Landa (see Landa, 1976
and Sharwood Smith, 1978 for further discussion) in which explanation is
broken down algorithmically into easy, highly structured stages giving the
relevant differentiations and decisions that the learner must make in order to
use the particular pattern or rule correctly. This elaborate manner of presentation can be done in a less explicit manner, that is, more covertly as Type A, or
there can be a teaching sequence in which the more explicit Type B explanations are followed up with less explicit versions (Type A) where the teacher's
direct assistance is gradually reduced via substitute symbolic devices (such as
Engels's mediators: see Engels, 1970; Sharwood Smith, 1978) that serve as
mnemonics and "summarizers" of what was previously explained in full and
explicit terms. These four basic types of consciousness raising, which summarize what are actually two dimensions along which it can vary, should together
provide evidence that what people sometimes call teaching *about* the language
can be accomplished in a great number of ways ranging from covert clues
"hidden" in the input organized for the learner to abstract statements and
varying also in the time and space devoted to drawing attention[3] to the
structures in question.

The problem of whether learners should themselves be able to verbalize
rules (see Lawler and Selinker, 1971), or to use Bialystok's term, articulate (see
Bialystok, 1981), is another matter. Consciousness raising can clearly be accomplished without requiring of learners that they talk about what they have

become aware of. It seems fairly certain that only some learners are able to do this anyway. One of the major flaws in the grammar-translation method, whatever its goals, may indeed have been to emphasize this rather special metalinguistic ability. Another flaw may have been the extent to which emphasis was placed on the rote learning of rules and vocabulary out of context. There may be a place for getting learners to articulate rules, but this should be tied to the type of learner and the general learning context. There may even be a place for some rote learning. But it is also clear that these questions should be considered apart from the general consideration of whether or not to draw the learner's attention to structural regularities in the course of teaching. This aspect of the grammar-translation method may stand up better to criticism than the other two.

Teaching about the language is currently relevant to the kind of debate going on in second language acquisition concerning the role explicit and implicit knowledge play in developing the competence of the learner. There has been a tendency to lay stress on the natural language-learning ability that every human being has, irrespective of color or class. The ability to analyze language in a conscious manner is seen as a different kind of skill, fostered in formal classroom teaching (by association an educated middle class phenomenon); hence the apparent attractiveness[4] of the creative construction hypothesis developed by Dulay and Burt and others which emphasizes the universal developmental patterns supposed to exist in second language acquisition over and above those patterns which are due to various differences in learners' language backgrounds. It seems reasonable to suppose that there are universal patterns, but their extent and significance are still a subject of much discussion (see doubts raised in Rosansky, 1977; Larsen-Freeman, 1977; Hatch, 1978; Hyltenstam, 1978). Of greater interest here is the theory developed by Krashen which incorporates the notions of explicit knowledge and implicit knowledge, what he calls, respectively, *learned competence* and *acquired competence*. The evidence for the distinction is inferred or investigated via, among other things, studies on morpheme acquisition: differing language backgrounds seem to play no real role when the learner has to perform spontaneously without focussing on form; learned competence (explicit knowledge) is tapped only when there *is* time and focus on form (see Krashen, 1979; Sharwood Smith, 1979, 1980). This theory is dynamic or flexible in the sense that it is under constant revision and more recent versions have played down the generality of learned competence (not everybody has it) and its importance (it does not aid acquisition).

Krashen's recent versions of the model are significant for teaching in that there is absolutely no "interface" between the two types of knowledge. If a given learner "learns" a rule at one stage and then, at a later stage gives evidence of being able to use it swiftly and without reflection, we are not permitted to say that learned knowledge has been transferred to acquired knowledge. Rather, the learner has in the intervening time, acquired the rule by another (intuitive) route; that is, in the course of exposure to the target language, the acquisition device has been stimulated to (re)construct the target rule from the data and not via some kind of "osmosis" obtaining between the two knowledge sources in the mind of the learner. Thus there are rules which learners "learn" (consciously) and rules which learners "acquire." From learner performance in tests and interviews we may observe that some rules are acquired but the learner is quite unable to account for them in any explicit way, that is, they are not part of learned competence. In other cases, rules are verbalized by the learners but may not turn up in spontaneous speech, and in other cases rules may turn up in spontaneous speech and also in the explicit verbalizations. This and other research (see Bialystok, 1979, e.g.) is strongly suggestive of the fact that the two knowledge sources exist. In Krashen's view, what is here called "consciousness raising" would be a luxury of highly dubious value since he holds that:

1. Learners can only profit from learned knowledge after a certain age, that is, roughly puberty (see Krashen, 1979, p. 153).
2. Learned knowledge is normally only accessible given time and focus on form.
3. Some learners hardly ever (and some never) use learned knowledge (see also Lawler and Selinker, 1971, for a related discussion).

There is also the point that only certain easy rules can become part of the learner's "mental baggage" (see McLaughlin, 1978, p. 319): that is, there are capacity restrictions on the Monitor. It would seem that, following this line of thinking, time taken up to make learners aware of linguistic regularities would be better spent fostering acquisition (see Fig. 4–2) without consciousness raising.

There have been other attempts to specify the role of explicit and implicit knowledge in second language performance which have not adopted the extreme "no interface" position taken by Krashen. McLaughlin, in a critical review of Krashen's model (in McLaughlin 1978), claims that the relevant phenomena can be more economically accounted for by using an information-processing model along lines favored by cognitive psychologists. In McLaughlin's suggested account, there are two types of performance behaviors depending upon whether "controlled processes" are being used or "automatic processes." The general idea is that one first begins slowly, haltingly, sometimes with a great deal of conscious awareness and then, in the course of time, we are able to automatize the whole process and execute the relevant programs and routines swiftly and without reflection. Krashen's reaction to this (see

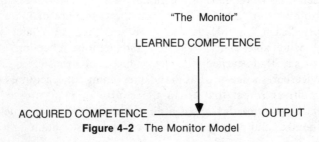

Figure 4-2   The Monitor Model

Krashen 1979) is to categorize this as a "learning precedes acquisition" account, which is not allowed in Krashen's model, since learned knowledge acts as a "Monitor," that is, a corrective mechanism with acquired output as its input. Krashen claims that strings (utterances) are always initiated by *acquired* competence (that is L2 competence or, where there are gaps, perhaps L1 acquired competence). In Krashen's view, McLaughlin's ideas are just speculations whereas Krashen's are at least, he claims, supported by empirical evidence; at least the question as to how learners seem to be able to perform automatically in the target language without being able to give any account of the rules does indeed need to be answered. We may note in passing that the fact that learners are not able to verbalize rules or even indicate in some indirect ways facts about the target language does not mean that at some time in their learning career they were not dimly or very clearly aware of structural problems to be overcome.

Whatever the view of the underlying processes in second language learning, it is quite clear and uncontroversial to say that most spontaneous performance is attained by dint of practice. In the course of actually performing in the target language, the learner gains the necessary control over its structures such that he or she can use them quickly without reflection. Now let us suppose, looking at Figure 4–3, that some aspects of second language performance can in principle be planned from the start entirely on the basis of explicit knowledge: a good oral example of this would be preparing a short question, a speech or telephone conversation where certain things can be predicted in advance. You know what you will have to say. You have attended an effective course of formal instruction giving you a range of procedures which allow you to put together utterances in a completely conscious manner. Let us also suppose that this type of activity is repeated again and again. In such situations, it is surely reasonable to suppose that a certain number of structures planned and performed slowly and consciously can eventually develop into automatized behavior. Utterances initiated by explicit knowledge (see arrow no. 1) can provide feedback into implicit knowledge. A good example would be placing the verb at the end of a subordinate clause in German; bad examples would be linguistic phenomena so complex and diffuse as to defy pedagogically attractive explanation: here conscious attention may be evoked but with no productive result.

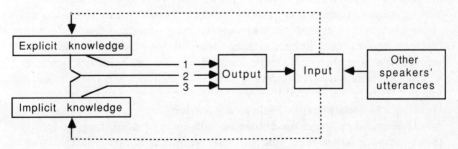

Figure 4-3 Linguistic input and output: three potential sources of feedback

The exclusive use of explicit knowledge is inevitably going to be restricted, especially where "hard rules" are involved. It may be considerably more likely in *foreign* language learning where the learners are of appropriate age and maturity and their instruction is exclusively formalistic, that is, focussing on Type D teaching. However, the point at issue here is not whether it is frequent but rather whether it is in principle possible. This is presumably an empirical question, and experiments using learners' introspections might help to shed light on this. But even when we consider situations where learned knowledge and acquired knowledge interact to produce utterances (see arrow 2 in Fig. 3), the ultimate, unified results are presumably available to the speaker as potential feedback into acquired (as well as learned) knowledge. Thus utterance arrived at partly via explicit knowledge can come to affect implicit (acquired) knowledge. This means that, when considering the input to either of the two knowledge systems, we should include not only incoming utterances from other speakers or writers but also the utterances produced by the learner. The verb placed consciously at the end of the clause under orders from the Monitor can become part of a total utterance produced in some natural or naturalistic context. If the utterance is judged successful (see Vigil and Oller, 1976; Sharwood Smith, 1979), it is reasonable to assume that it can partake in the general input into either of the knowledge sources. The flow of information from one source to others is formalized, in Figure 3, as a process mediated by the learner's own output. In this model this is represented as a potential movement via output without specifying at the moment whether only the final or latter stages of the process of production are involved or whether any intermediate output during utterance planning might be involved as well. The model represents the storage and movement of linguistic information, but it is assumed that a full account should formalize the role of the assessment made by the learner of the cognitive and affective impact of his or her utterances and any feedback where the learner has observed and is sensitive to assessment by interlocutors.

In conclusion, consciousness raising cannot or should not be treated simplistically. In the same way extremist approaches to language teaching, whether or not they are based on such hypotheses and others, neither reflect the great truths nor indeed the practice and interpretation by the average language teacher. While the empirical evidence for the impermeability and primacy of the acquisition device in the second or foreign language learner is hotly contested, there is every reason to accept the older, intuitively attractive version which says that explicit knowledge may aid acquisition via practice; learners who cannot articulate rules may still have access to the relevant information in explicit knowledge; learners who do not have such access may well *at one time* have had access to such information when the relevant rule had not yet been automatized; learners who do not appear to automatize rules that they have had in explicit knowledge for long periods of time may simply not be disposed to spend the extra time and energy transferring the information to implicit knowledge: that is, fossilization has occurred in that part of their learning development where "learning" has in fact preceded acquisition.

This account does not exclude pure acquisition but it allows for more than what either Krashen seems to allow for or indeed what recent approaches to language teaching methodology seem to allow for. There is nevertheless no reason to assume that consciousness raising by the teacher and conscious learning by the learner cannot be investigated in a systematic way using some less simplistic model as a guide.

NOTES

1. This paper is a much extended and adapted version of a paper given at the 2nd Annual Conference on "l'acquisition d'une langue étrangère: problèmes et perspectives" entitled: "Alternative perspectives on the notion 'explicit knowledge' in second language learning" at the University of Paris-Vincennes, April 1980. The paper has hopefully benefited from useful comments made during the discussions. Thanks are due to Vivian Cook, Eric Kellerman, Bill Littlewood, Barry McLaughlin, and Clive Purdue, among others, who attended the Colchester Second Language Acquisition Workshop, 1st June, 1980.
2. An interesting example of this technique, in a strictly learner-research context, is the test in Bialystok and Fröhlich (1980) designed to assess inferencing ability by indirectly suggesting cross-language correspondences between Danish and English using pairs such as *hvad-what*.
3. For a corresponding discussion of the different degrees of consciousness or attention in the learner, see Tarone (1979).
4. Kellerman makes a similar inference in his article, "Transfer or no transfer, where we are now," (1979) in *Studies in Second Language Learning* 2(1):38.

QUESTIONS FOR DISCUSSION

1. Discuss the usefulness of making the target language system explicit for the learner with reference to different aspects of that system (different areas of the grammar, the lexicon, phonology, pragmatics, etc.). In each case, discuss how elaborate you think the explanations and descriptions should be (cf. Fig. 1).
2. The point was made in the Bialystok paper that "we know more than we can tell" and also that "concepts are not encoded as words." What relevance do those observations have to Sharwood Smith's discussion here of the practice of rule articulation in consciousness raising?
3. Discuss any parallels and contrasts you may find when comparing the distinctions proposed in the Bialystok paper with the ideas put forth in this paper.
4. Both Krashen and Sharwood Smith assume two different types of knowledge. Discuss the difference(s) between these two perspectives.

REFERENCES

Bialystok, E. 1978. A theoretical model of second language learning. *Language Learning* 28:69–84.
Bialystok, E. 1981. Some evidence for the integrity and interaction of two knowledge sources. In R. Andersen (ed.), *New Dimensions in Second Language Acquisition Research*. Rowley, Mass.: Newbury House.

Bialystok, E., and M. Frölich, 1980. Oral communication strategies for lexical difficulties. *Interlanguage Studies Bulletin* **5**:1–31.

Engels, L. 1970. The function of grammar in the teaching of English as a foreign language. *ITL, A Review of Applied Linguistics* **10**:11–24.

Faerch, C., and G. Kasper. 1980. Processes and strategies in foreign language learning and communication. *Interlanguage Studies Bulletin* **5**:47–119.

Hatch, E. 1978. Apply with caution. *Studies in Second Language Acquisition* **2**:123–143.

Hyltenstam, K. 1978. Variation in interlanguage syntax. Working Paper no. 18, Phonetics Laboratory, Department of General Linguistics, Lund University.

Krashen, S. 1979. A response to McLaughlin, "The monitor model, some methodological considerations." *Language Learning* **29**:151–167.

Landa, L. 1976. *Instructional Regulation and Control.* Englewood Cliffs, N.J.: Educational Technology Publications.

Larsen-Freeman, D. 1977. An explanation for the morpheme orders of ESL. In E. Hatch (ed.), *Second Language Acquisition.* Rowley, Mass.: Newbury House.

Lawler, J., and L. Selinker. 1971. On paradoxes, rules, and research in second language learning. *Language Learning* **21**:27–43.

McLaughlin, B. 1978. The Monitor Model, some methodological considerations. *Language Learning* **28**:309–322.

Rosansky, E. 1977. Explaining morpheme acquisition orders: Focus on frequency. In G. Henning (ed.), *Proceedings of the Second Los Angeles Second Language Research Forum.* Los Angeles: UCLA English/TESL Department.

Sharwood Smith, M. 1978. Applied linguistics and the psychology of instruction: *Studies in Second Language Acquisition* **1**:91–115. A case for transfusion? In this volume.

Sharwood Smith, M. 1979. Optimalizing interlanguage feedback in the foreign language learner. *Studies in Second Language Acquisition* **2**:17–29.

Sharwood Smith, M. 1980. On the Monitor Model. *Cornucopia* **1**.

Tarone, E. 1979. Interlanguage as chameleon. *Language Learning* **29**:181–193.

Vigil, N., and J. Oller. 1976. Rule fossilization: A tentative model. *Language Learning* **26**:281–295.

5
Some Theories
of Communicative
Competence

Michael Canale
Merrill Swain
The Ontario Institute for Studies in Education

In order to arrive at a theory of communicative competence that is suitable for our research purposes, it is useful to consider in some detail some of the theories of communicative competence that have been proposed. There are many different ways in which these theories can be classified and presented; we have chosen to begin with what we consider to be theories of basic communication skills and work up to more comprehensive and integrated theories. It should be made clear that our classification of the different theories to be considered is based solely on the *emphasis* which each puts on grammatical competence, sociolinguistic competence, other areas of competence, and their components; there are few models of communicative competence that neglect important aspects of communication completely. In this section, then, we will present several representative theories and examine their aims, theoretical bases, and some empirical data bearing on each, where available. We will also discuss some advantages and disadvantages of these theories with reference to second language approaches for general programs.

THEORIES OF BASIC COMMUNICATION SKILLS

Theories of basic communication skills, more so than the other types of communicative theories we will examine, seem to be designed with general second language programs in mind. A theory of basic communication skills

"Theoretical Bases of Communicative Approaches to Second Language Teaching and Testing" by Michael Canale and Merrill Swain, 1980, *Applied Linguistics*, vol. 1, no. 1, pp. 8–24. Reprinted with permission of Oxford University Press.

can be characterized as one that emphasizes the minimum level of (mainly oral) communication skills needed to get along in, or cope with, the most common second language situations the learner is likely to face. Thus Savignon (1972) is concerned mainly with the skills that are needed to get one's meaning across, to do things in the second language, to say what one really wants to say. Schulz (1977) expresses a similar concern. Van Ek (1976) states as the general objective for the "threshold level" for general second language programs that "the learners will be able to survive (linguistically speaking) in temporary contacts with foreign language speakers in everyday situations, whether as visitors to the foreign country or with visitors to their own country, and to establish and maintain social contacts" (pp. 24–25). Much of the research on basic communication skills tends to put less emphasis on other aspects of communicative competence such as knowledge of the appropriateness of utterances with respect to sociocultural context (e.g., Rivers, 1973; Schulz, 1977; and some of the early research discussed by Paulston, 1974) or knowledge of discourse (e.g., Savignon, 1972; Van Ek, 1976). Furthermore, some of the communicative approaches based on this work do not emphasize grammatical accuracy (e.g., Palmer, 1978; Savignon, 1972).

It is not always clear just what skills are included in theories of basic communication skills. For example, Savignon (1972) makes explicit reference only to grammatical skills (e.g., pronunciation, vocabulary), communicative tasks with respect to particular communicative functions (e.g., greeting, leave taking, information getting, information giving), and other factors such as willingness to express oneself in the second language, resourcefulness in making use of limited grammatical skills, and knowledge of kinesic and paralinguistic aspects of the second language (e.g., facial expressions, gestures). The criteria she adopts for evaluating the communicative performance of her students include effort to communicate, amount of communication, comprehensibility and suitability, naturalness and poise in keeping a verbal interaction in hand, and accuracy (semantic) of information. However, she provides no description or specification of the grammatical and other skills required in, say, information getting, nor is there any empirical justification of the criteria for evaluation.

Van Ek (1976) provides perhaps the clearest statement of basic communication skills that we have come across. His model emphasizes "language functions" (or communicative functions) and "notions," and considers only in second place what language forms must be known to give expression to these functions and notions. He supplies lists of general language functions (e.g., imparting and seeking factual information, getting things done by some one, socializing), specific language functions (e.g., under the general heading "imparting and seeking factual information" are included identifying, reporting, correcting, and asking), general notions (e.g., existential, spatial, temporal), specific notions (e.g., names, addresses, likes and dislikes), topic areas (e.g., personal identification, house and home, travel, food and drink), settings (e.g., home, school), and roles (e.g., stranger, friend). All of these factors are involved in determining the particular inventories of vocabulary, structures, and grammatical categories that he proposes. But in spite of these specifications, there are serious gaps in the description of certain skills. For example, there is no description of any rules of language use bearing on appropriateness of utterances, even though factors such as role, topic, setting, notion, and function are considered in the model.

As concerns the theoretical bases of theories of basic communication skills, we think it is important to consider two principles: (1) that these theories can be said to specify a minimum level of communication skills and (2) that more effective second language learning takes place if emphasis is put from the beginning on getting one's meaning across and not on the grammaticalness and appropriateness of one's utterances.

Consider (1). There is no clear sense in which any theory of language that we are familiar with specifies what minimum level of skills is necessary to communicate in a given language. Notions of a minimum level based on language varieties such as pidgins and creoles (cf. Bickerton, 1975; Hymes, 1971, e.g.) are of no clear relevance, since these language varieties are generally not mutually comprehensible with the superordinate and subordinate languages they are based on. Furthermore, the notion of a minimum or threshold level as used by Van Ek (1976), for example, is in no way clearly related to the notion of a threshold level as it is understood by psycholinguists such as Cummins (1979). In this latter's work it is suggested that there may be threshold levels in the native language that the learner of a second language must attain in order to avoid cognitive disadvantages, and that must be attained in the second language to allow the potentially beneficial aspects of bilingualism on cognitive development and educational achievement to develop. Cummins (1979) mentions no attempts to characterize the psycholinguistic notion of threshold level in the manner in which Van Ek (1976) characterizes the communicative notion, and it is not clear whether a description of the former notion would be more or less comprehensive than the latter or in what ways the two descriptions would overlap. It would certainly be worthwhile to investigate the notion of threshold level that Cummins proposes in more detail before deciding whether or not to adopt certain aspects or all of Van Ek's model. For example, a close examination of the communicative competence of the immersion students discussed by Swain (1978) might be carried out with reference to Van Ek's model. Such an examination might be especially relevant and instructive since the immersion studies described by Swain (1974, 1978) are cited by Cummins (1979) as evidence for the positive effects that bilingualism can have on cognitive functioning and academic achievement.

Consider now (2), the view that more effective second language learning takes place if emphasis is placed immediately on getting one's meaning across rather than on the grammaticalness and appropriateness of one's utterances. With respect to emphasis on meaning over grammaticalness, it is quite reasonable to assume that since in acquiring a first language the child seems to focus more on being understood than on speaking grammatically, then second language acquisition might be allowed to proceed in this manner. Furthermore, since in first language acquisition most parents and peers seem to be more interested in finding out what a child has to say than in how he/she says it, then the second language teacher might assume a similar role to provide a more natural context for second language learning. However, although both neurological (e.g., Lenneberg 1967; Penfield and Roberts, 1959) and cognitive (e.g., Piaget, 1954) theories suggest that similarities might be expected to exist in acquiring first and second languages in childhood, the onset of lateralization (Scovel, 1978) and of formal operations (Krashen, 1975; Rosansky, 1975) in early adolescence significantly affects the means by which new language data are processed and stored. Effective teaching of a second language should take this into account by modifying the presentation of the material to suit the dominant processing mechanisms of the learner.

Thus although the view that second language teaching should mirror parental "teaching" of the first language may be appropriate with respect to young learners of a second language, we hesitate to endorse it in relation to adolescent and adult learners for several reasons. First, although it is clear that certain learner errors are the same in first and second language acquisition (cf. Dulay and Burt, 1974, e.g.), others are clearly not—for example, interlanguage transfer (cf. Canale, Mougeon, and Beniak, 1978; Schachter and Rutherford, 1979, e.g.). Thus not all the grammatical inaccuracies a second language learner makes are necessarily those that a native speaker of the second language is likely to overlook, either because the latter does not expect them or finds it otherwise difficult to process them for meaning. Second, it is not clear that adolescent and adult second language learners themselves are prepared or willing at the early stages to put emphasis exclusively on getting their meaning across. Davies (1978) summarizes a number of studies of adolescent and adult second language learners that suggest that receptive skills should be emphasized at the early stages of introductory classes but that production skills should not. Savignon (1972) found that college students in her experimental class in which emphasis was put on getting one's meaning across rather than on grammaticality, showed a significant drop in integrative motivation (i.e., the desire to think and act like a native speaker of French) when compared with groups of students in which emphasis was not put on getting one's meaning across. She comments that "it may be hypothesized that the initial difficulty as well as shock experienced by some in being asked to perform like native Frenchmen was responsible for the decrease in integrative orientation" (p. 60). Third, it is not clear that second language learners will develop grammatical accuracy in the course of their second language program if emphasis is not put on this aspect from the start. It may be that certain grammatical inaccuracies will tend to "fossilize"—that is, persist over time in spite of further language training—more when grammatical accuracy is not emphasized at the beginning, resulting in a more or less perma-nent classroom "interlanguage," that is, a language system that may satisfy basic communicative needs in the classroom but does not correspond entirely to the language systems used by native speakers of the second language (cf. Selinker, 1974; Selinker, Swain, and Dumas, 1975; Swain, 1974, for discussion of these notions). There are no data from later stages of study available on the groups Savignon (1972) examined, but there are some data from studies of primary immersion programs suggesting that even with young children, grammatical accuracy in the oral mode does not improve much after a certain stage, perhaps when the learners have reached a level of grammatical accuracy adequate to serve their communicative needs which, importantly, do not typically include interaction with native French-speaking peers (cf. Harley and Swain, 1978).

As to the other aspects of (2), that is that emphasis should be put on getting one's meaning across rather than on the sociocultural appropriateness of utterances, two comments seem relevant. First, it may well be the case that there are more or less universal conditions of appropriateness that hold for the common communicative functions that a second language learner in the early stages of a program is likely to be concerned with (cf. Widdowson, 1975, on this point). For example, it is reasonable to assume that the appropriateness conditions for giving a command in any language include the speaker's belief that the hearer has the ability and right to see that the command is carried out, that the speaker has the right to give a command to the hearer, and so forth. Of course, certain aspects of the appropriateness conditions for a given communicative function will not be universal; our point, however, is that second language learners may already have acquired an adequate knowledge of appropriateness conditions for their basic communicative needs in the second language just by having acquired such knowledge for communicative needs in the first language.

Second, it is not clear that native speakers of the second language expect second language learners at the early stages of a program (or even at later stages) to have mastered sociocultural rules bearing on appropriateness. Perhaps of relevance here are B. J. Carroll's (1978) tentative findings suggesting that native speakers of a language are more tolerant of second language learners' "stylistic failures" (e.g., not understanding stylistic features or not using appropriate language—cf. Munby, 1978, p. 92) than of their grammatical inaccuracies. However, it is also not clear how widely native speakers vary in their tolerance of sociocultural failures, what sociocultural contexts can be associated with different levels of tolerance, and so forth. Nor is it clear whether tolerance of grammatical inaccuracies that do not interfere too much with meaning is higher or lower than tolerance of sociocultural failures. Answers to such questions are important if second language learners' and teachers' expectations of tolerance to grammatical and sociocultural inaccuracies are to correspond to actual levels of tolerance shown by different groups of native speakers of the second language.

There are some empirical data from the field of language testing bearing on theories of basic communication skills. We think it is instructive to consider those data that concern the extent to which grammatical competence is acquired in second language courses organized on the basis of these theories and the extent to which communicative competence is acquired in courses organized on the basis of theories of grammatical competence.

Although it is a frequently expressed opinion that grammatical competence is not a good predictor of communicative competence (cf. Upshur, 1969, e.g.), one of the first empirical studies dealing with this question in a rigorous manner is that of Savignon (1972). She studied the communicative skills and grammatical skills of three groups of college students enrolled in an introductory audiolingual French course in the United States. All three groups received the same number of hours of instruction in the standard (formal and grammatical) program, but one group had an additional class-hour per week devoted to communicative tasks (where the emphasis was mainly on getting one's meaning across); the second group devoted an additional hour to a "culture lab" program; and the third spent an additional hour in a language laboratory program. We will refer to these as the communicative competence (CC) group, the culture group, and the grammatical competence group respectively. She found that although there were no significant differences among groups on tests of grammatical competence, the CC group scored significantly higher than the other two groups on four communicative tests she developed. The first test was a discussion in French between a student and a native speaker of French on one of three topics, the second an information-getting interview in which the student had to find out as much information as possible about the native speaker by asking him questions, the third a reporting task in which the student had to discuss a given topic first in English, then in French, and the fourth a description task in which the student had to describe an ongoing activity. The criteria of evaluation for these tests have been mentioned. The total testing time for each student was thirty minutes. She claims that "the most significant findings of this study point to the value of training in communicative skills from the very beginning of the [foreign language] program" (Savignon 1972, p. 9).

Another study reporting that grammatical competence is not a good predictor of communicative skills is discussed by Tucker (1974). He and several students conducted an experiment in both Cairo and Beirut. Two groups of subjects were selected: one group had scored very high (95th percentile) in English language proficiency as demonstrated on the Michigan Test of English Language Performance and the Test of English as a Foreign Language, and the other group had scored much lower (60th percentile) on these tests. In one of the communicative tests given to these subjects, the testee was asked to describe an object or picture so that a listener on the other side of an opaque screen could identify the object or picture from among an array of such items before him. On three of four such communicative tests, no significant difference was found between the performance of these groups of subjects. That is, "the individuals who were relatively low in their measured proficiency in English (i.e., their ability to manipulate grammatical transformations and so on) were able to communicate as effectively and as rapidly in English as were the individuals of high measured proficiency in English" (Tucker, 1974, p. 219).

Similar findings are reported by Upshur and Palmer (1974). In their study, the measured linguistic accuracy of Thai students who had learned English through formal classroom training was not found to be a reliable predictor of their measured communicative abilities.

It seems that an appropriate conclusion to draw from these three studies is that focus on grammatical competence in the classroom is not a sufficient condition for the development of communicative competence. It would be inappropriate, however, to conclude from these studies that the development of grammatical competence is irrelevant to or unnecessary for the development of communicative competence (given that all the subjects in each study did have grammatical training).

Savignon's (1972) reported finding that the CC group did just as well on the grammatical tests as the other two groups suggests that attention to basic communication skills does not interfere in the development of grammatical skills. Two other studies dealing with language-testing data are relevant to this finding. Schulz (1977) reports on a study of two groups of students of introductory French differing in that one group was given only communicative tests (developed by her) and the other was given only grammatical tests. She found that the former group did no better than the latter group on overall communicative posttests and performed at a significantly lower level on overall grammatical posttests. Thus her findings suggest that a communicative approach that is implemented in the classroom through a testing program but not through teaching or syllabus design is no more effective than a grammatical approach in developing grammatical skills. Palmer (1978) studied two groups of students of English who differed in that one group's classroom materials were modified to communication tasks while the other group's materials were kept standard (e.g., dialogues, grammar exercises, listening comprehension exercises). He found that the first group scored significantly lower than the second group on one of the grammatical tests (viz., a pronunciation test) but performed at the same level as the second group did on all other grammatical tests and on all communicative tests administered. He is careful to point out, however, that the teaching objectives for both groups of students dealt with language use skills, that the communicative tasks did not involve language use for personal or realistic needs, and that the students in the standard program were involved in quite a bit of conversation in English with the instructor (the author) outside the classroom. Thus it is not clear that the two groups differed in any substantive sense with respect to the amount of attention devoted to the development of communicative competence. It would therefore be inappropriate to interpret Palmer's findings as evidence that attention to basic communication skills interferes in the development of grammatical skills, or for that matter, that using communicative materials in the classroom does not enhance communicative skills. It may be helpful to summarize certain aspects of our view of theories of basic communication skills at this point.

First, there seem to be no strong theoretical reasons for emphasizing getting one's meaning across over grammatical accuracy at the early stages of second language learning. In fact, there seem to be a number of reasons for not doing so, as we pointed out. These findings must not be taken to mean that grammatical accuracy should be emphasized over getting one's meaning across, however. There is evidence against this view from a number of sources (aside from the well-known and warranted frustration on the part of students and teachers as concerns strictly grammatical approaches). Oller and Obrecht (1968) found that the effectiveness of pattern drills is significantly increased when the language in the drill is related to communication. Their conclusion is that from the very beginning of a second language program, aspects of grammatical competence should be taught in the context of meaningful communication. Oller and Obrecht (1969) report a similar finding in another study. Thus some combination of emphasis on grammatical accuracy and emphasis on meaningful communication from the very start of second language study is suggested. It must be noted that there is certainly no reason to focus on all aspects of grammar before emphasis is put on communication, nor does there seem to be a reason to focus on aspects of grammar that are not immediately related to the learner's second language communication needs at a given stage of instruction (cf. Belasco, 1965, on this point).

Second, there appears to be some reason to emphasize getting one's meaning across (or communicating) over explicit concerns about appropriateness at the early stages of second language study. The primary motivation for this view is the assumption that the appropriateness conditions that hold for the most common communicative functions differ little from language to language in certain fundamental respects. This is certainly a conservative and reasonable assumption, one that would have to be confronted with falsifying evidence before a more complicated hypothesis was advanced. Certainly these appropriateness conditions may be considered to be more universal than certain aspects of grammatical competence that are crucial to the verbal expression of meaning (e.g., vocabulary), and which may be quite arbitrary from one language to another. Of course many questions bearing on this view (such as the ones raised above concerning tolerance of errors in language use) remain to be studied. But it seems quite reasonable, in our opinion, to hold off on explicit emphasis on sociocultural aspects of language use at the early stages of second language study in general programs. Instead, one might begin with a combination of emphasis on grammatical accuracy and on meaningful communication, *where such communication is generally organized according to the basic communication needs of the learner* and the communicative functions and social contexts that require the least knowledge of idiosyncratic appropriateness conditions in the second language.

Finally, it would seem that unless a (basic, at least) communicative approach is adopted for the classroom, there is little reason to expect that students will acquire even basic communication skills in a second language. Grammatical approaches that incorporate only a communication-based testing component (e.g., Schulz, 1977) or communicative tasks where no personal or realistic communication takes place (e.g., Palmer, 1978), would seem to be no more (or less) effective than an unmodified grammatical approach for developing communicative competence, and in fact, they may be less effective than an unmodified grammatical approach in developing grammatical competence (e.g., Schulz, 1977). However, basic communicative approaches such as the one adopted by Savignon (1972) would seem to be just as effective as grammatical approaches in developing grammatical competence and more effective than grammatical approaches in developing communicative competence.

SOCIOLINGUISTIC PERSPECTIVES ON COMMUNICATIVE COMPETENCE

Research on communicative competence from sociolinguistic perspectives has been of a more theoretical and analytic nature than work on basic communication skills. Although there have perhaps been few direct applications of this research to general second language programs (cf., however, Kettering, 1974; Paulston and Bruder, 1976; Paulston and Selekman, 1976), the work of Halliday and Hymes in particular has inspired many of the communicative approaches that have been proposed. It is worthwhile then to examine some of the assumptions and components of their theories of language in its social context.

Two aspects of Hymes's research are of particular interest: his theory of communicative competence and his analysis of the ethnography of speaking. Hymes (1972) has rejected the strong version of competence for language that Chomsky (1965) adopted—where this competence is equivalent to grammatical competence—and proposed a theory of competence that includes the language user's knowledge of (and ability for use of) rules of language use in context. The actual theory of communicative competence that he suggests is comprised of knowledge (and abilities) of four types:

1. Whether (and to what degree) something is formally *possible*;
2. Whether (and to what degree) something is *feasible* in virtue of the means of implementation available;
3. Whether (and to what degree) something is *appropriate* (adequate, happy, successful) in relation to a context in which it is used and evaluated;
4. Whether (and to what degree) something is in fact done, actually *performed*, and what its doing entails (Hymes, 1972, p. 281, his emphasis).

Communicative competence is thus viewed by Hymes as the interaction of grammatical (what is formally possible), psycholinguistic (what is feasible in terms of human information processing), sociocultural (what is the social meaning or value of a given utterance), and probabilistic (what actually occurs) systems of competence. Thus a given utterance may be, for example, ungrammatical with respect to a particular grammar (e.g., *the was cheese green* with respect to Standard Canadian English), unacceptable or awkward in terms of a particular perceptual strategy (e.g., *the cheese the rat the cat the dog saw chased ate was green* with reference to a perceptual constraint on processing multiple center-embedded clauses), inappropriate in a particular social context (e.g., saying *good-bye* in greeting someone), or rare in a particular community or situation (e.g., saying *may god be with you* instead of *good-bye*, *bye-bye*, or the like in ending a routine telephone conversation). Earlier we expressed the opinion that it is not necessary to include psycholinguistic competence in one's model of communicative competence; we will maintain this opinion, although there seems to be little at stake on this point for second language teaching since perceptual strategies, memory constraints, and the like would seem to impose themselves in a natural and universal manner rather than require conscious learning on the part of a student. However, the inclusion of probabilistic rules of occurrence in Hymes's model seems to be an important aspect of language use that is ignored in almost all other models of communicative competence (however, Widdowson, 1978, mentions this factor). Knowledge of what a native speaker is likely to say in a given context is to us a crucial component of second language learners' competence to understand second language communication and to express themselves in a nativelike way (cf. Morrow, 1977; Oller, 1979, for related discussion).[1]

Hymes has spearheaded most of the recent work that is devoted to the description of sociocultural competence—that is, the basis for judgments as to the appropriateness of a given utterance in a particular social context. He has proposed the phrase *ethnography of speaking* (Hymes, 1964, 1967, 1968), to refer to the system of factors and rules that make up the structure of speaking or communication in a group and that are the basis for the social meaning of any utterance. We will be concerned here primarily with the components of speech events.

Hymes (1967) employs the notion of *speech event* to refer to activities or aspects of activities that are governed directly by rules of language use. For example, a speech event such as a private conversation would have rules of use associated with it that differed from those associated with a church sermon. A major aspect of the ethnography of speaking is the analysis of speech events in terms of their constitutive components. These are participants (e.g., speaker and hearer, sender and receiver), setting (i.e., physical time and place), scene (i.e., psychological or cultural setting), the actual form of a message (i.e., a linguistic description of the message), topic (i.e., what the message is about), purpose (i.e., goal, intention), key (e.g., serious, mock), channel (e.g., oral, written), code (i.e., language or variety within a language), norms of interaction (e.g., loudness of voice, when and how to interrupt, physical distance between participants), norms of interpretation (i.e., how different norms of interaction or violations of them are interpreted), and genre (e.g., casual speech, poem, prayer, form letter).

According to Hymes, these components of speech events are crucial to the formulation of rules of language use and to the analysis of the social meaning of utterances. Although some progress toward these ends has been made within Hymes's framework (cf. in particular Ervin-Tripp, 1972; Hymes, 1967; and references cited in both articles), many of the basic issues remain to be clarified. For instance, it is not clear that all of these components are always crucial in all speech events (as pointed out by Hymes, 1967). Allen and Widdowson (1975) point out that "utterances can take on an enormously wide

range of meanings in different contexts" and that "not only is there a difficulty
in establishing how *many* contexts to consider when specifying the range of
appropriateness of an utterance, but there is the problem of knowing how
much of the context is relevant" (p. 88, their emphasis). Hymes (1967) suggests
that hierarchies of precedence among components may emerge but notes that it
is not clear that any ranking of components can yet be established. Walters
(1978) reviews a variety of research studies showing that contextual factors
such as setting, topic, and the sex, age, and race of the participants are the most
salient in their effect on variation in requests, but there is much less research on
variation in the expression of other communicative functions. Van der Geest
(1978) reports on a communication analysis system that takes into consideration such factors as situation variables, role variables, communication variables, and syntactic variables; he stresses, however, that only a relatively small
part of communication is able to be handled within this system. Furthermore,
it is not clear how rules of language use should be expressed formally (though
see the work and suggestions of Ervin-Tripp, 1972; Hymes, 1972). It is quite
reasonable to conclude with Hymes (1967), Morrow (1977), Stratton (1977),
Walters (1978), and Widdowson (1975), among others, that relatively little is
known about how social context and grammatical forms interact. Nonetheless,
we find the notion of sociolinguistic competence to be a crucial one in a theory
of communicative competence and particularly deserving of research with
respect to second language teaching and testing.

　　Consider now the work of Halliday on sociosemantic aspects of language
and language use. One of the most significant aspects of his research has been
the development of a "meaning potential" approach to language, primarily at
the clause level rather than at the discourse level (cf., however, Halliday and
Hasan, 1976). Halliday (1973, 1978) views language essentially as a system of
meaning potential—that is, as sets of semantic options available to the language user that relate what the user can do (in terms of social behavior) to what
the user can say (in terms of the grammar). The process involved in language
production is one in which a social system determines sets of behavioral
options (what speakers can do) which are realized as sets of semantic options
(what they can mean, or the meaning potential) which in turn are realized as
sets of grammatical options (what they can say). Halliday (1973, 1978) has
suggested that his approach to linguistic interaction is not unlike that advocated by Hymes (1972, e.g.), where the notion of a socially constrained meaning potential is similar to Hymes's notion of communicative competence.[2]

　　We find it reasonable to distinguish the three levels of options in Halliday's model; however, there are some points to consider with respect to the
direction of influence from level to level. As concerns the claim that grammatical options are the (direct) realization of semantic options, there is little ground
for disagreement. It is one of the axioms of modern linguistics that any human
language can express any meaning in some way. To our knowledge there is no
convincing evidence for the alternative views that semantic options are determined by grammatical options or that certain meanings are inexpressible (as
opposed to not normally expressed) given the grammars of certain languages.

Munby (1978) has taken the significance of this claim for pedagogical purposes to be the theoretical support it gives to program designers, materials and test developers, and teachers to approach the development of grammatical competence from the standpoint of meaning, from the very beginning. We agree that meaningful communication should be emphasized as a means of facilitating the acquisition of grammatical competence from the beginning, but nonetheless maintain that meaningful (verbal) communication is not possible without some knowledge of grammar. It may be more realistic to view the normal process at the beginning of such learning as one in which what can be said (grammatical options) determines in some what can be meant (semantic options) in the second language. That is, the meanings (and perhaps some of the social behavior options) that one is able to exploit through the second language are restricted by the grammatical means of expression that have been mastered. Given this latter perspective on second language learning, it is not surprising to find that many of the students in Savignon's (1972) communicative competence class—where emphasis was put on getting one's meaning across—emphasized their difficulties in thinking of the right vocabulary and structures on her tests of communicative competence. Nonetheless, it is quite possible that at later stages of second language learning, in particular after a good basic command of grammar has been acquired, grammatical options are more of a direct realization of semantic options rather than the reverse. It is possible that one way to facilitate and perhaps speed up the onset of this normal interaction between semantic options and grammatical options is to try to base the specification of the grammatical options to be learned on the particular communicative needs of the learner. This possibility is suggested by the plausible assumption that there is a close relationship between the learner's communicative needs and those semantic options (and social behavior options) that he/she is most likely to express.

Let us turn now to Halliday's claim that semantic options are the realization of social behavior options. This view seems to be reductionist in at least two ways. First, it is obvious that semantic options are constrained by certain aspects of human cognition. Halliday would certainly admit this point but has maintained (e.g., in Halliday, 1978) that his orientation and goals in linguistics are socially, not psychologically, oriented. Second, we see no compelling reason to give primacy to social behavior options over semantic options in characterizing what one can mean in a language. We would certainly not agree that one is limited to expressing semantically only what social conventions, for example, allow; one may choose to violate or ignore such conventions. In fact until it is shown that there are any strong social limits on what one may choose to mean, Halliday's position would not seem to differ substantively from the opposite position, namely, that meaning options determine social options. Furthermore, language can be used with little or no reference to social context in many different ways: for example, in honest self-expression, in organizing one's ideas, and in creative uses of language (cf. Chomsky, 1975, for related discussion). It is not clear why, then, semantic options must be viewed exclusively as the realizations of social behavior options. Halliday has made this point:

> We would not be able to construct a sociosemantic network for highly intellectual abstract discourse, and in general the more self-sufficient the language [the more it creates its own setting . . .] the less we should be able to say about it in these broadly sociological, or social, terms. [Halliday, 1973, cited in Munby, 1978, p. 14]

It seems clear that a theory of natural language semantics must make reference to social behavior options if it is to be of relevance to a theory of communicative competence; but such social options do not seem sufficient to account for the sets of intentions or other semantic options available to the language user.

In summary, the sociolinguistic work of both Halliday and Hymes is important to the development of a communicative approach in that they have been concerned with the interaction of social context, grammar, and meaning (more precisely, social meaning). We find that there is still little known about rules of language use and about the manner in which and extent to which semantic aspects of utterances are determined (and grammatical forms selected) on the basis of social context. Nonetheless, work in these areas is crucial to the statement of specifications, objectives, and evaluation criteria within a communicative approach.

INTEGRATIVE THEORIES OF COMMUNICATIVE COMPETENCE

The theories of communicative competence that we have examined to this point have focussed mainly either on the minimum (oral) communication skills needed to cope in a second language situation (e.g., Savignon, 1972; Van Ek, 1976) or on the interrelation between language and social context (e.g., Halliday, 1973; Hymes 1967). These theories cannot be considered to be integrative in that they devote relatively little attention to how individual utterances may be linked at the level of discourse and do not provide an integration of the different components of communicative competence. In our view, an integrative theory of communicative competence may be regarded as one in which there is a synthesis of knowledge of basic grammatical principles, knowledge of how language is used in social contexts to perform communicative functions, and knowledge of how utterances and communicative functions can be combined according to the principles of discourse. Such theories are discussed in the work of, for example, Allen (1978), Allen and Widdowson (1975), Candlin (1978), Morrow (1977), Munby (1978), Stern (1978), Widdowson (1975, 1978), and Wilkins (1976). These theories might also be viewed as integrative in that they focus on speaking, listening, writing, and reading rather than on a subset of these skill areas. The most recent and comprehensive of such theories that we have examined is that proposed by Munby (1978). Since a review of Munby appears in this issue we will focus only on general aspects of his framework, discussing other studies as they relate to it.

The theoretical framework that underlies Munby's model of communicative competence consists of three major components: a sociocultural orientation, a sociosemantic view of linguistic knowledge, and rules of discourse. The

sociocultural component is based quite heavily on the work of Hymes discussed in the preceding section, and there is little that we can add here.

We also have little to say about the discourse component in Munby's
model, both because we are still relatively unfamiliar with the work in this field
and because there seems to be no theory of discourse that one can turn to with
confidence. In our opinion, the clearest and most directly applicable description of discourse for second language teaching is that discussed by Widdowson
(1978). He makes a fundamental distinction between *cohesion* and *coherence*
in spoken or written discourse. Cohesion is a relational concept concerned with
how propositions are linked structurally in a text and how the literal meaning
of a text is interpreted. In the work of Halliday and Hasan (1976), five main
types of cohesion are isolated: anaphoric reference (e.g., use of pronouns to
refer to something mentioned previously, as in *I gave IT to THEM*; substitution, which is quite similar to the first type (e.g., substitution of *one* for *a book*
in *Mary has a book. I wish I had one*); ellipsis, that is, omission of a grammatical element that has been expressed already (e.g., *John doesn't have a book,
nor do I*, where *have a book* is not repeated); conjunction, which involves the
use of such grammatical connectors as *soon* (temporal), *and* (additive), *although* (adversative); and lexical cohesion (e.g., direct repetition of the same
term to refer to the same object rather than the use of different terms to refer to
the same object). Coherence is concerned with the relationships among the
communicative values (or contextual meanings) of utterances. Widdowson
(1978, p. 29) provides the following example to illustrate this notion:

    A. That's the telephone.
    B. I'm in the bath.
    A. O.K.

Although there is no overt signal of cohesion among these utterances, they do
form coherent discourse to the extent that A's first proposition has the value of
a request, that B's remark functions as an excuse for not complying with A's
request, and that A's final remark is an acceptance of B's excuse. Note how
important the notions of setting, role of participants, goals, and so forth are in
arriving at a coherent interpretation of these utterances (e.g., consider the
setting to be the subway as opposed to a home).

Other approaches to the analysis of discourse are reported in the literature and deserve mention. Among the studies that approach discourse as part
of a theory of social interaction are those on conversational analysis (e.g., Fine,
1978; Goffman, 1978; Grice, 1975; Labov and Fanshel, 1977; Sacks, Schegloff,
and Jefferson, 1974), analysis of classroom discourse (e.g., Chaudron, 1977;
Herman, forthcoming; Sinclair and Coulthard, 1975), the definition and classification of speech acts (e.g., Austin, 1962; Searle, 1976), the role of discourse
routines in language acquisition (e.g., Bates, 1976; Bruner, 1978) and in interpretation of utterances (e.g., Candlin, 1978), and the relation between the
choice of utterances and social status (e.g., Olson, 1978). More formal linguistic approaches are reflected in the work of Harris (1952) and Hurtig (1977) as

well as in work on artificial intelligence (e.g., Shank and Nash-Webber, 1975, and references cited there). In addition to Halliday and Hasan (1976), an approach from the viewpoint of stylistics has been adopted by Benson and Greaves (1973) and is reflected in the work of Allen and Widdowson (1974). Representative work from a variety of research perspectives is presented by Freedle (1977) and Grimes (1975). It is not unfair to say that all of this work is still at an embryonic stage.

As concerns the sociosemantic component of Munby's theoretical framework for communicative competence, several points warrant discussion. First, Munby adopts the theoretical position suggested by Halliday (1973) that we discussed in the preceding section—that is, the view of language as semantic options derived from social structure. Our reservations about this position concern its application to communicative approaches to second language teaching. In particular, we do not accept the view that grammatical options in the second language are best handled at the *early* learning stages as arising only from semantic options and indirectly from social options. Although Munby does suggest that considerations of appropriateness and generalizability of grammatical forms should be involved in determining actual grammatical options, these criteria, and the process suggested, seem inadequate. For example, nowhere is reference made to the relative grammatical complexity of forms as a constraint on the semantic options and social behavior options that may be selected, or even as a constraint on the grammatical options selected via his processing model. We think that at some point prior to the final selection of grammatical options, semantic options, and social behavior options, grammatical forms must be screened in terms of the following: (1) grammatical complexity (e.g., the structures and lexical items that must be mastered to produce a given form spontaneously); (2) transparency with respect to the communicative function of an utterance (e.g., *I suggest you try the fish* is a more clear-cut and obvious grammatical encoding than *Have you never tried our fish?*, *The fish is nice*, etc. if one is a waiter in a restaurant trying to make a polite, deferential, and encouraging suggestion to a customer concerning what to order); (3) generalizability to other communicative functions; (4) the role of a given form in facilitating acquisition of another form; (5) acceptability in terms of perceptual strategies; and (6) degree of markedness in terms of social and geographical dialects (cf. Johnson and Morrow, 1978, and Morrow, 1977, for additional criteria and discussion).

Our concern with grammatical complexity (among other criteria) is closely related to perhaps the most common and significant concern with respect to communicative approaches: What is the optimum combination of attention to grammar and attention to other communication skills? Van Ek (1976) has pointed out quite explicitly that the objective of his threshold level approach is only part of a second language program:

> It is obvious, then, that the present [threshold level] objective cannot be offered as *the* objective of foreign language teaching. It is merely offered as the *minimum objective for the teaching of* (*mainly oral*) *foreign language communication.* As

such it can, in most cases, only be one part of a more comprehensive foreign language curriculum. [p. 17, his emphasis]

Various combinations of emphasis on grammatical skills and on other communication skills are suggested by Alexander (1976), Johnson (1977), and Wilkins (1978), among others, but no empirical data on learner performance under different treatments exist. Most of the communicative materials that have appeared recently (e.g., Edelhoff et al., 1978; Johnson and Morrow, 1978) tend to organize the syllabus primarily on the basis of the functions to be carried out, but do provide drills whose focus is a particular grammatical point. An example of a grammatical approach that provides drills whose focus is particular communication points may be the approach used by Savignon (1972) discussed earlier. There is no obvious way in which one could make comparisons of the effectiveness of Savignon's approach with respect to the type of approach suggested by Edelhoff et al. or by Johnson and Morrow (assuming that empirical data from tests or other instruments were available on this latter approach) without information on the similarities and differences between the groups at the pretreatment stage, information on the instruments, and so forth.

Our thinking, then, is that there is an overemphasis in many integrative theories on the role of communicative functions and social behavior options in the selection of grammatical forms and a lack of emphasis on the role of factors such as grammatical complexity and transparency. Perhaps the major problem of such a distribution of emphasis at the early stages of second language learning is that the grammatical forms to be mastered will not necessarily be organized or presented in an effective manner. As Johnson (1977, 1978) and Morrow (1978) have pointed out, it seems unlikely that a syllabus organized along communicative lines can be organized equally well along grammatical lines. Thus Johnson (1977) writes:

It seems reasonable to expect sentences which form a homogeneous functional grouping to be grammatically unlike. The choice of a functional organization therefore seems to imply a degree of structural "disorganization," to the extent that many structurally dissimilar sentences may be presented in the same unit, while what may be taken to be key examples of particular grammatical structures will be scattered throughout the course. [p. 669]

Furthermore, it is not clear that the types of communicative approaches that advocates of integrative approaches envision would lend themselves equally well to the teaching of different areas of grammar; for example, although vocabulary and certain aspects of morphology and syntax might be organized quite naturally in terms of communicative functions, other areas of grammar—phonology, morphological features such as gender distinctions, verb classes (e.g., -er, -ir, -re verbs in French), and so on—might not be served so well by an organization based on functions. It is perhaps because most applications of communicative approaches have been directed at advanced levels of second language learning (cf. Wilkins, 1978, among others, on this point) that there is a tendency to accord grammatical factors a secondary role in the organization of communicative syllabuses.

From a purely theoretical point of view, there are at least three basic assumptions that may be largely responsible for an overemphasis on communicative functions in communicative syllabus organization.

First is the assumption that the essential purpose of language is communication. This seems to be a fundamental assumption in speech act semantics (cf. Searle, 1969, e.g.) and in many theories of communicative competence (e.g., Campbell and Wales, 1970; Habermas, 1970). As has been pointed out by a number of linguists (e.g., Chomsky, 1975; Fraser, 1974; Halliday, 1978), there is little reason to view (externally oriented) communication as more essential than other purposes of language such as self-expression, verbal thinking, problem solving, and creative writing. Furthermore, it is not clear how crucial the communicative role of language is with respect to Cummins's (1979) notion of threshold level or Bruner's (1976) notion of analytic competence (cf., however, Bruner, 1978, for further comments). Nonetheless, the communicative purpose would seem to be the most practical concern for a general second language program (cf. Clark, 1972), and an approach focussing on this purpose may help to develop more positive learner attitudes toward second language learning (cf. Palmer, 1978).

Second, the assumption that grammatical form follows the communicative purpose or use of language is often taken as the main reason for adopting an approach based on communicative functions (cf. Fawcett, 1975). However, such an assumption is in our view inadequate as the basis for syllabus organization for several reasons. First, it is difficult to isolate the individual purposes of language or the ways in which different purposes interact; thus even if one were to assume that communication is the essential purpose of language (an assumption that we would not support), it would be misleading to associate certain language forms with this purpose exclusively since communication is not the *only* purpose of language. Slobin (1977) has pointed out that the goals or uses of language may conflict with one another, and there is as yet no theory of language, language acquisition, or language change that allows one to predict with any certainty when a given purpose will take precedence over another. Second, the position that form follows purpose implies a teleological point of view (i.e., that a given form exists because it is *needed* for a given purpose) that is as questionable in linguistics as it is in biology and evolution (cf. Lenneberg, 1964). Third, as was mentioned in our discussion of Halliday's (1973) sociosemantic approach to language, the opposite view—namely, that use serves grammatical form—is perhaps a more realistic one to adopt with respect to *second* language acquisition in the *early* stages. This opposite view even has some support in studies of first language acquisition at the early stages. Thus, although young children do not seem to acquire forms that they do not need (cf. Bates, 1976; Halliday, 1975, e.g.), they nonetheless may use a single form for many different communicative functions—where this form may be more easily acquired and in some sense "simpler" than the forms used most often by older speakers to convey these other functions (cf. Bloom, 1970; Slobin, 1971).

Finally, Widdowson (1978) has made the assumption that in normal communication one is concerned with aspects of language use and not with aspects of grammatical usage. This is certainly a reasonable assumption as regards normal communication between native or nativelike speakers of a language, although we assume that there is some attention to grammatical usage when native speakers of different dialects or registers communicate. Certainly knowledge of how to adjust (in both reception and production) to other varieties of a language is an important part of communicative competence in that language (cf. Hymes, 1972; Segalowitz, 1973, e.g.). However, there is some reason to question Widdowson's assumption as it applies to the beginning second language learner. First, this type of learner will most likely be unable to devote much attention to the task of how to use language until he/ she has mastered some of the grammatical forms that are to be used. That is, it may be difficult to focus simultaneously on use and usage, particularly at early stages (cf. Stern, 1975). Savignon's (1972) communicative competence group indicated this in their evaluation of their own performance on the communication tests she administered, as we mentioned. Second, B. J. Carroll's (1978) tentative findings on the tolerance levels of native speakers to grammatical errors and use errors in the speech of nonnative speakers (which we also mentioned earlier) would suggest that native speakers pay more attention to second language learners' grammatical usage than to their sociolinguistic use of language. In spite of these reservations, we think it is reasonable and important to adopt the position that second language learning will proceed more effectively when grammatical usage is not abstracted from meaningful context (as pointed out by Macnamara, 1974; Oller and Obrecht, 1968, e.g.). This seems to be what Widdowson had in mind in making the assumption that use, not usage, is focussed on in normal conversation. Thus he states:

> By focussing on usage, therefore, the language teacher directs the attention of the learner to those features of performance which normal use of language requires him to ignore. . . . The way he is required to learn the foreign language conflicts with the way he knows language actually works and this necessarily impedes any transfer [of knowledge of language use] which might otherwise take place. By effectively denying the learner reference to his own experience the teacher increases the difficulty of the language learning task. A methodology which concentrates too exclusively on usage may well be creating the very problems it is designed to solve. [Widdowson, 1978, pp. 17–18]

To summarize, then, we find that there is little theoretical motivation for the overemphasis on language functions and lack of emphasis on grammatical complexity and the like that is characteristic of Munby's model of communicative competence and of the organization of many communicative approaches. It seems that factors such as grammatical complexity should be considered in the process of specifying the grammatical forms and communicative functions that relate to learners' sociolinguistic needs.

NOTES

1. As Daina Green (personal communication) has pointed out to us, the relationship between appropriateness and probability of occurrence in Hymes's model is not clear. We share her view that if a given form is relatively infrequent in a certain context, then it is also more likely (statistically) to be inappropriate in this context. However, she agrees with us that the relationship between appropriateness and probability is by no means straightforward, since it is quite normal to find a written form used appropriately in a context in which it has possibly never occurred previously; for example, the present sentence has quite likely never been written before, but in the present context it is nonetheless appropriate, we think.

2. Widdowson (personal communication) has suggested that there is a possible discrepancy between the views of Hymes and Halliday, which can lead to what in his view is a misunderstanding about the relationship between grammatical competence and "ability to use language." He states:

   Hymes, essentially, looks at language and use in correlational terms—certain forms are used for certain functions because they are. There are rules of grammar here and rules of use there. . . . Halliday looks at language and use in integrational terms—certain forms are used for certain functions becaus they have the potential to be so used. The rules of grammar adumbrate rules of use, so to speak, and these include both conceptual (ideational) and communicative (interpersonal/textual) functions.

   Our own view is that the models of language and communication proposed by Hymes and Halliday are more similar than Widdowson's above characterization would imply, but that Hymes (especially Hymes, 1972) adopts a more psychological approach and Halliday a more sociological one. See Halliday (1978, pp. 37–38) on this last point.

QUESTIONS FOR DISCUSSION

1. Canale and Swain subdivide *communicative competence* into three contributing competences—grammatical, sociolinguistic, and strategic. With reference to one or more textbooks with which you are familiar (as either teacher or learner), discuss to what extent the goals of the pedagogical material are consistent with the nature of these three competences.

2. Mentioned in the Introduction to Part II were some experiments conducted by Reber et al. (1980) that may be relevant to consciousness raising (CR) in pedagogy. Recall, however, that the experimental stimuli were not samples of natural language. Having now read the Canale and Swain paper, do you imagine that the Reber et al. findings would likely be interpreted by Canale and Swain as evidence in support of grammatical CR? Why (not)?

3. Canale and Swain state that in many integrative theories of communicative competence the role of communicative function has been overemphasized. What does this mean? Do you agree with it? Are there any problems with the use of the term *communication* in discussions of pedagogical goals?

REFERENCES

Alexander, L. G. 1976. Threshold level and methodology. In J. A. Van Ek (ed.), *Significance of the Threshold Level in the Early Teaching of Modern Languages.* Strasbourg: Council of Europe.

Allen, J. P. B. 1978. New developments in curriculum: the notional and the structural syllabus. Paper read at the TEAL Conference, Vancouver, B.C., March. Mimeo.

Allen, J. P. B., and H. B. Widdowson. 1974. Teaching the communicative use of English. *IRAL* **12**:1–21.

Allen, J. P. B., and H. G. Widdowson. 1975. Grammar and language teaching. In J. P. B. Allen and S. P. Corder (eds.), *The Edinburgh Course in Applied Linguistics,* Vol. 2. London: Oxford University Press.

Austin, J. L. 1962. *How to Do Things with Words.* London: Oxford University Press.

Bates, E. 1976. *Language and Context: The Acquisition of Pragmatics.* New York: Academic Press.

Belasco, S. 1965. Nucleation and the audio-lingual approach. *The Modern Language Journal* **49**:482–491.

Benson, J. D., and W. S. Greaves. 1973. *The Language People Really Use.* Agincourt, Ontario: The Book Society of Canada Ltd.

Bickerton, D. 1975. *Dynamics of a Creole System.* New York: Cambridge University Press.

Bloom, L. 1970. *Language Development: Form and Function in Emerging Grammars.* Cambridge, Mass.: MIT Press.

Bruner, J. S. 1976. Language as an instrument of thought. In A. Davies (ed.), *Problems of Language and Learning.* London: Heinemann.

Bruner, J. S. 1978. On acquiring the uses of language. Berlyne Memorial Lecture, University of Toronto, Toronto.

Campbell, R., and R. Wales. 1970. The study of language acquisition. In J. Lyons (ed.), *New Horizons in Linguistics.* Harmondsworth: Penguin Books.

Canale, M., R. Mougeon, and E. Beniak. 1978. Acquisition of some grammatical elements in English and French by monolingual and bilingual Canadian students. *Canadian Modern Language Review* **34**:505–524.

Candlin, C. N. 1977. Preface to M. Coulthard. *An Introduction to Discourse Analysis.* London: Longman.

Candlin, C. N. 1978. Discoursal patterning and the equalising of integrative opportunity. Paper read at the Conference on English as an International and Intranational Language, The East-West Center, Hawaii, April. Mimeo.

Carroll, B. J. 1978. *Guidelines for the Development of Communicative Tests.* London: Royal Society of Arts.

Chaudron, C. 1977. A descriptive model of discourse in the corrective treatment of learners' errors. *Language Learning* **27**:29–47.

Chomsky, N. 1965. *Aspects of the Theory of Syntax.* Cambridge, Mass.: MIT Press.

Chomsky, N. 1975. *Reflections on Language.* New York: Pantheon Books.

Clark, J. L. D. 1972. *Foreign Language Testing: Theory and Practice.* Philadelphia: The Center for Curriculum Development.

Cummins, J. 1979. Linguistic interdependence and the educational development of bilingual children. *Review of Educational Research.*

Davies, N. F. 1978. Putting receptive skills first—an experiment in sequencing. Paper read at the 5th AILA Congress, Montreal, August. Mimeo.

Dulay, H. C., and M. K. Burt. 1974. You can't learn without goofing. In J. C. Richards (ed.), *Error Analysis: Perspectives on Second Language Acquisition.* London: Longman Group Ltd.

Edelhoff, C. G. et al. 1978. *Übungstypologie zum Lernziel kommunikative Kompetenz.* Munich: Langenscheidt-Longman.

Ervin-Tripp, S. 1972. On sociolinguistic rules: alternation and co-occurrence. In J. J. Gumperz and D. Hymes (eds.), *Directions in Sociolinguistics.* New York: Holt, Rinehart and Winston.

Fawcett, R. 1975. Language functions and language variation in a cognitive model of communication. Mimeo.

Fine, J. 1978. Conversation, cohesive and thematic patterning in children's dialogues. *Discourse Processes* 1:247–266.

Fraser, B. 1974. Review of Searle, 1969. *Foundations of Language* 11:433–446.

Freedle, R. O., ed. 1977. *Discourse Production and Comprehension,* Vol. 1. Norwood, N. J.: Ablex Publishing Corporation.

Goffman, E. 1978. Response cries. *Language* 54:787–815.

Grice, H. P. 1975. Logic and conversation. In P. Cole and J. J. Morgan (eds.), *Syntax and Semantics,* Vol. 3: *Speech Acts.* New York: Academic Press.

Grimes, J. E. 1975. *The Thread of Discourse.* The Hague: Mouton.

Habermas, J. 1970. Introductory remarks to a theory of communicative competence. In H. P. Dreitsel (ed.), *Recent Sociology,* No. 2. London: Macmillan.

Halliday, M. A. K. 1973. *Explorations in the Functions of Language.* London: Edward Arnold.

Halliday, M. A. K. 1975. *Learning How to Mean: Explorations in the Development of Language.* London: Edward Arnold.

Halliday, M. A. K. 1978. *Language as Social Semiotic.* London: Edward Arnold.

Halliday, M. A. K., and R. Hasan. 1976. *Cohesion in English.* London: Longman.

Harley, B., and M. Swain. 1978. An analysis of the verb system used by young learners of French. *Interlanguage Studies Bulletin* 3:35–79.

Harris, Z. S. 1952. Discourse analysis. *Language* 28:1–30.

Hermann, J. forthcoming. Sociolinguistic description of the use of language in classrooms. *Journal of Pragmatics* 3:3.

Hurtig, R. 1977. Toward a functional theory of discourse. In R. O. Freedle (ed.), *Discourse Production and Comprehension,* Vol. 1. Norwood, N.J.: Ablex Publishing Corporation.

Hymes, D. 1964. Directions in (ethno-)linguistic theory. *American Anthropologist* 66(part 2):6–56.

Hymes, D. 1967. Models of the interaction of language and social setting. In J. Macnamara (ed.), Problems of bilingualism. *Journal of Social Issues* 23:8–28.

Hymes, D. 1968. The ethnography of speaking. In J. Fishman (ed.), *Readings in the Sociology of Language.* The Hague: Mouton.

Hymes, D., ed. 1971. *Pidginization and Creolization.* Cambridge: Cambridge University Press.

Hymes, D. 1972. On communicative competence. In J. B. Pride and J. Holmes (eds.), *Sociolinguistics.* Harmondsworth, England: Penguin Books.

Jakobovits, L. A. 1970. *Foreign Language Learning.* Rowley, Mass.: Newbury House.

Johnson, K. 1977. The adoption of functional syllabuses for general language teaching courses. *Canadian Modern Language Review* 33:667–680.

Johnson, K. 1978. The application of functional syllabuses. In K. Johnson and K. Morrow (eds.), *Functional Materials and the Classroom Teacher.* Reading, England: Centre for Applied Language Studies, University of Reading.

Johnson, K., and K. Morrow. 1978. *Communicate: The English of Social Interaction.* Reading: Centre for Applied Language Studies, University of Reading.

Kettering, J. 1974. *Communication Activities.* Pittsburgh: English Language Institute.

Krashen, S. 1975. The critical period for language acquisition and its possible bases. In D. Aaronson and R. Rieber (eds.), *Developmental Psycholinguistics and Communication Disorders.* New York: New York Academy of Sciences.

Labov, W., and D. Fanshel. 1977. *Therapeutic Discourse: Psychotherapy as Conversation.* Philadelphia: University of Pennsylvania Press.

Lenneberg, E. H. 1964. The capacity for language acquisition. In J. A. Fodor and J. J. Katz (eds.), *The Structure of Language.* Englewood Cliffs, N.J.: Prentice-Hall, Inc.

Lenneberg, E. H. 1967. *Biological Foundations of Language.* New York: John Wiley and Sons.

Macnamara, J. 1974. Nurseries as models for language classrooms. In S. T. Carey (ed.), *Bilingualism, Biculturalism and Education.* Edmonton: University of Alberta Press.

Morrow, K. E. 1977. *Techniques of Evaluation for a Notional Syllabus.* Study commissioned by the Royal Society of Arts. Reading: Centre for Applied Language Studies, University of Reading.

Munby, J. 1978. *Communicative Syllabus Design.* Cambridge: Cambridge University Press.

Oller, J. W., Jr. 1979. *Language Tests at School: A Pragmatic Approach.* London: Longman.

Oller, J. W., Jr., and D. H. Obrecht. 1968. Pattern drill and communicative activity: a psycholinguistic experiment. *IRAL* 6:165–174.

Oller, J. W., Jr., and D. H. Obrecht. 1969. The psycholinguistic principle of Information Sequence: an experiment in second language learning. *IRAL* 7:119–123.

Olson, D. R. 1978. Assent and compliance in children's language comprehension. In *TINLAP-2.* New York: Association for Computing Machinery and Association for Computational Linguistics.

Palmer, A. S. 1978. Measures of achievement, communication, incorporation, and integration for two classes of formal EFL learners. Paper read at the 5th AILA Congress, Montreal, August. Mimeo.

Paulston, C. B. 1974. Linguistic and communicative competence. *TESOL Quarterly* 8:347–362.

Paulston, C. B., and M. N. Bruder. 1976. *Teaching English as a Second Language: Techniques and Procedures.* Cambridge, Mass.: Winthrop Publishers, Inc.

Paulston, C. B., and H. R. Selekman. 1976. Interaction activities in the foreign classroom, or how to grow a tulip-rose. *Foreign Language Annals* 9:248–254.

Penfield, W., and L. Roberts. 1959. *Speech and Brain Mechanisms.* Princeton, N.J.: Princeton University Press.

Piaget, J. 1954. *The Construction of Reality in the Child.* New York: Ballantine.

Rivers, W. M. 1973. From linguistic competence to communicative competence. *TESOL Quarterly* 7:25–34.

Rosansky, E. 1975. The critical period for the acquisition of language: some cognitive developmental considerations. *Working Papers on Bilingualism* 6:92–102.

Sacks, H., E. A. Schegloff, and G. Jefferson. 1974. A simplest systematics for the organization of turn-taking for conversation. *Language* 50:696–735.

Savignon, S. J. 1972. *Communicative Competence: An Experiment in Foreign-Language Teaching.* Philadelphia: Center for Curriculum Development.

Schachter, J., and W. E. Rutherford. 1979. Discourse function and language transfer. *Working Papers on Bilingualism* **19**:1–12.

Schulz, R. A. 1977. Discrete-point versus simulated communication testing in foreign languages. *The Modern Language Journal* **61**:94–100.

Scovel, T. 1978. The recognition of foreign accents in English and its implications for psycholinguistic theories of language acquisition. Paper presented at the 5th AILA Congress, Montreal, August.

Searle, J. R. 1969. *Speech Acts.* Cambridge: Cambridge University Press.

Searle, J. R. 1976. A classification of illocutionary acts. *Language in Society* **5**:1–23.

Segalowitz, N. 1973. Communicative competence, linguistic variability, and second language learning. Montreal: Sir George Williams Faculty of Arts, Concordia University. Mimeo.

Selinker, L. 1974. Interlanguage. In J. C. Richards (ed.), *Error Analysis: Perspectives on Second Language Acquisition.* London: Longman.

Selinker, L., M. Swain, and G. Dumas. 1975. The interlanguage hypothesis extended to children. *Language Learning* **25**:139–152.

Shank, R., and B. Nash-Webber, eds. 1975. *Theoretical Issues in Natural Language Processing.* Cambridge, Mass.: Bolt, Beranek and Newman.

Sinclair, J. M., and R. M. Coulthard. 1975. *Towards an Analysis of Discourse: The English Used by Teachers and Pupils.* London: Oxford University Press.

Slobin, D. I. 1971. Development psycholinguistics. In W. O. Dingwall (ed.), *A Survey of Linguistic Science.* College Park: University of Maryland Press.

Slobin, D. I. 1977. Language change in childhood and in history. In J. Macnamara (ed.), *Language Learning and Thought.* New York: Academic Press.

Stern, H. H. 1975. What can we learn from the good language learner? *Canadian Modern Language Review* **31**:304–318.

Stern, H. H. 1978. The formal-functional distinction in language pedagogy: a conceptual clarification. Paper read at the 5th AILA Congress, Montreal, August. Mimeo.

Stratton, F. 1977. Putting the communicative syllabus in its place. *TESOL Quarterly* **11**:131–142.

Swain, M. 1974. French immersion programs across Canada: research findings. *Canadian Modern Language Review* **31**:117–129.

Swain, M. 1978. French immersion: early, late or partial. *Canadian Modern Language Review* **34**:577–585.

Tucker, G. R. 1974. The assessment of bilingual and bicultural factors of communication. In S. T. Carey (ed.), *Bilingualism, Biculturalism and Education.* Edmonton: University of Alberta Press.

Upshur, J. A. 1969. Measurement of oral communication. In H. Schrand (ed.), *IFS Dokumentation, Leistungmessung im Sprachunterricht.* Marburg/Lahn: Informationzentrum für Fremdsprachenforschung.

Upshur, J. A., and A. Palmer. 1974. Measures of accuracy, communicativity, and social judgments for two classes of foreign language speakers. In A. Verdoodt (ed.), *AILA Proceedings, Copenhagen 1972*, Vol. III: *Applied Sociolinguistics.* Heidelberg: Julius Groos Verlag.

Van der Geest, T. 1978. Communicative analysis system. Paper read at the 5th AILA Congress, Montreal, August.

Van Ek, J. A. 1976. *Significance of the Threshold Level in the Early Teaching of Modern Languages.* Strasbourg: Council of Europe.

Walters, J. 1978. Social factors in the acquisition of a second language. Paper read at the 5th AILA Congress, Montreal, August.

Widdowson, H. G. 1975. Two types of communication exercise. In H. G. Widdowson (ed.), *Explorations in Applied Linguistics*. London: Oxford University Press.

Widdowson, H. G. 1978. *Teaching Language as Communication*. London: Oxford University Press.

Wilkins, D. A. 1976. *Notional Syllabuses*. London: Oxford University Press.

Wilkins, D. A. 1978. Approaches to syllabus design: communicative, functional or notional. In K. Johnson and K. Morrow (eds.), *Functional Materials and the Classroom Teacher: Some Background Issues*. Reading: Centre for Applied Language Studies, University of Reading.

6
Psychological Constraints on the Teachability of Languages

Manfred Pienemann
University of Sydney

RESEARCH QUESTION AND RELATED STUDIES

The question underlying this study is whether the process of natural L2 acquisition can be influenced by formal instruction.[1] Our research is intended to contribute to making explicit the view that all instances of language acquisition are subject to the same processing constraints. This study is not concerned with properties of *formal* language learning and their dependence on principles of natural acquisition as are the other studies in the field, which will be outlined below. Rather, it takes the reverse view and investigates the influence of instruction on *natural acquisition processes*. Consequently, the data are drawn from an experiment in which we tried to force other than "natural" learning processes in learners' natural acquisition of a second language (for further details see the following section). Thus the underlying question is: Can processes of natural acquisition be influenced (in other than the "natural way") by formal instruction?

It seems to me that this question is of outstanding importance for two reasons: (1) If we follow the above hypothesis about common principles for formal learning and natural acquisition, L2 curricula must be based on these

This research was funded by the Cornelsen-Foundation (Cornelsen Stiftung im Stifterverband fur die Deutsche Wissenschaft). This is a revised version of a paper presented at the Second European–North American Workshop of Cross-Linguistic Second Language Acquisition Research, Gohrde, West Germany, 1982. Reprinted with permission from *Studies in Second Language Acquisition*, vol. 6, no. 2, pp. 186–212.

principles. This is especially apparent if L2 development takes place in a context where natural acquisition is the predominant source for the linguistic development (as is the case with most immigrant workers and their children in Europe). Under this condition it is of immediate importance to discover in what way possible pedagogical options for L2 curricula are restricted by principles of language acquisition; that is, whether the effect of formal instruction is *exclusively predetermined* by acquisition principles or whether (and if so, in what way) acquisition processes can still be manipulated by the means of instruction. (2) The second reason is directly connected to the latter question. By investigating to what extent acquisition processes can be manipulated by instruction, we can specify some of the properties of those factors which are hypothesized to constrain language learning (and possibly also teaching).

The question underlying this research is *one* special case of the general view that *all instances of language learning, change, loss and so forth might be determined by the same factors* (*in the individual*). This main line of research is represented by the first left "node" in Figure 1, which gives an overview of the related research. Such a research perspective has been worked out by several scholars from different theoretical points of view (esp. Wode, 1981; Slobin, 1973, 1975; Felix and Wode, 1983).

The number of studies which have been conducted in this framework (with particular reference to formal L2 learning) is relatively small. Leaving aside theoretical differences in the explanation of acquisition processes for the moment (for discussion see esp. Berman, 1982; Clahsen, 1982; Felix, 1982), we can differentiate two approaches (within this "branch"), which also reflect some of the differences of the underlying question (cf. Figure 6–1).

One of them is my approach, the other is represented by the work of Felix and Simmet (Felix, 1978, 1981; Felix and Simmet, 1981; Hahn, 1982) which has been carried out within the tradition of the "integrated perspective of language acquisition" (cf. Wode, 1981). These authors primarily compare the structures of utterances which appear under conditions of formal instruction with the types of structures known from natural acquisition. In this research they found a considerable number of structural parallels and similar learning strategies, although the learners had been exposed to an input sequenced in contradiction to findings from natural L2 acquisition. As these similarities of structures appear in the two different types of language acquisition (although the input was substantially different) the authors have a relatively strong empirical basis for concluding that the principles underlying natural acquisition also apply to the formal learning of a language.

The strength of this argument is reduced somewhat by the following two weaknesses: (1) The data from formal instruction are not related to individual learners of the longitudinal observation. So the comparison of structures from different acquisitional types is (in this work)[2] not a comparison of acquisitional sequences, but rather of error types to natural orders of acquisition. (2) The conclusion that the principles of natural acquisition also apply to formal L2 learning only states the general role of those principles in formal learning, but it does not make explicit the way formal L2 learning is constrained by them.

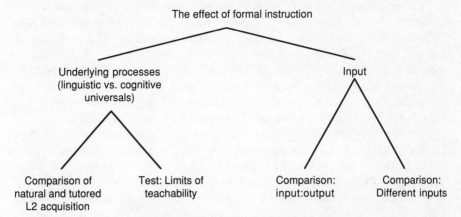

Figure 6-1 Characterization of related research

The primary difference between the above-mentioned research and the other main line of investigation I want to characterize (cf. Fig. 6–1) is that the former concentrates on underlying acquisition principles in different types of acquisition whereas the latter is concerned with the question to what extent acquisition/learning processes depend on the structure of formal input. Obviously, this question is related to investigations into input in *natural* acquisition. This research again is—as I will show in some more detail in a later section—related to a nonnativist view on first language acquisition which investigates the role of "motherese" (cf. Snow and Ferguson, 1977).

Many of the studies in this area were comparisons of two or more of the following variables:

1. the language to which the learner is exposed
2. the language he produces
3. the language of learners with a different input
4. the order of accuracy in natural acquisition
   (cf. Lightbown, 1983, 1987; Long, 1982)

A widespread research method among these studies (which is also common in L1 research, cf. Snow and Ferguson, 1977) is to compare the *frequency* of structures in the input language with their frequency/accuracy in the output. Consequently, the effect of input is measured in a quantitative manner (cf. also the study by Dietrich, Kaufmann, and Storch, 1979).

The results of these studies have not always been in agreement with each other. However, on the basis of a review of 13 empirical studies, Long (1982) points out that in systematizing these studies according to the absolute and relative effect of input and to the amount of natural versus formal input, a general tendency can be found which indicates a positive effect of instruction for L2 acquisition.

In this context I want to point to a general weakness of this "branch" of research. On the basis of the methods which are applied (esp. measuring frequency/accuracy), only a very specific type of question can be answered, namely, *how much* effect instruction has on the interlanguage. As the effect is measured on the basis of linguistic units which are not clearly related to acquisition processes, the focus of these studies is on *learning success* and not on *acquisition processes* (cf. also the critique of acquisitional criteria and morpheme order studies in Meisel, Clahsen, and Pienemann, 1981).

"Input" is also the heading of another line of research which is more clearly rooted in behaviorist learning psychology and which has been conducted in Germany for a number of years (cf. Jungblut, 1974; Heuer, 1976; Vogel and Vogel, 1975; Hüllen and Jung, 1979; discussion see Hahn, 1982). The overall question of this research is "What is the optimal input for learning purpose x?" To some extent this question is also addressed in the line of research outlined earlier (cf. Long, 1982).

However, here the question is not *what types of structures* in the input have the optimal effect on the learner's L2 development, but what is the *optimal way of presenting* any set of structures which has been selected as a learning objective independently of the actual state of the learner's interlanguage. Concentrating exclusively on the formal learning situation (i.e., normal foreign language classes), these studies investigated correlations between external variables such as teaching method, teaching material, teacher's behavior, and so on, and learning success in terms of error-free L2 learning.

The general tendency of this line of research is to hypothesize that the formal setting of tutored L2 learning allows for language-learning processes which are structurally different from natural L2 acquisition and which can be controlled by the appropriate structure of the input. As the learning process is a priori regarded to be fully dependent on input variables, the question "whether teaching makes a difference" does not arise. Instead, research in this framework is devoted to the search for the optimal teaching method.

Summarizing, the present research differs from previous studies in that it does not compare interlanguage patterns or learning success resulting from formal and informal learning. Instead it examines directly in a relatively controlled experiment whether the constraints imposed on natural acquisition can be eliminated by means of formal instruction.

* * * * *

[The following is a summary, by the editors, of sections 2 (Research Design) and 3 (Results) of Pienemann's paper. This paper concludes with sections 4 and 5 as they were originally.]

As informants, Pienemann used ten Italian children of migrant workers, aged seven to nine years, attending elementary school in Munich in an Italian-language class with supplementary instruction in German as a second language. Samples of their interlanguage were recorded before and after periods of formal instruction for the purpose of analyzing the changes that occurred.

The learning objective, and hence the structural domain under scrutiny in the experiment, was that of German word order. Specifically, Pienemann examined acquisition of the German *inversion* rule, with the developmental stages preceding it identified as follows:

- 1st stage: Canonical word order
  die Kinder spielen mim ball
  (the children play with the ball) [as in Standard German (SG)]
- 2nd stage: Adverb preposing (ADV)
  da Kinder spielen
  (there children play) [SG: "there play children"]
- 3rd stage: Particle shift (PARTICLE)
  alle Kinder muss die pause machen
  (all children must the break have) [as in SG]
- 4th stage: Inversion (INVERSION)
  dann hat sie wieder die Knoch gebringt
  (then has she again the bone brought) [as in SG]

It is important to recognize that the aggregate of word order possibilities in German is the result of interplay among any or all of these four rules.

The learning objective for the experiment was INVERSION and, specifically, whether or not it can be taught in advance of natural acquisition. Data were gathered by means of three interviews of the informants by the investigators and two hidden recordings of the informants sandwiched around two periods of instruction.

Sample results were reported for two of the informants (Giovanni and Teresa), both of whom (as with the other eight) had attained the stage prior to INVERSION. The same classroom instruction ostensibly resulted in attainment of INVERSION for one informant though not the other. Since all other so-called learner-external factors had been controlled for, the differential had to be attributable to a learner-internal factor—namely, the successful informant's readiness to learn INVERSION. Thus the same input produced different results because only in one case had the learner acquired the prerequisites for the corresponding learning process. (See Tables 6-1 and 6-2.)

* * * * *

THE TEACHABILITY HYPOTHESIS

The analysis in the preceding section has shown that a given linguistic structure cannot be added through instruction to the learner's interlanguage at any desired point in time in his/her acquisitional career. Rather the influence of formal instruction is constrained in a specific way: for instance, INVERSION which is acquired later than PARTICLE cannot be learned by any means without prior learning/acquisition of the developmentally earlier structure (PARTICLE).

Table 6-1 TERESA

	hidden recording I	interview I	instruction (copula)	interview II	instruction (INVERSION)	interview III
ADVERB	X	X		X		X
PARTICLE	(O,)	O,		O,		O,
INVERSION	O,	O,		O,		0,83
'INVERSION'						
da is	(X)	X		X		X
was/wo is?	(X)	X		X		X
da V	(X)	(X)				

Table 6-2 GIOVANNI

	hidden recording I	interview I	instruction (copula)	interview II	instruction (INVERSION)	interview III	hidden rec. II	hidden rec. III
ADVERB	X	X		X		X	X	X
PARTICLE	.047	0.31		0.14		0.50	0.61	0.56
INVERSION	.017	0.11		0.20		(0.67)	1.	0.67
'INVERSION'								
da is	X	X		X		X		X
jez is	X						X	X
wo is?						X	X	X
VERB & COMPLEMENT SEPARATED	0.	0.		0.		(0.5)	0.29	0.36

91

In this section I will outline an explanation of the constrained effect of formal instruction on L2 acquisition. What has to be explained is a learning process. Therefore the explanation has to be aimed at psychological plausibility.[3] In order to attain this goal I will build up my considerations on an explanation of acquisitional processes which is based on a psychologically plausible model of sentence processing.

The explanatory approach to L2 acquisition which I refer to has been worked out by the ZISA research group in various publications (cf. Clahsen, 1978, 1980, 1981, 1982). It is relying on a model of sentence processing as has been developed by Bever (1970), Fodor, Bever, and Garrett (1974), Bever and Townsend (1979), and Forster (1979). For the purpose of this paper it is necessary to sketch this position briefly.

The model of sentence processing which I mentioned allows for two different ways of mapping configurations of the underlying structure on surface forms: (1) through an autonomous linguistic level of processing containing a grammatical processor which is task-specific and (2) through an additional problem-solving component (GPS) which is not task-specific.

This has two important implications:

1. The strategies which are contained in the GPS "allow *direct* mappings between underlying structure and surface forms, thus short-circuiting the grammatical processor" (Clahsen, 1982, p. 3; emphasis added).
2. As the GPS is not task-specific "certain (complex) linguistic structures cannot be processed by the strategies of the GPS" (Clahsen, 1982a, p. 4).

Here we have to consider that it is a general finding of research into sentence comprehension and production that processing capacity—in syntax—"results from reorderings and restructurings of various levels of underlying linguistic units" (Clahsen, 1982, p. 4). Therefore, researchers working in this framework conclude that the strategies of the GPS require less processing capacity than grammatical procedures. Against this background the authors quoted assume—in one way or another—a developmental principle which predicts that "rules which require a high degree of processing capacity are acquired late" (Clahsen, 1982, p. 4).

Within this framework Clahsen proposes a set of processing strategies which are based on the findings from the cited empirical research into sentence processing and which allow precise predictions about the order of acquisition of L2 structures. The basic idea of this approach is a consequent application of what has been outlined so far: as strategies require less processing capacity than grammatical operations, the learner will first produce structures which conform to these strategies. Among grammatical processes such will be acquired first which require the lowest processing capacity. For a number of structures Clahsen establishes a hierarchy of processing complexity which derives from the number of strategies violated when producing these structures and from the memory load involved in the grammatical operations. His predictions turned out to be correct in longitudinal and cross-sectional studies.

For the purpose of the present study, I quote those of Clahsen's strategies which explain the order of acquisition of the structures which are relevant in our study (i.e., ADVERB, PARTICLE, and INVERSION):

1. Canonical Order Strategy (COS)
   "In underlying sequences $[x_1 + x_2 \ldots x_n]^c_x[\ ]^c_{x+1} \ldots [\ ]^c_{x+n}$
   in which each subconstituent $x_1, x_2 \ldots x_n$ contributes information to the internal structure of c_x, no subconstituent is moved out of c_x, and no material from the subsequent constituents $c_{x+1}, c_{x+2} \ldots c_{x+m}$ is moved into c_x" (Clahsen, 1981, p. 5).
2. Initialization/Finalization Strategy (IFS)
   "In underlying sequences [X Y Z], permutations are blocked which move X between Y and Z and/or Z between X and Y" (Clahsen, 1981, p. 5).

Leaving aside the other evidence for these strategies quoted in the before-mentioned literature, I briefly want to mention that strategy (2) is supported by mnemonical investigations, which found that elements in the final and initial position in a sentence can be memorized best (cf. Neisser, 1967).

If we now compare strategies (1) and (2) with the three acquisitional stages ADVERB, PARTICLE, and INVERSION, which are essential in this context, it is apparent that ADVERB requires the lowest degree of processing capacity, because it is in line with both strategies as the following drawing indicates:

$$NP + V + X + \boxed{PP}\ ^4$$

The rule PARTICLE can be illustrated as follows[5]:

$$NP + \begin{Bmatrix} Aux \\ Mod \end{Bmatrix} V + X$$

As this illustration shows, this rule violates strategy (1). The same is true for INVERSION[6]:

$$X + NP + [V + NP]_{VP}\ Y$$

The crucial difference between the last two rules is that PARTICLE moves an element into the salient final position: a permutation which is *not blocked* by strategy (2). INVERSION, however, *does* violate strategy (2) and thus requires the highest processing capacity of the three rules.

So, what PARTICLE and INVERSION have in common is that they represent grammatical procedures which interrupt basic linguistic units and thus violate strategy (1). They differ in the respect that PARTICLE moves the crucial element into an "easier" position than INVERSION does. As the procedure underlying PARTICLE requires the same processing prerequisite as one of the crucial procedures underlying INVERSION (namely, the ability to interrupt basic linguistic units), the learner has already acquired one necessary processing prerequisite for INVERSION at the stage PARTICLE while the other (= moving the verb into a less salient position) still has to be acquired.

This explains why it is not possible to reverse the order of acquisition of these two rules or to skip PARTICLE; as one of the processing prerequisites for INVERSION is also the prerequisite for PARTICLE, the learner would automatically be in the position to process PARTICLE as soon as he/she can handle the procedures underlying INVERSION. Thus INVERSION cannot be instructed without simultaneously introducing the crucial processing prerequisite for PARTICLE.

Furthermore, the processing prerequisites underlying INVERSION cannot be learned in any desired order, since violating strategy (2) presupposes that (1) can be violated, too, because moving the verb into an internal position (= 2) requires (in the case under discussion) that basic units be interrupted (= 1). For this reason the interruption of basic units must be learned first.

If we assume that the L2 learner has to abandon the strategies in successive steps, Giovanni was optimally equipped for the learning of INVERSION, since he had already command of the processing prerequisite to be learned first, whereas Teresa would have to learn both prerequisites during the experiment. Teresa would have been best equipped for the learning of processes which only violate strategy (1) but not (2) (like PARTICLE or the above-mentioned subject-final-strategy) at the actual stage of her interlanguage during the experiment (= ADVERB), because she could only produce structures which conform to both strategies. The instruction did not bring about such learning, however, because it concentrated on INVERSION, thus demanding a procedure which violates both strategies simultaneously.

Such a prediction of the point in the L2 development when PARTICLE can be learned best through instruction is exactly in line with the central hypothesis of this paper. This says that an L2 structure can only be learned through instruction if the learner's language is close to the point when this structure is acquired in the natural setting; and Teresa's interlanguage in fact was at the stage prior to PARTICLE.

In this section we have so far been dealing with the theoretical explanation of one special instance of this general hypothesis concerning the learning of INVERSION. The preceding prediction is another concrete case within our hypothesis concerning the learning of PARTICLE that deserves to be justified theoretically.

In the same manner as the processing procedures underlying PARTICLE contain a processing prerequisite for the subsequent stage, this also holds for ADVERB and PARTICLE: it is characteristic of PARTICLE that it violates the Canonical Order Strategy. Logically, before this strategy can be violated in a systematic way, the learner must have made a hypothesis about the underlying word order of the L2. As Meisel (1980) and Clahsen, Meisel, and Pienemann

(1983) show, learners from Romance languages do so by transferring the underlying SVO-order of their first language. This process of non-surface transfer can be witnessed at the two initial acquisitional stages which precede PARTICLE: the learners start out with an exceptionally strict SVO-order (cf. Clahsen, 1981, 1982; Clahsen, Meisel, and Pienemann, 1983; Pienemann, 1981). This initial word order in the acquisition of German as L2, which conforms to both above strategies, is the characteristic of the two stages preceding PARTICLE.

The processing procedure underlying PARTICLE (moving the uninflected part of a complex verbal group into final position) only functions on the basis of the learner's initial hypothesis about the word order of the L2. If the learner were to start out with an underlying SOV-order he/she would have to produce rather different processing procedures, since in this case for the same surface structure (e.g., NP + Aux + NP + V) the inflected part of the verbal group would have to be moved into sentence internal position, a procedure which violates both processing strategies. From this we can conclude that the acquisition of word-order rules would be structured quite differently, if the learner were to start out with an SOV-hypothesis. This is in fact the case in the acquisition of German as L1. Here the learner starts out with an underlying SOV-order and thus acquires the separation of discontinuous elements (PARTICLE) and INVERSION at the same stage (cf. Clahsen, 1982a). The reason for this is that on the basis of this underlying word order both operations require the same degree of processing complexity, because in both cases the finite verbal element has to be moved into sentence internal position, which violates both strategies.

So far we have been dealing with three acquisitional stages which are represented by three permutation rules of German. I have given empirical and theoretical evidence which makes explicit the teachability hypothesis that is behind this paper for these acquisitional stages. So, up to this point in our argumentation our hypothesis has been operationalized on the basis of some specific acquisitional stages. If we want to generalize this hypothesis and at the same time have it testable in other structural domains than the ones investigated, it is necessary to clarify which device will be used to measure the learner's development in his/her L2.

I shall base the teachability hypothesis on the levels of processing capacity rather than on specific linguistic structures which appear in certain acquisitional sequences. The reason for this is the following: if the hypothesis were related to surface phenomena such as acquisitional sequences, we would not automatically be justified in assuming for any given acquisitional sequence that inherent stages always be interrelated in such a way that a given stage contains processing prerequisites for the following stage. Rather, it would be necessary to prove separately for each acquisitional sequence to which the hypothesis would be applied that the stages are interrelated in the way outlined previously. Since such a proof—within the framework we have relied on so far—would have to be based on the processing complexity the corresponding structures involve, I decided to base my hypothesis directly on this abstract level. As the overall pattern of levels of processing complexity could be shown to underlie quite a number of further acquisitional sequences (see below), this can be regarded as a reliable basis for generalizing the hypothesis.

From the approach outlined earlier, Clahsen (1981) infers three levels of processing complexity which the learner has to overcome successively when acquiring the word-order rules of German main clauses:

I. The learner conforms to both above strategies.
II. The learner violates COS but not IFS.
III. The learner violates COS and IFS.

In this abstract formulation it is apparent that at each stage a necessary prerequisite for the following stage is developed: in order to conform to the COS-strategy the learner is forced to establish a fixed word order (= stage 1). This is the prerequisite for any type of systematic violation of this order, which appears at stage II. The interaction between stages II and III is obvious, since the violation of COS is the prerequisite for the simultaneous violation of both strategies (for the interrelation between COS and IFS see previous discussion).

So, the fact that at each stage prerequisites for the subsequent stage are developed is not an incidental feature of the structures investigated, but it is produced by the learner who successively overcomes the processing restrictions represented in the stages I to III. This view is strongly supported by the fact that these stages of processing complexity are also the underlying pattern in the acquisition of quite a number of other permutation rules. Figure 6–2 summarizes these rules in their order of acquisition from the top to the bottom. ADVERB, PARTICLE, and INVERSION have been mentioned before. SVO refers to the canonical order of the first stage[7]; ADV-VP refers to an optional permutation which moves a PP into a position right of the finite verbal element. TOPI stands for another optional permutation which moves an object NP into initial position. Neg + V is an "unacceptable" interlanguage structure in German. The other Neg-rule moves Neg into final position[8] (for detailed information see Clahsen, 1981, 1982a; Meisel, 1980; Clahsen, Meisel, and Pienemann, 1983).

For the acquisition of the rules listed in Figure 2 Clahsen (1981) has shown the following: (a) all rules on stage I conform to both above strategies; (b) the rules on stage II violate the COS-strategy but not the IFS-strategy; (c) all rules on stage II violate both strategies.

Now recall that in the INVERSION case our argument was that Giovanni was able to learn INVERSION because he had already command of prerequisites for processing this structure which Teresa did not have as a learner from the ADVERB-stage. As at each of the stages I to III processing prerequisites for the subsequent stage are developed, our initial line of argumentation can be applied to all structures represented in Table 1. Thus we can predict that a learner at one of the stages I to III can only learn such structures through instruction which are in line with the restrictions of the following stage. Therefore Figure 6–2 represents a broad basis for testing our hypothesis.

Stages	V	PP	NP	Neg
I	SVO	ADVERB	—	Neg + V
II	PARTICLE	—	TOPI	Neg-END

Figure 6–2

Besides the evidence I have presented for the formal learning of INVERSION there are some further pieces of empirical evidence in our data which favor this hypothesis. The first type of additional evidence concerns the structure of our informants' interlanguage. If the idea underlying Figure 6–2 is correct, we should find that Teresa has not acquired any of the structures from stage II or III but only structures from stage I, since we argued that her interlanguage conforms to the restrictions of stage I. This is exactly what we find in the analysis of her interlanguage: as mentioned before, PARTICLE is not applied although she produces contexts for application (cf. Table 1) and INVERSION is not actively applied. Apart from this the only other rule which appears is Neg + V as the following example sentences illustrate:

19. *ich nicht spreche*   (Teresa)
    (I not speak)
20. *du nix essen die mann*   (Teresa)
    (you not eat the man)
21. *die kinder nix komm*   (Teresa)
    (the children no come)

According to Figure 6–2 this is precisely the type of negation structures which must be expected at stage 1 for sentence negation.[7]

Parallel to Teresa, we would predict Giovanni's interlanguage to have the following features before the instructional experiment: PARTICLE, TOPI, and Neg-END but not INVERSION and ADV-VP. This prediction is correct for PARTICLE and INVERSION. The following example sentences indicate that this is also correct for TOPI [cf. sentence (22)] and Neg-END[8] [cf. sentences (23) and (24)].

22. *der große bälle er hat gemacht*   (Giovanni, int. II)
    (the big balls he has made)
23. *der schulbus is nich gekommen*   (Giovanni, int. II)
    (the school bus has not come)
24. *der kann nich sprechen*   (Giovanni, int. II)
    (he cannot speak)

As ADV-VP is an optional rule we cannot rely on obligatory contexts to detect whether this rule is definitely acquired or not. But since there is no instance of a sentence internal position of a prepositional phrase throughout all the interviews before the crucial instruction, we can safely conclude that this rule is not acquired before this decisive point in time.

This brings us to the other type of evidence for our hypothesis which concerns the *development* of Giovanni's interlanguage: as Giovanni proceeded from stage II to III the application of ADV-VP should no longer be blocked after this progress in his L2 development. And in fact there are some instances which indicate that Giovanni starts to apply ADV-VP from the fifth recording on. Two examples are given:

25. *ich kann schon trinken*   (Giovanni, int. V)
    (I can already drink)
26. *der is da oben verstecken*   (Giovanni, int. V)
    (it/he is up there hidden)

As the prepositional phrases which appear right of the finite verbal element in Giovanni's interlanguage are restricted to short adverbs and as the number of such instances is rather small in a considerable corpus, we may assume that the acquisition of ADV-VP is in its very beginnings (cf. Clahsen, Meisel, and Pienemann, 1981).

So the prediction that ADV-VP can be acquired once a learner has proceeded to stage III can roughly be verified. However, the question remains unanswered whether the acquisition/learning of these rudiments of ADV-VP is a result of the instruction or of natural acquisition. Probably this cannot definitely be answered on the basis of the available evidence, but I would like to give the following tentative interpretation: The instruction had the effect that the processing restrictions of stage II could be overcome. For the acquisition of ADV-VP, however, the learner needed some evidence that such a structure exists in his target language. Since this evidence was not provided in a systematic way in the instruction, the learner must have drawn it from some natural input to which he was exposed. In order to gain further evidence the teachability hypothesis will have to be tested with other structures in an experimental setting.

In summary, I have given in this section a theoretical explanation for the observation we made in the preceding section: in the mixed setting of natural and formal L2 acquisition a certain linguistic structure (INVERSION) could only be added to the interlanguage by formal instruction, if the learner was close to the point where this structure was acquired in a natural setting. On the basis of studies of sentence processing I have shown that the learner at the lower stage (ADVERB) has to learn/acquire the processing prerequisite for the stage prior to INVERSION before he/she can process the crucial operation underlying INVERSION.

Since these teachability constraints of INVERSION could be explained on the basis of the processing restrictions which are successively abandoned during the acquisition process, our teachability hypothesis was generalized on the basis of the levels of processing complexity underlying a number of acquisitional sequences thus being testable for further structures. This operationalized formulation of our hypothesis could be supported by some additional evidence from the data discussed in this paper.

DISCUSSION

In this section I will discuss some issues concerning the teachability hypothesis developed above which deserve further clarification. Let us first return to the question from which this study has started out—namely, whether natural L2 acquisition can be influenced by formal instruction.

In earlier studies this question has been investigated from different theoretical positions presupposing different ways of interpreting it (cf. the first section). So we have to indicate which interpretation we refer to, because in this broad formulation the question cannot be answered unequivocally from our data, which contain effects as well as noneffects.

As the teachability hypothesis is a special instance of the view underlying this study that all kinds of language development are dependent on a set of shared principles, this study is based on a special interpretation of this question—namely, whether the process of natural acquisition can be *altered* by instruction. This should not be misinterpreted as a merely technical question, since the order of acquisition is the surface manifestation of underlying acquisition principles. Therefore, if it is impossible to alter this order, we may conclude that instruction cannot influence the underlying acquisition process.

Judging from the findings of our experiment, the answer to this specified formulation of the question is definitely negative: although a structure from stage x can successfully be instructed at stage x-2, thus seemingly shortcutting the "natural" order of acquisition, this learning cannot result in actual use of the structure in normal speech (inside or outside the classroom) since processing it is not possible on the basis of the procedures available to the learner at this point in the development. Teresa's nonacquisition though successful instruction of INVERSION at the stage ADVERB illustrates this point clearly.

So the teachability hypothesis negatively marks off the possible influence of instruction on the acquisition process. However, this negative definition does not imply that formal instruction has no influence on acquisition whatsoever: as previously indicated, instruction can improve acquisition with respect to the speed of acquisition, the frequency of rule application, and the different contexts in which the rule has to be applied, *if* the interlanguage development fulfills the requirements for such an influence.

This, of course, only goes part way toward answering the question under discussion because many resulting questions have remained unanswered; above all how the (conscious or unconscious) knowledge given in the instruction is transmitted into the language-processing system. This transmission of knowledge is in fact implicitly one of the main issues of theories of language teaching, and there is a long tradition of competition between the different methods of transmission, which we know as the foreign language teaching methods.

A crucial assumption underlying all these methods is that language is teachable and that linguistic structures can be taught in many different orders, the most optimal of which has to be selected from a didactic perspective. In the past this assumption has naively been deduced from different learning theories which were not specifically based on the learning/acquisition of language (cf. Vogel and Vogel, 1975). Our findings as well as other studies (cf. Felix, 1981; Felix and Simmet, 1981; Hahn, 1982) have provided strong counterevidence against this assumption. Therefore, language-teaching methods of every different kind should be closely reexamined for psychological validity.

However, our hypothesis itself does not imply an alternative suggestion for an optimal teaching method, the obvious reason being that it only negatively defines the margin within which instruction in whatever method may have an effect. In order to develop psycholinguistically founded language-teaching methods it will be necessary to investigate much more neatly the process of transmission of rational knowledge to the unconscious system of language processing.

The second issue is concerned with the explanation of the teachability constraints described earlier. The teachability hypothesis is based on the processing prerequisites for the structure which has to be learned. From this perspective we can decide whether the speaker of a certain interlanguage is prepared for the learning of a given structure or not.

Within Krashen's (1981, 1982) theory there is a hypothesis which implies a similar prediction about what can be taught to learners of a second language. In the following paragraphs I will demonstrate that the two hypotheses are based on different theoretical assumptions which are not compatible.

Krashen's hypothesis is based on the claim that "children progress [in their language development] by *understanding* language that is a little beyond them" (Krashen, 1981, p. 126). This is known as the so-called $i + 1$ hypothesis, i representing the actual stage of acquisition and 1 indicating the subsequent step of acquisition. According to Krashen the child can understand the crucial new items from $i + 1$ by the aid of context. From this Krashen concludes that formal instruction can influence (in the sense of support/promote) L2 acquisition if it contains comprehensible input.

So, similar to the teachability hypothesis this approach predicts that at stage i elements from $i + 1$ can be learned best. The $i + 1$ hypothesis, however, is less specific in its scope, since it does not imply that *no other* elements than those from $i + 1$ can be learned at stage i and transmitted to the acquired system. Thus it does not address the question whether the process of L2 acquisition can be steered by formal instruction, which is the main concern of the teachability hypothesis. In Krashen's work the $i + 1$ hypothesis is a central part of the definition of the requirements for formal input to the "optimal": in order to promote language acquisition, formal instruction has to provide input containing $i + 1$.

This is not the place to discuss the $i + 1$ approach from a teaching point of view (for discussion see Pienemann, 1986). Rather, I will concentrate on the crucial psycholinguistic assumption on which it is built. This is the assumption that "children progress by *understanding* language that is a little beyond them" (Krashen, 1981, p. 126), "where 'understand' means that the acquirer is focused on the meaning and not on the form of the message" (Krashen, 1982, p. 21).

Bearing in mind that the $i + 1$ hypothesis is at the core of Krashen's theory from which he derives far-reaching conclusions for formal instruction, it is only very vaguely based on empirical research:

1. The $i + 1$ hypothesis cannot be operationalized or tested, since i, $i + 1$, and so forth are not defined in Krashen's work at all.
2. The claim that input containing $i + 1$ promotes language acquisition is derived from the assumed learning-aid-effect of tuned input to the language-learning child. It is, however, questionable whether care-taker talk—not to speak of natural L2 input—is in fact tuned to the level of the child's L1 production. Krashen writes that "we see posi-tive, but not strikingly high correlations between linguistic input com-plexity and linguistic competence in children" (1981, p. 102; Newport, Gleitman, and Gleitman, 1977; Cross, 1977). However, these positive correlations which are listed in Krashen's book (1981, p. 126) are selected from a larger number of almost equally distributed *negative and positive* (or zero) correlations in his studies.
3. There is not much research into the interaction between comprehen-sion and production in L2 acquisition (or in language acquisition in general) which is based on longitudinal comparative studies, but exist-ing findings strongly contradict Krashen's acquisition-by-understand-ing claim, since comprehension and production were found not to develop as mirror images of each other but as separate abilities (cf., e.g., Bever, 1981; Bloom and Lahey, 1978). Not only may the gap between comprehension and production be more than one acquisi-tional stage, but there is strong evidence that the interaction between the two sides of language processing does not necessarily have to be such that comprehension precedes production. Rather, it is possible that children *produce* items first and only in a later stage understand them (cf. Bloom and Lahey, 1978).

Besides this, in Krashen's hypothesis the role of nonlinguistic factors in comprehension is seen as a static one, adding the specific information of $i + 1$ to the learner. However, the nonlinguistic factors which contribute to produc-ing and understanding messages play significantly different roles in the two processes and undergo several changes during the acquisition (cf. also Schöler, 1982; Strohner and Nelson, 1974).

As a final issue I briefly want to touch upon what implications our findings have for the theory of foreign language instruction. This matter is dealt with more explicitly in another paper (cf. Pienemann, 1986).

The results I presented here very clearly demonstrate what has been claimed by universalist researchers before (cf. Hahn, 1982; Felix, 1981; Wode, 1981): if formal input is constructed in contradiction to natural sequences, it impedes rather than promotes language acquisition. There are two obvious though opposite conclusions which have been drawn from this finding. One is that the formal instruction of syntax can be abandoned, since the child's language acquisition is self-regulating anyway (Dulay and Burt, 1973). The other is that formal input should be presented in the natural order of acquisition (cf. Krashen, Madden, and Bailey, 1975).

Both proposals are short-sighted: giving up the instruction of syntax is to allow for the fossilization of interlanguages in a simplified form (cf. Pienemann, 1978). Such a fossilization often appears with the natural L2 acquisition in minority groups (cf. Meisel, Clahsen, and Pienemann, 1981). Of course, it is unclear whether fossilization can be avoided by instruction, but abandoning the instruction of syntax at this point in time is not to care about how this question can be solved.

Teaching syntax along the line of the natural order seems to imply that markedly deviant transitional structures like ADVERB without INVERSION have to be taught, too. At the time being it is simply unknown what effect such a procedure would have on language acquisition. Of course, this problem could be solved without intricate teaching experiments, if it is possible to base the structure of formal input on the natural order in such a way that teaching deviant forms can be avoided. But this, too, is an unsolved problem.

Additionally, if teaching is intended to be based on the process of natural acquisition, it has to be taken into account that—depending on the learner type—learning problems which appear at a given acquisitional stage can be solved in different structural ways ranging between "deviant" and standard-oriented (cf. Meisel, Clahsen, and Pienemann, 1981; Pienemann, 1981). Thus it has to be decided which of these transitional solutions of learning tasks has to be adopted for instruction. This brings us to another problem—namely, whether the different types of transitional solutions, which are bound to specific learner types, can be manipulated by instruction aiming at efficiency, nondeviant competence, and so on (for discussion see Pienemann, 1984).

These remarks are intended to illustrate that applying L2 research is not just writing acquisitional orders into new curricula. Solving a number of severe and psycholinguistically relevant problems is a necessary part of application. Besides this it seems evident to me that a concrete proposal for application has to be embedded into some approach to language teaching. However, what I think is far out of reach is a "psycholinguistic method" of L2 instruction. After the waves of "direct method," "language lab," and so forth, the teacher should be saved from another "instant application." For the development of instructional methods which are above cooking-recipe status, problems must be solved whose outlines we may only just have discerned.

NOTES

1. This research was supported from many sides. My thanks go to the Bavarian Department of Education for the permission to conduct the experiment, to the Institute of German as a Second Language at the University of Munich for their invaluable support, and to the University of Passau for the use of facilities in the analysis of data. Invaluable comments on ideas and on an earlier version of this paper came from Harald Clahsen, Rainer Dietrich, Sascha Felix, Kenneth Hyltenstam, Jürgen Meisel,

and Howard Nicholas. This work could not have been produced without the patient constructive support from my colleague Angela Hahn. My thanks also go to Claudia Wimmer and Jan Wilts who have spent a lot of time on organizing, transcribing, and analyzing, not to forget Martin Fee, John Halliday, and Michael Knight for lending me their native speaker competence.

2. T. Pica's (1982) work, which was not available at the time I wrote this paper, is in fact a comparison of acquisitional sequences in both types of acquisition (M. Long, personal communication). For the time being I can only include references to her work in the bibliography, which I received after the manuscript was finished.

3. The term *psychological plausibility* is used here in order to indicate that the explanations of learning processes we would like to provide should be based on linguistic operations which do not contradict psycholinguistic findings about the mental processes involved in language processing. This does not imply, however, that the operations discussed below have been proved to be mentally *real* (cf. Clahsen, Meisel, and Pienemann, 1983).

4. All the following descriptions are based on an underlying SVO order for the interlanguages being described. This assumption for the underlying word order is justified in some detail in Clahsen et al. (1983). The main point of this argument is that (a) there is no evidence for SVO order in the data (i.e., all interlanguages conform to an SVO order in the initial stages), (b) that it is plausible to assume some sort of transfer for this initial word order, since the L1s of the corresponding learners are Romance languages, which follow an underlying SVO order.

5. This is only one of the structural descriptions of the rule, which can also be aplied to separable verbs.

6. This illustration, too, only refers to *one* possible structural description for the rule.

7. In Figure 2 ADVERB and SVO appear at the same stage, although these structures are acquired successively by child learners (cf. Pienemann, 1981). The reason for this way of presenting stages of acquisition is that the structuring principle in Figure 2 is not the pure temporal order of acquisition alone but primarily the processing complexity involved in these structures as measured in the way outlined earlier. Therefore, Figure 2 does not say anything about the temporal relation between the structure at each stage. But, of course, it implies that all structures at stage III are acquired before the structures at stage II; which are in turn acquired before the structures at stage I.

8. Note that in sentences in which Neg-End is applied the negating element does not necessarily have to appear in final position since there are other permutations which may be applied after Neg-End and which also move an element into final position [e.g., PARTICLE, as indicated by example sentence (23)] (cf. Clahsen, Meisel, and Pienemann, 1983, 121ff.).

QUESTIONS FOR DISCUSSION

1. Although many of the papers in this section make use of much the same technical terminology, not all the papers necessarily use these terms in the same sense. Consider, for example, the meaning of the word *strategy* for Bialystok and for Pienemann. What does *strategy* mean for these two authors, and in which sense(s) (if any) does *strategy* have a relevance to pedagogical consciousness raising (CR)?

2. Pienemann faults much of the second language acquisition literature for too much attention to learning success and not enough on acquisition processes. Could the Canale and Swain paper be criticized for the same reasons, or are there broader concerns that should also be taken into consideration?

3. What special problems for pedagogical CR can you foresee that might be posed by Pienemann's teachability hypothesis? How much of what you do with grammatical CR falls within the constraints imposed by the teachability hypothesis?

4. Can Pienemann's claim (i.e., his teachability hypothesis) be used in support of arguments *for* CR in language pedagogy? Could it also be used *against* CR? Explain how a yes answer to both questions might be possible.

REFERENCES

Andersen, R., ed. 1983. *Pidginization and Creolization as Language Acquisition.* Rowley, Mass.: Newbury House.

Andersen, R., ed. 1984. *Second Languages: A Cross-Linguistic Perspective.* Rowley, Mass.: Newbury House.

Berman, R. 1982. Cognitive principles and language acquisition. Paper presented at the Second European-North American Workshop on Cross-Linguistic Second Language Acquisition Research. Göhrde, West Germany, August.

Bever, T. 1970. The cognitive basis for linguistic structures. In J. Hayes (ed.), *Cognition and the Development of Language.* New York: Wiley.

Bever, T. 1981. Normal acquisition processes explain the critical period for language learning. In K. Diller (ed.), *Individual Differences and Universals in Language Learning Aptitude.* Rowley, Mass.: Newbury House.

Bever, T., and D. Townsend. 1979. Perceptual mechanisms and formal properties of main and subordinate clauses. In W. Cooper and E. Walker (eds.), *Sentence Processing: Psycholinguistic Studies Presented to Merrill Garrett.* New York: Academic Press.

Bloom, L., and M. Lahey. 1978. *Language Development and Language Disorders.* New York: Wiley.

Clahsen, H. 1978. Syntax oder Produktionsstrategien? Zum natülichen Zweitspracherwerb der Gastarbeiter. In R. Kloepfer et al. (eds.), *Bildung und Ausbildung in der Romania*, Vol. 2. München: Fink.

Clahsen, H. 1980. Psycholinguistic aspects of L2 acquisition: word order phenomena in foreign workers' interlanguage. In S. Felix (ed.), *Second Language Development: Trends and Issues.* Tübingen: Günter Narr.

Clahsen, H. 1981. The acquisition of German word order: a test case for cognitive approaches to L2 development. In R. Andersen (ed.), *Pidginization and Creolization as Language Acquisition.* Rowley, Mass.: Newbury House.

Clahsen, H. 1982a. Autonomy and interaction in (second) language acquisition research: evidence for an integrativist position. Paper presented at the Second European–North American Workshop on Cross-Linguistic Second Language Acquisition Research. Göhrde, West Germany, August.

Clahsen, H. 1982b. Spracherwerb in der Kindheit. In *Eine Untersuching zur Entwicklung der Syntax in der Kindheit.* Tübingen: Günter Narr.

Clahsen, H., J. Meisel, and M. Pienemann. 1983. *Deutsch als Zweitsprache: Der Spracherwerb ausländischer Arbeiter.* Tübingen: Günter Narr.

Cooper, W., and E. Walker, eds. 1979. *Sentence Processing: Psycholinguistic Studies Presented to Merrill Garrett.* New York: Academic Press.

Cross, T. 1977. Mother's speech adjustments: the contribution of selected child listener variables. In C. Snow and C. Ferguson (eds.), *Talking to Children: Language Input and Acquisition.* Cambridge: Cambridge University Press.

Dietrich, R., T. Kaufmann, and G. Storch. 1979. Beobachtungen zum gesteuerten Fremdsprachenerwerb. *Linguistische Berichte* **64**:56–81.

Dulay, H., and M. Burt. 1973. Should we teach children syntax? *Language Learning* **23**:235–252.

Felix, S. 1978. Zur Relation zwischen natürlichem und gesteuertem Zweitsprachenerwerb. In R. Kloepfer et al. (eds.), *Bildung und Ausbildung in der Romania,* Vol. 2. München: Fink.

Felix, S. 1981. The effect of formal instruction on second language acquisition. *Language Learning* **32**:87–112.

Felix, S. 1982. *Psycholinguistische Aspekte des Zweitsprachenerwerbs.* Tübingen: Günter Narr.

Felix, S., and A. Simmet. 1981. Der Erwerb der Personalpronomina im Fremdsprachenunterricht. *Neusprachliche Mitteilungen* **3**:132–144.

Felix, S., and H. Wode, eds. 1983. *Language Development at the Crossroads: Papers from the Interdisciplinary Conference on Language Acquisition at Passau.* Tübingen: Günter Narr.

Fodor, J., T. Bever, and M. Garrett. 1974. *The Psychology of Language: An Introduction to Psycholinguistics and Generative Grammar.* New York: McGraw-Hill.

Forster, K. 1979. Levels of processing and the structure of the language processor. In W. Cooper and E. Walker (eds.), *Sentence Processing: Psycholinguistic Studies Presented to Merrill Garrett.* New York: Academic Press.

Hahn, A. 1982. *Fremdsprachenunterricht and Sprachwerb: Linguistische Untersuchungen zum Gesteuerten Zweitsprachenerwerb.* Ph.D. dissertation, University of Passau.

Heuer, H. 1976. *Lerntheorie des Englischunterrichts: Untersuchungen zur Analyse Fremdsprachlicher Lernprozesse.* Heidelberg.

Hüllen, W., and L. Jung. 1979. *Sprachstruktur und Spracherwerb.* Düsseldorf.

Jungblut, G. 1974. Terminologie er Lehr-und Lernphasen im Fremdsprachenunterricht. *Linguistik und Didaktik* **17**:33–41.

Kloepfer, R., et al., eds. 1979. *Bildung und Ausbildung in der Romania,* Vol. 2. München: Fink.

Krashen, S. 1981. *Second Language Acquisition and Second Language Learning.* Oxford: Pergamon.

Krashen, S. 1982. *Principles and Practice in Second Language Acquisition.* Oxford: Pergamon.

Krashen, S., C. Madden, and N. Bailey. 1975. Theoretical aspects of grammatical sequencing. In M. Burt and H. Dulay (eds.), *On TESOL '75.* Washington, D.C.: TESOL.

Lightbown, P. 1983. Exploring relationships between developmental and instructional sequences in L2 acquisition. In H. Seliger and M. Long (eds.), *Classroom Oriented Research in Second Language Acquisition.* Rowley, Mass.: Newbury House.

Lightbown, P. 1987. Classroom language as input to second language acquisition. In O. Pfaff (ed.), *First and Second Language Acquisition Processes.* Rowley, Mass.: Newbury House.

Long, M. 1982. Does second language instruction make a difference? A review of research. *TESOL Quarterly* **14**:388–390.

Meisel, J. 1984. Strategies of second language acquisition. In R. Andersen (ed.), *Second Languages: A Cross-Linguistic Perspective.* Rowley, Mass.: Newbury House.

Meisel, J., H. Clahsen, and M. Pienemann. 1981. On determining developmental stages in natural second language acquisition. *Studies in Second Language Acquisition* 3:109–135.

Neisser, U. 1967. *Cognitive Psychology.* New York: Appleton.

Newport, E., H. Gleitman, and L. Gleitman. 1977. Mother, I'd rather do it myself: some effects and non-effects of maternal speech style. In C. Snow and C. Ferguson (eds.), *Talking to Children: Language Input and Acquisition.* Cambridge: Cambridge University Press.

Pica, T. 1982. The role of linguistic environment in second language acquisition of the English indefinite article. Unpublished manuscript, University of Pennsylvania.

Pienemann, M. 1978. Erwebssequenzen und Lernprogression: Überlegungen zur Steuerung des Zweitspracherwerbs. In R. Kloepfer et al. (eds.), *Bildung und Ausbildung in der Romania,* Vol. 2. München: Fink.

Pienemann, M. 1981. *Der Zweitspracherwerb ausländischer Arbeitkinder.* Bonn: Bouvier.

Pienemann, M. 1984. The effect of instruction on learners' orientations in L2 acquisition. Unpublished manuscript, University of Sydney.

Pienemann, M. 1986. Learnability and syllabus construction. In K. Hyltenstam and M. Pienemann (eds.), *Modelling and Assessing Second Language Acquisition.* Clevedon: Multilingual Matters.

Schöler, H. 1982. *Zur Entwicklung des Verstehens inkonsistenter Äusserungen.* Fechtenheim: Fischer.

Slobin, D. 1973. Cognitive prerequisites for the development of grammar. In C. Ferguson and D. Slobin (eds.), *Studies of Child Language Development.* New York: Holt, Rinehart and Winston.

Slobin, D. 1975. Language change in childhood and history. *Working Papers of the Language Behavior Research Laboratory,* No. 41. Berkeley: University of California.

Snow, C., and C. Ferguson, eds. 1977. *Talking to Children: Language Input and Acquisition.* Cambridge: Cambridge University Press.

Strohner, H., and K. Nelson. 1974. The young child's development of sentence comprehension: influence of event probability, non-verbal context, syntactic form and heir strategies. *Child Development* 45:567–576.

Vogel, K., and S. Vogel. 1975. *Lernpsychologie und Fremdsprachenerwerb.* Tübingen: Günter Narr.

Wode, H. 1981. *Learning a Second Language. I. An Integrated View of Language Acquisition.* Tübingen: Günter Narr.

7
Consciousness Raising and Universal Grammar

William Rutherford
University of Southern California
Michael Sharwood Smith
Rijksuniversiteit, Utrecht

In this paper we will examine the role of consciousness raising (CR) in the acquisition of grammatical structure. By *consciousness raising* we mean the deliberate attempt to draw the learner's attention specifically to the formal properties of the target language. We will, in particular, question a current assumption that formal grammar has a minimal or even nonexistent role to play in language pedagogy and that theoretical linguistics has virtually nothing to contribute to what goes on in the classroom. We will in fact sketch out what the nature of such a contribution might be.

If there is one thing taken for granted today in language teaching methodology, it would seem to be that teachers should give preeminence to creating an environment in the classroom which approximates to the real-life communicative use of language. Teachers have been encouraged for some time to discard textbooks which draw attention to the grammatical forms of the target language, such attention being excluded ostensibly for its "nonnaturalistic" character—that is, because it is atypical of so-called normal everyday spontaneous language behavior. In one quite well-known approach, for example, teaching materials that do provide for explicit CR are converted to assignments for outside the classroom as a means of motivating those types of learners who derive a sense of security from knowing *about* the language (Krashen and Terrell, 1983). It is not claimed, however, that CR plays any direct role in the development of L2 linguistic competence.

"Consciousness Raising and Universal Grammar," by William E. Rutherford and Michael Sharwood Smith, 1985, *Applied Linguistics*, vol. 6, no. 3, pp. 274–282. Reprinted with permission of Oxford University Press.

It would not be true, current fashion notwithstanding, to say that re-searchers in second language acquisition uniformly deny a role for explicit grammar in the development of target language competence. Bialystok (1981), for example, has proposed a framework in which what we here call CR does play, or can play, a part. Sharwood Smith (1981a) called into question the simplistic view of CR in which intuitive, "natural" acquisitional processes are compared with the highly conscious metalinguistic learning of rules and para-digms, much like that associated with grammar-translation methodology. The conscious type of learning is assumed to be irrelevant to development of the spontaneous control of first or second languages and, in any case, is not available to the pre-adolescent child, according to standard Piagetian thinking. There are two ways of challenging the validity of such a rigid dichotomy. The first is to call attention to the metalinguistic activities that young monolingual or bilingual children indulge in during the acquisition of their first language(s) (Sharwood Smith, 1981a). Clearly, attention to the outer form of language is not the prerogative of the adolescent learner in a formal classroom context. Now admittedly, the role that such metalinguistic awareness plays in facilitat-ing acquisition is not clear. Furthermore, children do not themselves formulate anything but the simplest of rules to capture their metalinguistic insights. However, this is an open question and it cannot be assumed that attention to the form of language only comes in the formal classroom as an external "unnatural" requirement of the teacher or textbook.

The second challenge lies in the fact that CR is highly complex and variegated. The provision of rules of thumb—or, at an even more sophisticated level, of linguistic rules—is the extreme end of what is really a continuum. There are many ways of drawing attention to form without indulging in metalinguistic discussion. A simple example would be the use of typographical conventions such as underlining or capitalizing a particular grammatical sur-face feature, where you merely ask the learner to pay attention to anything that is underlined or capitalized. Another example would be the deliberate expo-sure of the learner to an artificially large number of instances of some target structure in the language on the assumption that the very high frequency of the structure in question will attract the learner's attention to the relevant formal regularities. In other words, CR can have *degrees* of explicitness. It can also have degrees of elaboration; that is, the teacher can spend more time, use more space, and go into more depth in drawing attention to some aspect of the target grammar, while keeping the degree of explicitness constant. However, we are not saying that either of these two aspects of CR will *automatically* ensure the acquisition of some structure—that is, that CR is a sufficient condition for acquisition to take place. There is enough evidence available to show that it does not, even if common sense fails to make this apparent. All that is being said is that when CR is being discussed, a very complex range of possibilities is at issue, not just the classroom articulation of rules and paradigms in the traditional manner.

We lack the research evidence for ruling CR out of court. The claim here, in fact, is that the more differentially CR is considered, the more it seems reasonable to treat the role of CR as a set of unresolved empirical questions. Another way of putting this is to say that we should seriously consider the following hypothesis, a slightly modified version of the Pedagogical Grammar Hypothesis (PGH) proposed by Sharwood Smith (1980)—namely:

> Instructional strategies which draw the attention of the learner to specifically structural regularities of the language, as distinct from the message content, will under certain conditions significantly increase the rate of acquisition over and above the rate expected from learners acquiring that language under natural circumstances where attention to form may be minimal and sporadic.

We would be the first to admit that there are questions being begged in this formulation. We will thus briefly consider what might be meant here by "certain conditions" on which the validity and comprehensibility of this claim rests.

Having stated our position, but before elaborating on it, we would like to focus briefly on one of its (obvious) assumptions—one that periodically comes up for discussion among language-learning researchers—namely, the relationship (if any indeed) between language pedagogy and formal linguistics.

In the era of what one might term *modern linguistics* (since, say, 1945), the large body of works on language pedagogy that claims to have been informed by linguistic theory have in common at least one overriding characteristic—namely, that linguistics was seen as the indispensable repository, so to speak, of the facts about language form that were to be imparted to the learner. That is, accounts of linguistic phenomena in formal terms were seen as candidates for dilution, simplification, or rephrasing in informal terms for the benefit of language teacher and/or learner. It is therefore not surprising that in the recent shift away from pedagogical attention to language form—a shift promulgated by a number of newly emergent methodologies—there should also occur some veiled (and not so veiled) criticism of linguistics per se, and emphatic reminders that theoretical linguistics after all has ostensibly very little to offer language pedagogy. Recent statements to this effect can be found, for example, in the writings of three of our most influential language-teaching specialists. In one of the articles of H. G. Widdowson we read that "applied linguistics ("as the theoretical branch of language teaching pedagogy") can only claim to be an autonomous area of inquiry to the extent that it can free itself from the hegemony of linguistics and deny the connotations of its name," and that "there is reason to suspect that a description [of language] deriving from linguistic theory is *not* the best suited one for language teaching" (1979, pp. 234–235). In the introduction to a section called "The Linguistic Background" in a book on language teaching edited by C. J. Brumfit and K. Johnson, these authors write that "linguistics . . . is by and large the study of language structure. Perhaps this is why transformational grammar, so revolutionary in linguistics, has had such little effect on language teaching: after all, the most it can offer is alternative strategies for teaching grammar— new ways of teaching the same thing" (Brumfit and Johnson, 1979, p. 3).

We find these sorts of statements questionable on three counts: the implied very simplistic notion of what linguistics is, the implied very impoverished notion of what "transformational" (i.e., generative) grammar is, and the implied misunderstanding of what can be done with formal principles of language organization in pedagogy. However, we do not wish that this criticism be taken as effort on our part to single out the authors in question; indeed, we would argue that their assumptions concerning limitations upon what a possible relationship between formal linguistics and language pedagogy could be are representative of a fairly wide sample of language-teaching professionals.

To say that linguistics is the study of language structure is like saying that astronomy is the study of stars or that chemistry is the study of elements. What is lacking, of course, is a statement of the goals one wishes to attain through such study, and for linguistics that goal is an understanding of the workings of the human mind—that is, linguistics as one of the cognitive sciences.

To suggest that the goal of generative research is to provide better and better descriptions of language structure is like saying that the goal of medical science is to provide better and better descriptions of disease symptoms. What is lacking here, of course, is a clear conception of the proper ultimate goal: the development of theories by which phenomena—constructs and processes— may be *explained*. In this light then, the descriptive goals become secondary.

Finally, to imply that the only value of formal linguistics in language pedagogy is that it can provide improved ways of teaching the inventory of familiar grammatical constructions is like saying that the value of music theory to actual performance is that it can improve one's scales and arpeggios. What is absent here is a proper understanding of just what it is that theory—in this case linguistic theory—can contribute to practice—in this case language pedagogy. It is this third misapprehension that leads us back to the substance of our paper.

Having already proposed that the PGH be taken as the point of departure, we need now to ask the obvious next question: On what basis does one decide what to call (and not to call) attention to? Following our discussion above we distinguish in general three different possible kinds of pedagogical decisions with regard to the role of grammatical consciousness in language learning: one can explicitly call attention to a grammatical feature and, if necessary, even articulate an informal pedagogical "rule" as an instructional aid; one can *implicitly* call attention to a grammatical feature through calculated exposure of the learner to crucial preselected data; and one can choose to ignore a grammatical feature altogether, thus neither suppressing it nor giving it prominence. An additional option cutting across the first two choices is that what is called attention to may be accomplished through degrees of *elaboration*. Decisions of these kinds (if indeed they are rendered at all) are usually made by language-teaching professionals on the basis of informal and ad hoc notions of "complexity" and "simplicity" born of long experience with language learners in settings of formal instruction. Without denying the value of such experience, it is nevertheless our contention that such decision making is important enough that we must also explore the theoretical underpinnings of pedagogical grammar (PG) by which these decisions may come about in principled fashion.

Our attempt to address the question of decision making in PG thus implies that one must have recourse to something like a model of PG, where one of the components of such a model—namely, that concerned with formal principles of language organization—derives from linguistic theory. Without trying here to work out the full details of a possible model of PG (but see Sharwood Smith, 1980, p. 45, for a first approximation), we will discuss the nature of its linguistic component and, ipso facto, the question of how linguistic theory might inform pedagogical decision making in a principled way. The principles whose potential utilization we will explore here are those embodied in modern generative theory and, in particular, "core grammar" and its associated theory of markedness (Chomsky, 1981a,b,c; White, 1983a, 1984a). It should be emphasized, however, that the issues we raise throughout this discussion are of a highly empirical nature, as already mentioned. At this stage, then, it is difficult to be more than simply programmatic.

The most recent instantiation of generative grammar (known as "government and binding") is a theory of Universal Grammar (UG). UG, in turn, "consists of a highly structured and restrictive system of principles with certain open parameters, to be fixed by experience. As these parameters are fixed, a grammar is determined, what we call a 'core grammar'" (Chomsky, 1981b, p. 38). We assume, then, following the authors cited earlier, that a core grammar for a given language thus determined will consist of, among other things, the constraints on the movement of elements within the sentence (i.e., constraints on alpha-movement), *rules of construal* that define how anaphors are to be interpreted, and the result of having set the parameters (e.g., word order, PRO-drop), with varying degrees of markedness. The (relatively unmarked) core is supplemented by a marked *periphery* containing language-specific rules, and surface-structure well-formedness will be attained through the effect of universal constraints and conditions on the output of derivations.

UG, or the set of formal constraints upon the ways in which a first language may be presumed to develop, is a biological endowment of our species. And there is as yet no reason to suppose that these constraints are not still in operation in adulthood, or for the acquisition of subsequent languages. Indeed, the research findings for UG in L2 acquisition that have appeared so far suggest that the constraints *are* still in place. For example, Ritchie (1978) effectively demonstrated that what we now call the "subjacency condition" (Chomsky, 1981c)—in 1978 Ritchie could only identify it as the "right roof constraint"—must be counted "among the principles which constitute the post-critical-period language acquirer's capacities for language acquisition" (Ritchie, 1978, p. 43). White (1983b) has provided some evidence that the resetting of a UG parameter (viz., PRO-drop) from the learner's L1 in the learning of L2 can affect the acquisition of a cluster of other L2 grammatical properties associated with that parameter. Schmidt (1980) showed that interlanguages obey universal constraints on the surface orders of canonical constituents in coordinate structures. Adjemian and Liceras (1984) argue that Anglophone adult learners of L2 French and Spanish, wherein interlanguage (IL) production does not reveal preposition stranding, perceive as marked the loss of oblique case assignment (Chomsky, 1982). Adjemian and Liceras presumably were limited to knowledge of an earlier formulation of the [ppP-ϕ] filter (preposition stranding), permitted in English but in few other languages—thus attesting to the still active role of UG in L2 acquisition (but see White, 1983a, for predictions that marked forms will be *preferred* by the learner under such conditions). Finally, Flynn (1984) has tried to show that language-learning sensitivity of the child to the principal recursion direction (i.e., left- or right-branching) of his or her L1 is still present in adult L2 acquisition. Other such studies are reported on in Gass (1984). It is our feeling that findings of this kind are of considerable importance for theoretical approaches to PG and, in particular, for principled guidance in decision making with regard to possible grammatical candidates for CR.

   We will assume as valid, then, the hypothesis that certain principles of UG remain constant for all language learners and that they need not be further considered for any active role in the delineation of PG. There are two aspects of such principles that we need to mention here: the nature of the principle itself, and the ways in which the principle applies to individual languages. The principles are the universal *conditions* and *constraints* on syntactic well-formedness that are presumed to hold for all languages—for example, subjacency (but see below), case assignment, the theta criterion, and so on. For example, we would claim, consistent with our hypothesis, that (attested) English IL production of a sentence like *He put the book* is to be interpreted not as failure to meet the theta criterion (the requirement that all thematic roles be assigned), but rather as improper subcategorization of *put*.

   The other aspect of these principles is to be found in the parameters, choice of bounding nodes, and so on, the nature of whose application or setting may vary across languages but where in the case of particular pairs of L1/L2 the application or setting is identical. Taking parameterization as our example—and, in particular, PRO-drop—there are pairs of languages whose setting of the PRO-drop parameter will be the same. Spanish and Italian would represent one such pair, for both of which PRO-drop entails "the possibility of empty subjects, of verb-subject word order, and of extraction of subjects out of embedded clauses containing complementizers" (White, 1984b, p. 7). Since the learning of either of these languages by speakers of the other involves no resetting of the PRO-drop parameter, we would hold that the parameter should play no active role in the construction of PGs for this pair of languages as L1/L2.

   There are, of course, aspects of UG *conditions* and *constraints* that vary with relation to specific languages and that also need therefore to be considered for purposes of PG. For example, while "subjacency"—that is, the stipulation that no constituent may move across more than one bounding node in any single rule application—is a condition that holds universally, what constitutes a "bounding node" will vary from one language to another, with far-reaching consequences for the shape of those individual grammars. [The bounding nodes in English, e.g., are claimed to be NP, S, and S-bar (Chomsky, 1981a); for Italian they are NP and S-bar (Rizzi, 1982).] Bounding nodes would therefore have an effect on the construction of PGs.

Once again, we suggest that where there is UG identity in a given set L1/L2 for those features of UG that vary across languages (e.g., parameter settings) and that become fixed in the course of (native language) experience, CR need not figure in the corresponding PG. The learner may not immediately recognize the relevant cross-linguistic identities between L1 and L2 but, again, priorities for CR should be elsewhere.

We turn our attention finally to the relationship between differential CR and differential aspects of contrasting UGs. Recall that the differential aspects of CR can occur on two distinct planes, one having to do with the *degree* of CR itself [viz., explicit (overt), implicit (covert), and zero], the other having to do with the extent of *elaboration* of CR. However, we will confine ourselves here to discussion of the first of the two planes—degree of CR—since the possible contribution of UG (if any) to decision making with regard to *how much* and *how elaborate* the data to provide for the learner is at present quite obscure.

Let us discuss the matter of differential CR within the context of parametric variation, wherein a given pair L1/L2 will specifically reveal activation or nonactivation of the PRO-drop parameter. Fitting this description, for example, would be the pair Spanish (activation)/English (nonactivation), and these will suffice here for purposes of illustration. It might be supposed that contrasting settings for PRO-drop will pose equivalent problems for speakers of either Spanish or English learning the other's language. Yet not only are there so far no acquisitional data to support such a guess, but in fact White (1984b) has claimed that UG, incorporating this concept of parameterization, makes a quite different prediction—namely, that the activated PRO-drop parameter in Spanish will pose a greater problem for Spanish speakers learning English than vice versa. This is due simply to the fact that the Spanish speakers have to notice *the nonoccurrence in English of missing pronoun subjects*, whereas the English speakers have only to notice their *occurrence* in Spanish. The evidence that something is possible in a given target language may in principle, if not in practice, consist of a single example, whereas the learner may need a great deal of exposure in order to come to the realization that a given construction type is not possible under any circumstances.

These observations have perhaps the following implications, then, for CR in PG. We would suggest that the different learning problems posed by the contrasting parameter settings discussed above point to decisions of CR in PG that likewise contrast as to explicitness. That is, CR for the learning by Spanish speakers of the nonoccurrence in English of missing pronoun subjects (i.e., their obligatory presence) will be *explicit*. CR for the learning by English speakers of the occurrence in Spanish of missing pronoun subjects (i.e., their optional presence) will be *implicit*.[1] The claims—that the different parameter settings will pose the difficulties cited and that the differential CR just described will aid the acquisition in question—need of course to undergo much empirical validation, as does the additional claim (White, 1983b, 1984b) that L2 acquisition of the *cluster* of properties associated with PRO-drop will automatically occur as a natural consequence of the resetting of the PRO-drop parameter by English speakers in the course of learning Spanish.

Implied throughout our discussion is an assumption that in recent years has often been discounted, if not even discredited—namely, that contrastive linguistics can be taken seriously and that it has an important role to play not only in L2 acquisition research but in language pedagogy as well. This newly emergent importance derives in large part from the solid grounding of contrastive research in current versions of linguistic theory that for the first time make it possible to compare languages not in terms of the operation of specific (and often poorly motivated) transformational rules, but rather in terms of the new differential application across all languages of a relatively small set of universal principles (cf. recent papers of White, 1983a,b, 1984,a,b; Flynn, 1984; Liceras, 1985). Contrastive research now proceeds, therefore, within a theoretically principled framework, and it is this fact alone that establishes its value for language pedagogy and strengthens the conditions for (essential) empirical testing of the PGH. Serious consideration of the PGH, then, as a set of empirical questions concerning differential CR, owes at least part of this seriousness to a linguistic theory that makes principled contrastive study actually possible.

It must be understood that what we have tried to set forth here is not so much a *claim* about CR (and much less ex cathedra pontifications to practicing teachers) as an outline of valid and plausible research programs for formal investigation of CR within a UG framework, leading to serious testing of the PGH and perhaps eventually to useful applications to classroom instruction. Nor do we intend that CR, of any kind, be understood as an alternative to so-called communicative language teaching or as a substitute for the attainment of communicative skills. CR is considered by us as a potential facilitator for the acquisition of linguistic competence and has nothing directly to do with the use of that competence for the achievement of specific communicative objectives, or with the achievement of fluency—that is, automatic control of structure. (Nor is there anything inherent in the notion of CR itself that immediately suggests how it is to be realized in all the many possible classroom situations.) As such, then, CR is to be seen as one part of a larger pedagogical context that embraces as well the other essentials for target language mastery. (We are not saying that UG is the *only* force determining candidates for CR in PG; rather, we would say that it may be the only *constant* force, other influencing factors, e.g., proficiency level, curricular objectives, affective variables, etc., appearing under particular circumstances.)

Once again, it is time for CR and the PGH to be subjected to empirical scrutiny. With recent advances in the delineation of UG, "there is no reason to assume that consciousness-raising by the teacher and conscious learning by the learner cannot be investigated in a systematic way" (Sharwood Smith, 1981a, p. 167). It is just such a "system" that we have argued for here.

NOTE

1. Hilles (1986) calls attention to UG research on the clustering of properties associated with a particular parameter and suggests that for pedagogical purposes the learning of one such property (e.g., "dummy" place holders in English) might serve as a "trigger" for the rapid learning of the rest of those properties (e.g., the fact that English, a non-PRO-drop language, cannot leave subject position unoccupied).

QUESTIONS FOR DISCUSSION

1. The Rutherford and Sharwood Smith paper, in discussing the possible value of UG for pedagogical decision making, assumes that UG is still operative with adult learners. If, as Bley-Vroman claims, this is no longer the case, what other kinds of questions would one now want to ask in the pursuit of principled decision making for pedagogical grammar?

2. Cited in the Rutherford and Sharwood Smith paper are references to work of other researchers that claims to provide evidence for the operation of UG in adult language learning—that is, that principles of UG do not appear to be violated in any of the interlanguage samples examined so far. Is it possible, however, that nonviolation of UG principles could equally be attributed to other sources as well—for example, classroom instruction?

3. If, as Corder says, teaching is a matter of providing the right data at the right time, then what kinds of data might serve to feed the hypothesis formation capacity of a speaker of (topic-prominent) Mandarin learning (subject-prominent) English? Would special efforts be required in the provision of such data?

REFERENCES

Adjemian, C., and J. Liceras. 1984. Accounting for adult acquisition of relative clauses: universal grammar, L1, and structuring the intake. In F. Eckman, L. Bell, and D. Nelson (eds.), *Universals of Second Language Acquisition.* Rowley, Mass.: Newbury House.

Bialystok, E. 1981. Some evidence for the integrity and interaction of two knowledge sources. In R. Andersen (ed.), *New Dimensions in Second Language Acquisition Research.* Rowley, Mass.: Newbury House.

Brumfit, C., and K. Johnson. 1979. The linguistic background. In C. Brumfit and K. Johnson (eds.), *The Communicative Approach to Language Teaching.* London: Oxford University Press.

Chomsky, N. 1981a. Markedness and core grammar. In A. Belletti, L. Brandi, and L. Rizzi (eds.), *Theory of Markedness in Generative Grammar.* Pisa: Scuola Normale Superiore di Pisa.

Chomsky, N. 1981b. Principles and parameters in syntactic theory. In N. Hornstein and D. Lightfoot (eds.), *Explanation in Linguistics.* London: Longman.

Chomsky, N. 1981c. *Lectures on Government and Binding.* Dordrecht: Foris.

Chomsky, N. 1982. *Rules and Representations.* Oxford: Blackwell.

Flynn, S. 1984. Similarities and differences between first and second language acquisition: setting the parameters of universal grammar. In D. Rogers and J. Sloboda (eds.), *Acquisition of Symbolic Skills.* New York and London: Plenum.

Gass, S. 1984. Language transfer and language universals. *Language Learning* 34:115–132.

Hilles, S. 1986. Interlanguage and the PRO-drop parameter. *Second Language Research* 2:33–52.

Krashen, S., and T. Terrell. 1983. *The Natural Approach: Language Acquisition in the Classroom.* Oxford, Pergamon.

Liceras, J. 1985. The role of intake in the determination of learners' competence. In S. Gass and C. Madden (eds.), *Input in Second Language Acquisition.* Rowley, Mass.: Newbury House.

Ritchie, W. 1978. The right roof constraint in an adult-acquired language. In W. Ritchie (ed.), *Second Language Acquisition Research: Issues and Implications.* New York: Academic Press.

Rizzi, L. 1982. *Issues in Italian Syntax.* Dordrecht: Foris.

Rutherford, W. In press. Aspects of pedagogical grammar. In W. Rutherford and M. Sharwood Smith (eds.), *Readings in Pedagogical Grammar.* Rowley, Mass.: Newbury House.

Rutherford, W. 1982. Functions of grammar in a language teaching syllabus. *Language Learning and Communication* 1:21–36. Reprinted in this volume.

Schmidt, M. 1980. Coordinate structures and language universals in interlanguage. *Language Learning* 30:396–416.

Sharwood Smith, M. 1980. The competence-performance distinction in the theory of second language and the Pedagogical Grammar Hypothesis. Paper presented at the Contrastive Linguistics Conference, Boszkowo, December.

Sharwood Smith, M. 1981a. Consciousness-raising and the second language learner. *Applied Linguistics* 2:159–168.

Sharwood Smith, M. 1981b. Notions and functions in a contrastive pedagogical grammar. In A. James and P. Westmay (eds.), *New Linguistic Impulses in Foreign Language Teaching.* Tübingen: Günter Narr. Reprinted in this volume.

White, L. 1983a. Markedness and parameter setting: some implications for a theory of adult second language acquisition. Paper presented at the 12th Annual University of Wisconsin–Milwaukee Linguistics Symposium, March.

White, L. 1983b. The PRO-drop parameter in adult second language acquisition. Paper presented at the Eighth Annual Boston University Conference on Language Development, October.

White, L. 1984a. Universal grammar as a source of explanation in second language acquisition. Paper presented at the 13th Annual University of Wisconsin–Milwaukee Linguistics Symposium, February.

White, L. 1984b. Implications of parametric variation for adult second language acquisition: an investigation of the PRO-drop parameter. Unpublished paper, McGill University.

Widdowson, H. 1979. *Explorations in Applied Linguistics.* London: Oxford University Press.

Activities for part one

1. Work out what you think would be the advantages and disadvantages of consciousness raising (CR) with respect to:
   a. learners in different age groups (preadolescent, adolescent, young adult, older adult, etc.),
   b. learners in different types of educational institutions,
   c. the typical time constraints in teaching programs familiar to you,
   d. the three types of competence discussed by Canale and Swain.
2. Sharwood Smith's paper proposed a set of coordinates (elaboration and explicitness) for a two-dimensional description of the possible varieties of CR. Using these same coordinates, plot the kind of pedagogical CR that you employ or that you have experienced as a learner in a formal instructional setting. Do any varieties of grammatical CR exist that are not captured by the Sharwood Smith grid?
3. Categorize the following two tasks, both involving speaking to a native speaker of a given target language, in terms of one or more of the models discussed so far:
   a. telephoning someone (whom you do not know) to make an airline reservation
   b. having an informal conversation at the beach with an old friend
   How do you think each of the authors would view these tasks?
4. The Pienemann study is based partly on research of Clahsen and Muysken to the effect that a child learning German as L1 and an adult learning it as L2 will initially hypothesize different basic word orders—namely, SOV for the child and SVO for the adult. Linguistically speaking, however, both orders figure in a description of German; that is, SOV is typically claimed to be the underlying order, whereas SVO is the surface order of main clauses. This kind of finding could be used in support of the claims advanced in the Bley-Vroman paper as to the different nature of L1 versus L2 learning. What other kind of evidence could bear on L1/L2 differences, and how would you go about testing it out?

two

WHAT IS PEDAGOGICAL GRAMMAR?

The discussion value of any worthwhile topic must obviously be related, among other things, to the clarity of one's concepts. It is therefore appropriate to ask what it is that we denote by the widely used citation *pedagogical grammar* (PG) because the term appears to occur with less than semantic consistency. Is PG, for example, a discipline, a formal abstraction, or a collection of facts about a particular language? If it is the latter, are such facts intended for digestion by curriculum designers, syllabus compilers, teachers, or learners? Or is PG all of these things? Is it possibly more than these? The papers in this section sort out the answers to some of these questions.

Perhaps the paper that addresses the PG identity issue most directly is Sharwood Smith's. Here we encounter the notion of "pedagogical processing," or a useful reference to the matter of by what means and in what form information about language and language learning may shape the pedagogical outcome. Sharwood Smith distinguishes between two kinds of pedagogically oriented language descriptions termed *concentrated* and *extended* (see also the Sharwood Smith paper in part four). *Concentrated descriptions* are metalinguistic statements or observations exclusive of learner variables that would otherwise be factored in. *Extended descriptions* are the on-line grammatical information tailored to the exigencies of particular learning situations. The former, then, serves as input to the latter. The process of deriving a PG, however, must be in accord with one overriding canon of educational psychology—namely, Bruner's "Apostel principle," whereby learning within any domain presupposes some prior knowledge of that domain. Sharwood Smith's application of the principle results in a four-stage learning construct consisting of the learner's experiential knowledge, its manifestation as notions and functions, their formal exponents in the native language, and their formal exponents in the target language. The author makes clear that PG is intended ultimately to facilitate the acquisition of target language grammatical competence. PG is thus the means to an end rather than the end itself, one of the principal themes to be found also in the first Corder paper.

Corder makes the useful point that the form of any PG will of necessity be a reflection of one's belief about the psychological processes of language learning. Thus, "a structuralist grammar consists essentially of a long list of word classes and a list of permitted sentence patterns. Such a model of grammar has also usually been associated with the psychological view of language as a habit structure and the learning of language as the acquisition of a set of habits" (p. 130). In stark contrast to this point, one of the more recent beliefs holds that grammatical competence in the acquisition of language by adults will be attained necessarily and sufficiently as the result of mere exposure to instances of the target language that are comprehended, much as (it is supposed) children acquire their native tongue. Attention to grammatical form would obviously have no place in such a notion of language learning, whose pedagogy was referred to many years ago as the "sunburn" method. But adults are not children (cf. Bley-Vroman's paper in part two), and a model of adult language learning for Corder would have to include the learner's testing of hypotheses about target language structure and their subsequent classroom confirmation or disconfirmation. This kind of feedback is usually the responsibility of either textbook or teacher, all the more so in a foreign language teaching setting where the classroom is the learner's only contact with the target language. It will often happen in fact that it is only the teacher who constitutes the repository for target language data and metalinguistic information—where, in effect, the PG, so to speak, turns out to be the teacher.

Not very long ago the language teacher, if asked to define the notion "pedagogical grammar," might have thought it a bit pointless, or better still, redundant. The answer could well have been something like "but language pedagogy is grammar," and of course we have a language-teaching methodology arising out of almost two millennia of grammar teaching to attest to it— grammar translation. We can therefore assume, recalling Corder's point, that whatever was being taught at any time during this vast period was doubtless an indication of what one then (unconsciously) conceived the language-learning process to be—namely, the learner's accumulation of grammatical information. But what was taught must also have reflected what one's concept was of language and its organizing principles. Certainly, casual inspection of any, or at least most, teaching materials that mention grammatical form, whether grammar based or not, leaves one with the distinct impression that language is made up of constructs (e.g., phonological, morphological, syntactic, discoursal, etc.) arranged in hierarchical fashion, with the teacher's task being to impart these entities directly to the learner. This is the view of language that is challenged in the Rutherford paper, which argues for a concept of PG that is consistent with more broadly conceived principles of language organization, where language is seen as less an assemblage of discrete units than the interplay of wide-ranging grammatical forces.

Several of the papers in part two—most notably Bialystok's—pointed toward a concept of L2 grammatical competence that encompasses not only the learner's (tacit) structural knowledge of the target language but also his or her *access* to that knowledge—that is, the learner's ability to bring that knowledge to bear on the need to use the new language in whatever capacity. It would follow then that any viable theory of PG would have to account for not only *what* the learner calls up in the act of deploying his or her grammatical resources but also *how* he or she is able to do so. One of the merits of the Widdowson paper is that it suggests an approach to PG that is consistent with the learner's need to maximize precisely this kind of access. One aspect of the approach would be represented by efforts to engage the learner, as Widdowson puts it, "in problem-solving tasks which require a gradual elaboration of grammar to service an increasing precision in the identification of relevant features of context" (p. 154). It is thus a conception of grammar as not so much the specification of permitted sentence patterns and participating word classes (recalling Corder's terms) as it is the "mediator" between bare lexicon and the necessary context within which the strung-out lexis must achieve meaning. One possible realization of PG in something very close to Widdowson's approach is seen in the Rutherford paper in part three.

We thus move a bit farther in this part toward identifying the kind of theoretical construct that PG will have to be—one that is articulated in terms, for example, of the Apostel principle, of metalinguistic knowledge, of knowledge accessibility, and of a theory of grammar that is consonant with notions of usability as well as learnability. The papers in this section collectively begin to suggest the outlines of a concept of pedagogical grammar that is shaped by partial answers to some of the seven questions posed in the introduction to this book.

8
Pedagogic Grammars

S. Pit Corder
University of Edinburgh

SCHOLARLY AND PEDAGOGIC DESCRIPTIONS

When we talk to someone we adapt our way of speaking to our hearer. We also select what we are prepared to talk about in the light of who our audience is. The atomic physicist does not talk to his wife about atomic physics in quite the same way as he does to his colleagues, and unless his wife happens to be a physicist also he may be wise not to talk to her about it at all. The way we talk about something is obviously dependent upon the knowledge of the subject our hearer already possesses. We may judge that he possesses sufficient knowledge of a general sort to warrant our embarking on the subject, in which case we shall attempt to use some sort of everyday terminology, with a lot of explanation and qualification, and hope to get our message across. This is the task which the scientific journalist faces when trying to "popularize" some recent discovery in science. If we judge our hearer simply does not have this general basic knowledge, we don't even broach the subject. On the other hand, if we know our audience to be specialists we freely use what the layman calls our "jargon," and in consequence get our meaning across more surely and economically.

The way the linguist, applied linguist, or teacher describes the grammar of a language is determined by his audience. All are describing the same "object," but the reasons they have for doing so are rather different. It is not

S. Pit Corder: *Introducing Applied Linguistics* (Penguin Education 1973). Copyright © S. Pit Corder, 1973. Reproduced by permission of Penguin Books Ltd.

only that their different audiences come with greatly varying knowledge of the subject but that the result they are trying to achieve is different. We can approach the same problems from the point of view of the reader, or "consumer." What does he read a description of the language for? There are a number of different sorts of consumers of grammars: linguists, students of linguistics, interested laymen, teachers of the language as a mother tongue, teachers of the language as a foreign language, students of the language as a foreign language. We might suppose that since the object being described is identical in every case, whoever is talking about it or whoever he is talking to, the differences in the descriptions would be rather matter of style than of content. But this is not quite the case. As we saw earlier, it is the "viewpoint which creates the object"; there are no "facts" in language itself; it is the linguist who "creates" them in his description; what is or is not relevant is determined by the theoretical approach adopted. What can be assumed or what must be explicitly stated depends on the knowledge of the reader, and what is included or omitted depends upon what the reader is meant to do with what he has learned.

A theoretical linguist writing a grammar of a language (or more probably a fragment of a grammatical description of a language) for other linguists is trying to show his readers that that analysis, based upon the particular theoretical model of language he favors, reveals properties in human language and, for that reason, in the particular language in question, which would not be revealed by some alternative and, in his eyes, inadequate theory of language structure. The object of the descriptive exercise is the evaluation or validation of a particular linguistic theory of language. This is explicitly stated in the preface to Lees's *The Grammar of English Nominalizations* (1963):

> There are many different reasons for engaging in technical linguistic research on natural language, but we view the following motivations as especially compelling. Only by studying the grammatical details of particular languages may we gain a deeper insight into the mechanisms underlying that most characteristically human type of behaviour, man's ability to communicate by means of language. [p. xvi]

A similar object lies behind Nida's *A Synopsis of English Syntax* (1960):

> The purpose of this analysis of English syntax is to demonstrate the application of descriptive techniques to the problems of syntax in the writer's own speech. [p. 1]

This introduction is followed by a section of 27 pages listing the theoretical inadequacies of earlier descriptions of the language.

Since the object of such "theoretical" linguistic descriptions is to validate a particular theory or aspect of a theory, or refute some alternative theoretical model, the linguist need only describe enough of the language in question to make his point. It is for this reason that we do not have any comprehensive theoretical linguistic descriptions of well-known languages at the present time. When a linguist does attempt to produce a comprehensive description, we find that his objectives are significantly different. They are not so much to elucidate the nature of a particular language as to teach a particular linguistic theory to students. Such a book is Paul Roberts's *English Syntax* (1964). Its subtitle is *An Introduction to Transformational Grammar*. And although the author states that it is intended "to give English speaking students a description of the syntax of their language" (p. 403), a close inspection shows that it provides much less information about the subject even than any of the shortened versions of the grammars by the great grammarians, such as Curme or Jespersen. The work is, in fact, an introduction to a particular model of syntax, taught inductively through its application to a particular language. In other words, it is not a grammar of English so much as a textbook of syntactic theory. The difference between a work of this sort and those first mentioned is not one of objectives but simply of audiences; in the first case professional linguists, and in the second case perhaps unwitting students of linguistics.

Most of what I have called the great scholarly grammars—Sweet, Jespersen, Curme, Poutsma, Kruisinga—addressed themselves to the educated general public. They were not writing for specialists. Their objectives were enlightenment of a general humanistic sort, the making systematic and explicit what every native speaker knows implicitly. These are summed up by Sweet (1891):

> We study the grammar of our own language for other objects than those for which we study the grammar of foreign languages. We do not study grammar in order to get a practical mastery of our own language, because in the nature of things we must have that mastery before we begin to study grammar at all. Nor is grammar of much use in correcting vulgarisms, provincialisms and other linguistic defects.
>
> The native language should be studied from the point of view of general grammar. We then learn to compare the grammatical phenomena of our own language with those of other languages . . . so we are better prepared for the divergent grammatical structures of other languages. In this way the study of English grammar is the best possible preparation for the study of foreign languages.
>
> Lastly, grammar satisfies a rational curiosity about the structure and origin of our own and other languages, and teaches us to take an interest in what we hear and utter every day of our lives. [pp. 5–6]

Sweet even more clearly than the others had a didactic purpose in writing his grammar, and this was of a rather specific kind.

But there is another class of comprehensive descriptions which has a more specific pedagogical objective. These are addressed not to the general interested layman but to some more narrowly defined professional group. For example, Owen Thomas (1965) addresses himself to the prospective teachers of the mother tongue:

It is my hope that teachers will learn something valuable about the nature of English from this text, and that this knowledge will improve their teaching and help their students.

I am personally and professionally interested in the problems of teaching English, and only peripherally interested in the problems of theoretical linguistics. To achieve my primary aim in the best way I know how I must risk offending those whose professional interest is in theory. I admire and respect them, but there is little I can do to enlighten them. [p. vii]

Similarly in Whitehall (1951):

Intended primarily for teachers and students of English composition, it may serve other readers—particularly those interested in literary exegesis—as a succinct, elementary linguistic introduction to English syntax.

I should hasten to add, however, that this book was not written with my fellow linguists in mind, that certain distributional methods fruitful in technical linguistics are not used here, and that pedagogical simplicity rather than linguistic consistency determine the inductive approach to the subject matter. [p. iv]

The authors of these latter grammars, then, specifically reject the notion that they are trying to teach linguistic theory. Indeed, they admit that the theoretical framework they adopt may be open to criticism for that reason. They accept that it may be necessary, for pedagogical purposes, to be eclectic in their theoretical orientation. They take the point of view that these considerations override theoretical coherence. In other words, theoretical eclecticism may be necessary when the objective of the grammar is to teach something other than linguistic theory.

We shall find that this standpoint is even more apparent when the descriptions of a language are intended for teachers of foreign languages or their pupils. The linguist who makes descriptions of parts of a particular language for other linguists is expounding general linguistic theory, or as Sweet called it, "general grammar." The grammarian writing descriptions of a language for the native speaker of that language, whether educated layman, teacher, or student, aims, on the other hand, to make explicit what every native speaker knows implicitly of his language. The writer of a grammar for teachers and students of foreign languages has rather different aims, to which I now turn.

GRAMMARS FOR FOREIGN LANGUAGE TEACHERS

Foreign language teachers may or may not be native speakers of the language they teach. If they are not native speakers they are normally expected to have what is called a *near-native* communicative competence in the language. Grammars written for their use will in part have the same objectives as those written for the native speaker, but since they will have had to learn the language as a second language and studied it descriptively as part of their training, the objects of grammars intended for their use will be less to make explicit what they know implicitly than to present the "facts" of the language in a form which will help them to present them to their own pupils. Pedagogic grammars of this kind, then, are in some degree textbooks in the methodology of grammatical presentation. However, because of the rapid advances in our understanding of the structure of particular languages which have resulted from recent linguistic research, we often find that these grammars also provide new information about the language besides indications of how to present it to their pupils. A good example of a pedagogic grammar intended for teachers of English as a foreign language, which has already been referred to, is Hornby (1954). In his preface he claims that the book is intended to "provide information for those who are studying English as a foreign language" (p. v). However, two pages later he says: "It is a sound principle not to present the learner with specimens of incorrect English" (p. vii). This clearly is addressed to the teacher and is a proposal about what I have called the methodology of grammatical presentation. The book is, as we saw already, accompanied by two volumes of methodological instructions on how to present the material described (Hornby, 1959).

But not all pedagogic grammars intended for teachers of foreign languages are so explicit in their methodological proposals. For the most part explicit suggestions on how to present syntactic data to the learner are found in books on teaching method. The methodological proposals in pedagogic grammar for teachers are more often implicit rather than explicit. In other words, the authors of such grammars have already organized the description or presented the data in a form which the teacher can use more or less directly in presentation to his own pupils. We could say that grammars of this sort present the facts of language in a "partially digested" form. The amount of "predigestion" will depend upon the amount of linguistic sophistication the author is presupposing in his reader. The reason that such predigestion is necessary at all is not so much that the author wishes to help the teacher in his teaching, but that he judges the teacher will not be able to follow a rigorous linguistic presentation of the material. This accounts for the fact that we cannot always distinguish between those pedagogical grammars which are intended for teachers of the mother tongue from those meant for foreign language teachers and, in extreme cases, from those suitable for the advanced foreign learner of the language. Only when teachers receive a grounding in linguistics as part of their initial training as teachers will the distinction between linguistic grammars and pedagogic grammars for teachers disappear.

We can sum up the contents of these two sections in Table 8-1.

GRAMMARS FOR LANGUAGE LEARNERS

All the examples of "grammars" so far referred to have been more or less comprehensive descriptions of a language enclosed within the covers of a single book. This book has carried an explicit title such as *English Syntax* or *A Grammar of English*. Older readers will remember, as learners of Latin or French (or some other language), possessing a "grammar" book with some

Table 8–1

Author	Reader	Object of "grammar"
Linguist	Linguist	To illustrate and validate a particular syntactic theory
Linguist	Student of linguistics	To teach syntactic theory inductively through its application to a particular language
Applied linguist	Educated native speaker	To systematize in linguistic terms the implicit knowledge of the reader
Applied linguist	Teacher of the mother tongue	To systematize the implicit or explicit knowledge of the reader in a form which is pedagogically appropriate for his (native speaker) pupils
Applied linguist	Teacher of a foreign language	To systematize the implicit or explicit knowledge of the reader in a form which is pedagogically appropriate for his (nonnative speaker) pupils

similar title, which was intended for reference purposes in addition, perhaps, to their regular textbook, or "method": *A Course in Elementary French* or *A Latin Primer*. Sometimes the course book itself incorporated some part of the grammatical descriptions of the language and provided exercise material on it. Alternatively, the *Shorter Grammar of Latin* itself contained exercise material for practice in the application of the grammatical rules. Typically, however, a set of books for students of a language, particularly a dead one, consisted of a trio: dictionary, grammar, and reader. This trio is associated particularly with a method of teaching usually known as the *grammar-translation* method, in which the main activities in the classroom were oral translation into English from the reader, the rehearsing of the conjugation of verbs and declension of nouns, while the main homework activities were written translations from "unseen" passages in the target language. The theoretical presuppositions (i.e., the framework for the grammatical descriptons, the various categories of a traditional "general grammar") were rarely discussed. The learner had, therefore, to discover for himself what was meant by such terms as *infinitive*, *participle*, *deponent verb*, *case*, *tense*, *number*, and so on. The teaching and learning of the theoretical foundations on which the description of the language was based were largely inductive and concentrated almost wholly on accidence and derivation. Very little was said about syntax. To this day I have only the haziest notion of the *function* of the "supine" in Latin, though I can still spout the supine form of any verb you care to mention, regular or irregular. Reference to my dogeared copy of *A Shorter Latin Primer* (Kennedy, 1906) tells me that: "the *verb* has (amongst other forms) two *supines* (verbal substantives)" and later, that "The supines are cases of a verbal substantive: amatum, *in order to love*; amatu, *for* or *in loving*." It turned out that there was another verbal substantive, the *gerund*. I did, it is true, eventually develop some functional concept of the verbal substantive and discovered how to use the gerund somewhat tentatively. I have never, to this day, found any use for the *supine*.

With changes in language-teaching methodology in more recent years, the way that information about the target language is distributed in the teaching materials has changed. It is now less often so neatly divided into "dictionary," "grammar," and "reader." Sometimes all these are rolled into one textbook, so that instead of concentrating all the grammatical information in one place, all the lexical information in another, they are spread over the whole course in several course books, interspersed with reading passages and practice exercises of various sorts.

But redistribution is not the only change that has taken place, nor is it really the most important. Far more significant is the way that the information about the target language is now given. It would not be an exaggeration to say that there was little difference fifty years ago between a "grammar" for learners of a second language and scholarly grammars intended for native speakers, except their scope. This is the distinction which Sweet proposed (1899):

> As regards fullness of treatment, there is an obvious distinction to be made between a grammar which is to be assimilated completely so that the learner at least practically knows it by heart, and the one which is only for reference.
>
> The latter will aim at being exhaustive wherever reasonable and practicable and will, perhaps, give information on a variety of subjects which would be omitted altogether in the learner's grammar. [p. 137]

This is, perhaps, one of the earliest references in English to the distinction which has now become commonplace, between a scholarly, or "linguistic," grammar and a "pedagogical" grammar. However, Sweet was a revolutionary in his own day in recognizing that it was not only in scope but also in presentation that what he called a "practical grammar" should differ from a "reference grammar." He exemplifies this thus:

> From the point of view of the practical study of languages, such a question as whether or not the prepositions are to be treated of in the grammar as well as the dictionary, and the further question whether all of them, or only some of them, are to be included in the grammar, must be answered by showing whether or not the acquisition of the language will be facilitated thereby. [p. 125]

Sweet clearly saw that the criterion for a pedagogic grammar for second language learners, his "practical grammar," was not "theoretical purity" but practical effect. This is still the problem of pedagogic grammars: how do we present the information about the structures of the language to the learner in such a way that it helps him to develop his communicative competence?

Sweet speaks about "assimilating the grammar completely" and "knowing it by heart." This might suggest the rote learning of paradigms and syntactic rules and their mechanical repetition. This was indeed part of the grammar-translation method at its most extreme. But a further reading shows quite clearly that by the notion of "assimilation" and "knowing by heart," he meant what would nowadays be called the "internalization of the rules of the grammar" or the "acquisition of competence," which shows itself as the ability to interpret and produce grammatical utterances. In other words, it is quite clear that Sweet had realized that the rules and categories the linguist uses to describe the grammar of a language were only a "way of talking" about what the native speaker "knows" and not a description of psychological entities and processes. This means that our pedagogical descriptions of the target language must be devised to help the learner learn whatever it is he learns but are not necessarily *what* he learns. Pedagogical descriptions are *aids* to learning, not the *object* of learning; so long as we keep that firmly in our minds we shall not get confused by the ambiguity of the expression "teaching grammar." The problem of devising an efficient pedagogical grammar is, then, more a psycholinguistic than a theoretical linguistic one. The form our pedagogical grammar takes will be dependent upon what we believe to be the psychological processes involved in language learning. I have suggested elsewhere that current theories fell somewhere on the continuum between pure deductive and pure inductive learning processes. If we apply the extreme inductive hypothesis to the learning of grammar, then pedagogic grammar would scarcely be distinguishable from reading materials or other "textual" data, written or spoken. Or, to put it another way, all we should need to do would be to "expose" the learner to plenty of uncontrolled, unorganized data for him to get to work on. This has been called the "sunburn" method. In theory at least this differs little from simply sending the learner to live in a country where the language is spoken. Most people would hardly regard this latter course as a form of "teaching," because what characterizes teaching is its methodical or systematic organization of the data for learning.

The classroom method in the most inductive approach, often known as the "structural method," has in practice been associated with a very high degree of control of the data, usually in a much more organized and restricted form than in other approaches, to the point that the learner may even be so "starved" of material to learn from that his progress is actually held up.

By rigid control of the data, I do not just mean the considerable degree of "idealization" to which it has been subjected. Anyone who cares to compare the dialogue in a play or novel with actual everyday conversation will realize that even the most "realistic" examples are still far removed from reality (cf. Abercrombie, 1963). The data supplied in pedagogic grammars and other textbooks under the rubric of "dialogues" are even more idealized. By rigid control I mean, rather, the strict limitation of the data to a single syntactic structure to be presented at one time. This control derives from the belief that the learner must not be "swamped" with too much data and that he must be given time to "absorb" each new pattern or category or whatever, before passing on to the next item. This notion is often expressed as learning the pattern until its production becomes "automatic." The extreme inductive approach has in practice usually been associated with a "structuralist" theory of syntax in which the structure of sentences is described in terms of permitted sequences of word classes rather than more abstract generative rules. A structuralist grammar of a language consists essentially of a long list of word classes and a list of permitted sentence patterns. Such a model of grammar has also usually been associated with the psychological view of language as a habit structure and the learning of language as the acquisition of a set of habits.

If this is the model of learning adopted there is not much that can be "said" about grammar, because of the low level of generalization of its statements. Consequently, "talking about" language is generally restricted or discouraged. A typical expression of this point of view is that of Fries and Lado (1957):

> "Knowing" grammar has most often meant the ability to use and respond to some fifty or sixty technical names and *talk about sentences* in terms of these technical names.
>
> The materials (in this book) rest upon the view that learning foreign language consists *not* in learning *about* the language but in developing a new set of habits. One may have a great deal of information about a language without being able to use the language at all. The "grammar" lessons here set forth, therefore, consist basically of *exercises to develop habits*, not explanations or talk about language. [p. v]

Here we have a case where a "pedagogical grammar" consists essentially of exercises rather than descriptions. Where these do occur they differ relatively little from those in "theoretical" grammars of the same persuasion. Compare Fries (1957) with the work just quoted (Fries and Lado, 1957).

However, there is no necessary or logical connection between an inductive approach to teaching and any particular grammatical model. One may believe that the learning of the grammar is fundamentally an inductive process, and yet believe that the most adequate accounts of the grammar of a language are, for example, transformational.

The difference in that case will be the way the data are selected and organized rather than how they are presented. One may still decide that descriptive statements about the language do not help the processes of learning, and therefore exclude them from the teaching materials. However, in practice, it turns out that there has been an association between a more deductive approach to teaching and the adoption of some sort of transformational account of the grammar. In other words, there is a strong tendency for those who regard such a model as descriptively more adequate to believe that language is not a matter of habit, but rather rule-governed behavior, and that inductive learning can be controlled or guided and made more efficient by statements, formal or informal, about the structure of the language—that is, by adopting a more deductive approach. Interestingly enough, Chomsky, who above all linguists is associated with transformational grammar, has taken the most extreme inductive stand in connection with foreign language teaching (1968):

> My own feeling is that from our knowledge of the organization of language and of the principles that determine language structure one cannot immediately

construct a teaching programme. All we can suggest is that a teaching programme be designed in such a way as to give free play to those creative principles that humans bring to the process of language learning, and, I presume, to the learning of anything else. I think we should probably try to create a rich linguistic environment for the intuitive heuristics that the normal human automatically possesses. [p. 690]

The most extreme form of the deductive approach was undoubtedly the grammar-translation method. Here it was assumed that what was learned was neither more nor less than the rules and categories of the linguistic description, that there was a complete identity between the linguistic categories and processes and the psychological categories and processes. Therefore the rote learning and subsequent repetition of the rules of the grammar was regarded as evidence that "internalization" of the rules had taken place. The learner who could best spout the conjugations and declensions, analyze sentences and parse words, must be the one who best "knew" the language. Unfortunately, it didn't always work out quite as simply as that in practice.

The conclusion we can draw from this discussion is that there is no logical connection between a particular psychological theory of how grammar is learned and any particular linguistic theory of language structure. The two are separate dimensions in which teaching materials may vary. This is expressed diagrammatically in Figure 8–1.

There is, however, an undoubted *historical* connection between them, such that primarily inductive learning theories tend to be associated with "structural" grammars and notions of language as a habit structure, and deductive learning theories with transformational models and the notion of language as rule-governed behavior. We must, it seems, return to Sweet's essentially pragmatic approach to pedagogic grammars in which the nature and use of the grammar must be determined by "whether or not the learning of the language will be facilitated thereby."

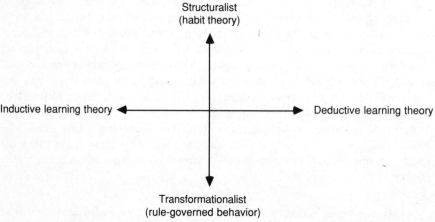

Structuralist
(habit theory)

Inductive learning theory ◄──────────────────► Deductive learning theory

Transformationalist
(rule-governed behavior)

Figure 8-1   Learning theory and language structure

DATA, DESCRIPTION, AND PRACTICE

Learning the grammar of a language is acquiring the ability to produce grammatically acceptable utterances in the language, however we choose to describe that ability, whether as a matter of habit or skill or knowledge of formation rules. Any teaching materials which are designed to develop that ability are, pedagogically speaking, "grammars." We must not expect any longer that these materials should necessarily resemble what are traditionally known as "grammars." But, as we have seen, there is more to learning a language than acquiring its "formation" rules. The learner has to be able to understand utterances in situations and himself speak and write appropriately. Not all elements in the teaching materials, therefore, have the function of teaching the grammar of the language. But with the distribution of the pedagogical grammatical element throughout all the teaching materials, it is no longer so easy to isolate those parts which have purely grammatical teaching functions from those whose aims are the development of the general ability to communicate. The teaching of grammar is intricately bound up with the teaching of meaning. It is not sufficient merely to enable the learner to produce grammatical sentences; he must know when and how to use them. The distinction between competence and performance is no longer seen as relevant. Grammatical ability is only one element contributing to communicative competence. This means that there is now an insistence on understanding the meaning of grammatical forms and that the teaching of grammar cannot be divorced from the teaching of meaning as it so clearly used to be both in the extreme deductive approach, the "grammar-translation" method, and also in the extreme inductive approach, the "structural method." What little we know about the psychological processes of second language learning, either from theory or from practical experience, suggests that a combination of induction and deduction produces the best results. We can call this a "guided inductive approach." Learning is seen as fundamentally an inductive process but one which can be controlled and facilitated by descriptions and explanations given at the appropriate moment and formulated in a way which is appropriate to the maturity, knowledge, and sophistication of the learner. In a sense, teaching is a matter of providing the learner with the right data at the right time and teaching him how to learn, that is, developing in him appropriate learning strategies and means of testing his hypotheses. The old controversy about whether one should provide the rule first and then the examples, or vice versa, is now seen to be merely a matter of tactics to which no categorical answer can be given. Giving a rule or description first means no more than directing the learner's attention to the problem or, in psychological terms, establishing a "set" toward, or readiness for, the task; giving the examples or the data first means encouraging the learner to develop his own mental set of strategies for dealing with the task.

The learner must have data on which to base his hypotheses about the semantic or syntactic functions of each new "item." He may or may not benefit by explicit descriptions and explanations about how it works. He must, in any case, develop hypotheses and be given the opportunity to test their correctness. This means he must be given the chance to make decisions or choices and consequently run the risk of making errors. The function of the teacher is to provide data and examples, and where necessary, to offer explanations and descriptions and, more important, verification of the learner's hypotheses (i.e., corrections). We can show the relation between these functions diagrammatically as in Figure 8–2. In the ordinary classroom lesson there is a constant switching from one activity to the next. In the same utterance the teacher may provide data and explanations while the learner may form a new hypothesis, test it, and have it verified by the teacher. I do not, of course, suggest that these are all conscious or deliberate processes in either teacher or learner.

This analysis suggests, then, that there are up to four fairly well-defined elements in the grammatical component of teaching materials: data and examples, descriptions and explanations, induction exercises, and hypothesis-testing exercises. Each component has a function in the learning process, but the sequence in which they occur in the textbook cannot be prescribed for all cases. Descriptive and explanatory material may precede a full display of the data or it may follow it. It may follow or precede the largely mechanical exercises which are meant to promote the inductive processes. It may be omitted altogether from the textbook material and be carried out by the teacher in the classroom. The induction and hypothesis-testing exercises may be mixed together in the materials. A summary of the structure of the pedagogical grammatical element in teaching materials is given in Figure 8–3.

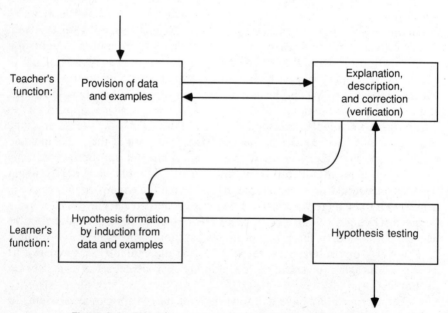

Figure 8–2 Teaching and learning activities in the classroom

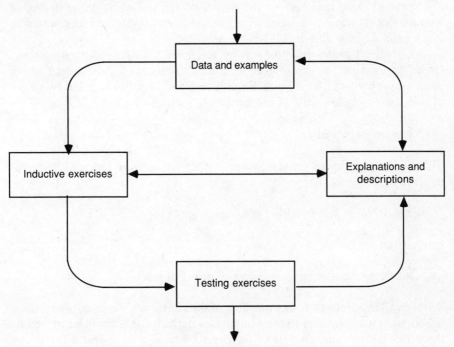

Figure 8-3 PG in teaching materials

EXPLANATIONS AND EXERCISES

We do not need here to go into a philosophical discourse on the distinction between explanation and description. In the classroom this is blurred by the fact that a description may often be used as an explanation, particularly when a learner wants to know why he has made a mistake. It is a descriptive statement about a language to say that the verb agrees in number and person with the subject; when a learner makes an error of concord, that description then becomes an explanation. It is an explanatory statement to say that concord marks a functional relation such as "actor" and "action." What we are here concerned with is the form that explanations may take. One of the main objections to using descriptions of the language is that the learner has to learn the "language used for making descriptions," he has to learn the meaning of such terms as *subject*, *object*, *agreement*, *concord*, *person*, and *number*. This is regarded by some people as an additional learning task over and above that of learning the language. It is regarded as justified, on the other hand, by those who accept a guided inductive approach if it helps the learner to make precisely those conceptual generalizations he has to make anyway. The question then becomes not so much *whether* we should teach him the descriptive terminology, but *which* terminology. If he has to acquire new concepts anyway, he might as well have some sort of a language for talking about them. The argument, then, is more about the nature of the terminology, its degree of formality or informality or scientific rigor, than about whether there should be any terminology at all.

I shall illustrate this problem by reference to a grammatical teaching "item" in English: "double object sentences." This is a highly simplified account of the problem. There is an English sentence pattern which has two noun phrases following the verb—for example:

I gave Mary a book

This can be generalized by stating the surface structure in terms of its grammatical constituents:

NP + VP + NP + NP

or their functions:

subject + verb + indirect object + direct object

We can call this Pattern 1. The meaning of the constituents is usually expressed in this way: subject refers to the person who performs the action expressed by the verb; indirect object refers to the person who is a recipient of the action expressed by the verb, and the direct object refers to the thing affected by the action expressed by the verb. There are alternative ways of expressing these relations between persons, things, and the action—for example,

I gave the book to Mary

We can call this Pattern 2. This sentence can still be regarded as a double object sentence because the meaning is the same, but it has a slightly different surface structure. The order of direct and indirect object is reversed, and the indirect object is realized by a prepositional phrase:

subject: NP + verb + direct object: NP + indirect object: to + NP

However, it depends upon which verb is chosen whether this alternative form of the sentence is possible. Some verbs are found with both patterns, some with only one or the other:

Give:	I gave Mary a book	Pattern 1
	I gave a book to Mary	Pattern 2
Ask:	I asked Mary a question	Pattern 1
	*I asked a question to Mary	Pattern 2
Explain:	I explained the problem to Mary	Pattern 1
	*I explained Mary the problem	Pattern 2

(Teachers of English as a second language will be thoroughly familiar with both these ungrammatical forms, which result from overgeneralization of a rule.)

If the indirect object is realized by a pronoun, the grammatical structures are unchanged, but if the direct object is realized by a pronoun, then only Pattern 2 is normally acceptable.

I gave a book *to her*   Pattern 1

I gave *her* a book   Pattern 2

*I gave Mary *it*   Pattern 1

I gave *it* to Mary   Pattern 2

Thus verbs which only occur in Pattern 1—for example, *ask*—cannot occur at all with a direct object pronoun:

*I asked Mary it   *I asked it to Mary

Finally, only Pattern 1 has a corresponding passive form with the indirect object as subject:

I gave *Mary* a book

Mary was given a book (by me)

I asked *Mary* a question

Mary was asked a question

This means that verbs which occur *only* in Pattern 2—for example, *explain*—have no corresponding passive form with indirect object as subject:

*Mary was explained the problem

These are the selected "facts" about double object sentences or, as has become evident, about verbs which take two objects. The question is: Can these facts be explained to the learner in some fashion or other without using even this somewhat restricted terminology as in the foregoing account? The answer is: probably, yes; by setting out examples of these sentences in such a way that he will be able to infer the rules. But as I have already pointed out, he must first understand the meaning of the different forms—that is, he must be able to infer from examples of the different sentences which constituent refers to the actions, which to the recipient of the action, and which to the object affected by the action. He must, in other words, be able to *segment* the sentence and assign a function to each segment. This is what the textual data is for and also the purpose of any translations which may be given.

As we saw, we had three classes of verbs to deal with: those which occurred in both Patterns 1 and 2 and those which occur only in Pattern 1 or Pattern 2. Our exposition must therefore be such as to enable the learner to

Table 8–2

	Pattern 1	Pattern 2
Verb class A	I *gave* Mary the book	I *gave* the book to Mary
Verb class B	I *asked* Mary the question	
Verb class C		I *explained* the problem to Mary

discover these subcategories. We shall need a matrix of the forms shown in Table 8–2 to show this.

Not all the information will necessarily be presented at one time. What is essential is that the *contrast* between the uses of verb classes A, B, and C should be established. This will not be achieved by treating the *give* and *ask* classes or the *give* and *explain* classes as one and the same. To do this would be to encourage precisely the overgeneralization which leads to the errors noted.

The establishment of a particular verb *class* can obviously not be done by using only one example—for example, *give* or *ask*. It is the task of what I have called the "inductive practice exercises" to establish the class membership of a number of verbs. This is usually done by several different sorts of exercise, basically all of a *substitution* type, in which the function may or may not be specified. Table 8–3 is a "generative" description in that it yields a large number of grammatically acceptable sentences. The learner can produce all of these by a process of selecting one item from each column in the sequence given. It is a purely *mechanical* operation and, if the lexical items are carefully chosen, can be performed without any understanding. In the example given it will, of course, generate a number of semantically unacceptable sentences—for example:

*I wrote Bill some sugar

In this form, then, *some* decisions of a semantic sort must be made. No syntactic decisions are needed. A most important substitution exercise in this pattern is the pronoun substitution exercise, shown in Table 8–4. It can only concern the indirect object at this stage:

Table 8–3

Subject	Verb (Class A)	Indirect object	Direct object
John	gave	me	the book
I	lent	you	a letter
We	offered	Bill	a present
The men	wrote	the girl	the pencil
Someone	sent	my friend	some sugar

Table 8–4

Mary She	gave	Bill him	a present

There are, of course, a number of other types of inductive exercises. A substitution practice of this sort may lead on to a completion exercise in which the learner is asked to supply a semantically acceptable form to fill one of the noun phrase slots:

_____ sent me a letter

I showed _____ the papers

He taught the pupils _____

Notice again no *syntactic* decisions are required, only semantic ones. What we cannot do at this stage is allow the learner a *free* choice of verb, because this involves both a semantic *and* a syntactic choice, which he is not yet ready to make.

At this point we may wish to introduce the student to Pattern 2 in connection with the same class of verbs. This can be done by transformation exercises. Again these are purely mechanical—for example:

She gave Bill a present   She gave a present to Bill

They sent us a letter   They sent a letter to us

(There are, of course, phonological problems here as well as problems about the appropriate use of these forms, but this is not part of the teaching of syntax.)

Two more sorts of transformation exercises complete a minimum list of inductive exercises on this pattern. The active-passive transformation:

She gave Bill a present   Bill was given a present

and the direct object pronominalization transformation which involves two operations, both purely mechanical:

She gave Bill *a present*   She gave it to Bill

What I have called inductive exercises are syntactically purely mechanical; they are what Dakin (1973) calls "meaningless exercises"—they involve no grammatical decisions, at least as far as the particular "item" being taught is concerned. (They may, of course, involve *some* syntactic choices, as in the case of the passivization exercise where appropriate tense, number, and participle forms are concerned, but knowledge of these is *presupposed*. Similarly, the pronominalization exercises presuppose the ability to substitute *him* for *Bill* or *the man*, and *it* for *the present*, etc.) It would be legitimate to ask what use an exercise is which requires apparently no thought and which can be performed without any need to understand the sentence. The answer must be that any exercise which *demands* no decision of a semantic or syntactic sort may be of little value for the teaching of grammar—it may be useful as a pronunciation practice. But so long as *some* decisions are involved, even if they are only semantic or concerned with syntactic processes already supposed to be known, then the student is *forced*, to some degree, to understand what he is doing, and in the process discover something about double object verbs, even if only the subcategory to which the different verbs belong.

So far I have only outlined the inductive exercises relating to one sub-category of verb and one sentence pattern. Clearly the same procedures must be applied to the other verb categories and the other pattern, where they are applicable. But now the difficulty arises. In some respects each of these verb categories overlaps—that is, *give* and *explain* both occur in Pattern 2 and *ask* and *give* in Pattern 1. How are we to make sure the learner does not overgeneralize and produce forms such as the following?

> *I explained him the problem
> *I asked the question to Mary

The answer is simply that he will surely do so, but that it is precisely the function of what I have called the hypothesis-testing exercises to overcome this. Hypothesis-testing exercises all have the characteristic that they force the learner to make syntactic choices, to differentiate what he has hitherto treated as the same, to make judgments about what is and is not acceptable. They are sometimes called *problem-solving* exercises for this reason. Dakin calls them "meaningful exercises." As I indicated on page 134, it is in these exercises that the teacher has an indispensable role to play. He, and only he, can provide the confirmation of the learner's hypotheses; only he can make judgments about the acceptability of the learner's sentences, the correctness of his choices.

Hypothesis-testing exercises simulate real-life language, because when we speak we make perhaps hundreds of decisions a second, each one of which may have syntactic or semantic consequences or be constrained in one way or another by the context. But choices are of two sorts. Those which involve making a decision between two forms which are given, and those which involve producing forms spontaneously. The former has some relation to the process of understanding language, the latter to producing it. So hypothesis-testing exercises are of two sorts. The first requires the learner to make choices between two or more given forms as to which is the acceptable one; these are called *recognition exercises*. The second type requires him to produce spontaneously the form which will make an acceptable sentence; these are called *production exercises*. The recognition type of exercise requires for success a less fully developed knowledge of the grammatical point being learned, and is therefore not such a stringent test of the learner's hypotheses or so full a confirmation of his knowledge. The productive type of exercise is the most demanding form and consequently is normally practiced last in the series before completely free or unguided production practice.

The fundamental form of the recognition exercise is a multiple choice. In the particular example we have been using, the learner can be required either to fit the correct pattern to a given verb or to fit an acceptable verb into a given pattern. The former type is both easier to devise and is probably psychologically a more "real" operation. The way the actual exercise is presented will, of course, vary. But these are the types of choices involved:

John explained   the problem to me
                 *me the problem

The problem was explained   to me
                                *me

It was lent   *Bill
            to Bill

                     *asked
The question was   *explained   him
                     given

What did you   *say   him?
               tell

Production exercises typically require the learner to supply something, to complete a sentence in an acceptable way:

I showed ——

What did you —— him?

Who did you —— the book to?

or to provide an appropriate response:

I've got a present

Who sent ——?

I know a good dentist

Who introduced ——?

Again, what are fundamentally "retrieval" exercises come in a great variety of forms in which varying amounts are to be supplied by the learner. In those illustrated, not only must a verb of the right subcategory be selected but also one which is semantically acceptable in the context. Or, alternatively, given a particular verb, not only must the correct pattern be selected but also semantically acceptable noun phrases.

TESTS AND EXERCISES

If an exercise is largely mechanical and can therefore be done without necessarily understanding fully what is going on, it cannot serve as a test of the learner's grammatical knowledge (though it may test his vocabulary). If he makes a grammatical error it must, therefore, be due to carelessness, not to lack of knowledge. Furthermore, all mechanical exercises have one and only one solution. This means that they do not require the presence of a teacher to monitor the results. A machine which has the answer programmed into it can do the job. For this reason, exercises done in the language laboratory are typically mechanical induction exercises. On the other hand, the problem-solving exercises may or may not have a unique solution. Recognition exercises do, and can, therefore, also be performed in the language lab or in programmed instructional material, but production exercises are open-ended; they have no unique solution. They require the presence of, or at least reference to, a teacher and cannot be satisfactorily "mechanized."

I made a distinction between mechanical exercises which are intended to promote the making of hypotheses or the discovery of rules and the hypothesis-testing exercises whereby the learner can check whether he knows the rules or how right his rules are. They tell him whether he still needs to work at the "item" or not. But they also tell the teacher whether the learner has yet learned this "item." This is why hypothesis-testing exercises look like objective test materials. There is no difference *in form* between the two things, only a difference in function. Exercises of this sort are designed to tell the learner about his knowledge and thereby help him to learn. Tests are intended to tell the teacher (or researcher) about what the learner knows. It is of no consequence, therefore, whether the learner does or does not make errors in his exercises, they are not meant to *measure* anything. It may, of course, be of consequence to both learner and teacher if he makes errors in his tests. They are intended to measure his knowledge for various purposes. It is because of the similarity in form between tests and exercises of this sort that both teachers and learners have, particularly in the past, confused the two functions.

THE TEACHER AS A "PEDAGOGICAL GRAMMAR"

Any or all of the component functions of a "pedagogical grammar" can be carried out without any printed or spoken teaching materials being imported into the classroom. In other words, the whole or any part of the teaching of grammar can be carried out by the teacher without the support of textual or recorded material. He can provide the data and examples orally or in writing. He can conduct the induction exercises orally, provide descriptions and explanations with the help of the blackboard, and carry out the hypothesis-testing procedures whether orally or in writing, providing correction and verification. The most difficult part for the teacher is to provide adequate quantities of well-conceptualized data. Hence, the virtual indispensability of textual material written or recorded. A well-qualified, energetic, and inventive teacher can be a living pedagogical grammar; what he can't so easily be, curiously enough, is the generator of abundant and appropriate textual data, in spite of the love that teachers are said to have for the sound of their own voices! But unfortunately not all teachers are well qualified, nor are they all endowed with unlimited energy and invention. This is one reason why they need the help of teaching materials. The question is: does the learner need a teacher at all if he has access to unlimited data and practice materials? In other words, can the live teacher ever be eliminated from the learning process? Apart from his general pedagogical and administrative duties, is the teacher indispensable? People do appear to learn languages by self-instruction, so the answer might appear to be no. But a closer analysis of self-instruction will show that this is not the case. There is one function of the teacher which cannot be provided by any teaching materials yet devised. The one thing a self-taught student cannot get from himself or his learning materials is final authoritative confirmation about his hypotheses. This can only be provided by someone who possesses a knowledge of the whole grammatical system, who can make precisely those intuitive judgments about the acceptability of utterances which characterize the "competence" of the native speaker. The data available to the self-taught learner, however extensive it may be, can only be a sample of the language. Search as he may through it he can never be sure to find in the data the example which will unequivocally confirm every hypothesis he may make about the grammar of the language. In the last resort he must have access to a native speaker (or as near-native an informant as he can get). The minimal irreducible and indispensable function of the teacher is to tell the learner what is or is not an acceptable utterance. We can call this his *monitoring function*. A learner cannot, in this sense, adequately monitor his own performance, whether receptive or productive. If he could, he would be a native speaker of the language!

Of course, producing acceptable utterances is not the whole of language learning. The learner must know when to select one or another in order to achieve his communicational ends. In other words, utterances must also be appropriate to the situation. This, too, requires monitoring. But the "speaking rules" of language cannot yet be described. What we cannot describe we cannot teach systematically. Thus the learning of the speaking rules is still a wholly inductive process. A native speaker can tell whether an utterance is appropriate or not; this was what we called *Sprachgefühl*. But he cannot say much about why a particular utterance is or is not appropriate. To acquire *Sprachgefühl* a learner requires plentiful contextualized language data and he needs a native-speaking informant to make judgments about the appropriateness of his utterances. But teaching the speaking rules is not part of a pedagogical grammar. Perhaps one day it will be, when we know a little more about how language is used.

QUESTIONS FOR DISCUSSION

1. In the Corder paper we have read that "pedagogical descriptions are *aids* to learning, not the *object* of learning." Is it possible to say how descriptions of a particular construct (e.g., relative clause) might differ as to whether or not they were intended as an aid to learning or the object of learning? Is there something unusual about conceiving a grammatical construct as an object of learning?

2. Corder cites four elements that figure in the design of grammar-based teaching materials: data and examples, description and explanation, induction exercises, and hypothesis-testing exercises. The latter (where the teacher's role is paramount) prescribe activity in which the learner is induced to apply judgments of grammaticality and, as such, are referred to by Corder as "problem-solving exercises." Is this the kind of problem solving that Bley-Vroman (Part II) claimed characterizes general adult learning, and if so, would you want to go on to say that Corder's thoughts on what could constitute a pedagogical grammar (PG) are consistent with Bley-Vroman's general characterization of adult language learning?

3. Among the various kinds of consumers of grammars cited by Corder are "teachers of the language as a foreign language" and "students of the language as a foreign language." Why is a distinction being drawn here between teachers and students? That is, why couldn't one PG suffice for teachers *and* students in any given learning situation? If they do need to be differentiated, in what ways should this be accomplished?

4. Corder cites Sweet's belief that the nature and use of PG should be determined by "whether or not the learning of language will be facilitated thereby." Is this just another way of saying "do whatever seems to work," or is there more to it than this? How would one go about determining that the learning of some part of a language was indeed facilitated by PG and not by something else (e.g., a positive attitude)?

5. There is a widespread assumption that pedagogical consciousness raising (CR) (perhaps in its narrower sense of "teaching grammar") entails the use of descriptive terminology. Corder assumes this also where the question for him is "not so much *whether* we should teach [the student] the descriptive terminology, but *which* terminology" (p. 135). Do you share these assumptions? Can one not hold such assumptions but still believe in the need for pedagogical CR? How is this possible?

6. Corder's paper finishes with the following statements: "[A native speaker] cannot say much about why a particular utterance is or is not appropriate [*Sprachgefühl*]. To acquire *Sprachgefühl* a learner requires plentiful contextualized language data and he needs a native-speaking informant to make judgments about the appropriateness of his utterances. But teaching the speaking rules is not part of pedagogical grammar. Perhaps one day it will be, when we know a little more about how language is used" (p. 143). But fourteen years have now elapsed since Corder's important paper was published. Have we now learned enough about the nature of these speaking rules—that is, how language is used—to justify their incorporation in PG? If so, how do we go about doing it?

REFERENCES

Abercrombie, D. 1963. Conversation and spoken prose. *English Language Teaching* **18**:10–16.

Chomsky, N. 1968. Noam Chomsky and Stuart Hampshire discuss the study of language. *Listener*, May, pp. 687–691.

Dakin, J. 1973. *The Language Laboratory and Language Teaching*. London: Longman.

Fries, C. 1957. *The Structure of English*. London: Longman.

Fries, C., and R. Lado. 1957. *English Sentence Patterns*. Ann Arbor: University of Michigan Press.

Hornby, A. 1954. *Guide to Patterns and Usage in English*. Oxford: Oxford University Press.

Hornby, A. 1959. *The Teaching of Structural Word and Sentence Patterns*. Oxford: Oxford University Press.

Kennedy, B. 1906. *A Shorter Latin Primer*. London: Longman.

Lees, R. 1963. *The Grammar of English Nominalizations*. The Hague: Mouton.

Nida, E. 1960. *A Synopsis of English Syntax*. Norman, Okla.: Summer Institute of Linguistics.

Roberts, P. 1964. *English Syntax*. New York: Harcourt, Brace and World.

Sweet, H. 1891. *New English Grammar*, Part I. Oxford: Oxford University Press.

Sweet, H. 1899. *The Practical Study of Languages*. London: Dent.

Thomas, O. 1965. *Transformational Grammar and the Teacher of English*. New York: Holt, Rinehart and Winston.

Whitehall, H. 1951. *The Structural Essentials of English*. New York: Harcourt, Brace and World.

9
Grammar, and Nonsense, and Learning

H. G. Widdowson
University of London

The title of this paper is a quotation, as you might perhaps suspect. It comes from a song in Goldsmith's play *She Stoops to Conquer*, sung by Tony Lumpkin, a character who misspends much of his time in a tavern called The Three Pigeons.

> Let schoolmasters puzzle their brain
> With grammar, and nonsense, and learning.

In Tony Lumpkin's judgment, good liquor is much to be preferred to all this. But we cannot afford to be so self-indulgent and dismissive. Over recent years schoolmasters and schoolmistresses and others concerned with the teaching of languages have puzzled their brains about the role of grammar in learning. Some have concluded that it has no real role at all and that learning can manage without it; others have persisted in a more traditional view that language learning is essentially the same as the learning of grammar. What, then, is the relationship between the two?

Tony Lumpkin associates grammar with nonsense. He is not alone. No less a person than J. R. Firth, not someone, one supposes, who would have rejected all learning in favor of the bottle, observes that grammarians "make regular use of nonsense." He gives the example: "I have not seen your father's pen, but I have read the book of your uncle's gardener" (1957, p. 24). This,

Note: An earlier version of this paper was read at the Fifth National LEND Conference in Rimini, November 1985, and published in the proceedings. Printed by permission of the author.

though exemplifying the syntax of English, is in Firth's view nonsensical as an expression of meaning. So, he asserts, are other rather less extreme examples including the following, all of which appear as instances of English in books by reputable grammarians:

> The farmer killed the duckling.
>
> Pussy is beautiful.
>
> The lion roars.

Firth's strictures would, of course, apply equally to a very large number of sentences appearing in language-teaching textbooks and practiced by pupils. In this case, nonsense is not only associated with grammar but learning as well.

What Firth is pointing out is that sentences as artificial constructs for exemplifying linguistic forms do not have to meet the same conditions of making sense as do expressions naturally used in the service of communication in context. They have no "implication of utterance": whatever meaning *potential* they might have is remote from any realization since the contexts which would provide the occasion for their use are of unlikely occurrence. Many people concerned with language teaching have, of course, come to a similar conclusion. In consequence, there has arisen a deep distrust of sentences and, by association, of the grammar they exemplify, even to the extent of supposing that meanings can be achieved without recourse to grammatical means at all. The mistake here is to equate grammar with the devices used to exemplify its formal properties. Grammar is not just a collection of sentence patterns signifying nonsense, something for the learners' brains to puzzle over.

What then is it? What is this thing called "grammar"? It is obviously important that we should have some clear idea about the nature of the phenomenon as an aspect of language, not just as a preliminary but as a prerequisite for determining how it should figure in pedagogy. What, then, is grammar? One obvious way of finding out is to look up the term in a dictionary. David Crystal has produced a work which ought to be particularly well suited to our purpose. It is called *A First Dictionary of Linguistics and Phonetics* (Crystal, 1980). Two pages are devoted to the entry *grammar*. Unfortunately they leave us little the wiser about its essential nature. It is, we are told (among other things), "a systematic description of a language," "the way words, and their component parts, combine to form sentences," "a device for generating a finite specification of the sentences of a language." So grammar is the name we give to the knowledge of how words are adapted and arranged to form sentences. But what are sentences? And what are they used for? Why do words have to be subjected to adaptation and arrangement in this way?

There are, after all, occasions when words do very well on their own. Consider the classic case of the surgeon performing an operation and the utterances he addresses to his assistants: "Scalpel!" "Swab!" "Clamp!" No sign of grammar here: no interrogative forms, modal verbs, question tags; no sentences at all. Just words. The reason why communication is achieved here by lexical means only is of course because the context of shared knowledge makes it possible to use minimal cues. The conceptual or lexical meaning is sufficient for its indexical purpose on this occasion. The words are themselves sufficient as pointers to required meaning. Grammatical elaboration would be redundant. Indeed it would be dangerous: it would make communication less effective, the operation less efficient, and put the patient in peril. By the time the surgeon had produced his complete sentence, the patient might well have bled to death: a victim of verbosity.

In this case, then, words alone are enough to indicate meaning because of the high degree of contextual determinacy. On other occasions, of course, on most occasions indeed, we cannot count on the context complementing words so closely, occasions when more precision is needed to identify the *contextual* features which are to be related to the *conceptual* meaning of the words. And this is where grammar comes in. Consider again the sentence that was cited earlier:

The farmer killed the duckling.

Stripped of its grammatical appendages and reduced to lexical essentials this appears as three words:

farmer kill duckling

The very conceptual meaning of these three lexical items in association allows us to infer a sort of unfocused proposition: a process *kill*, two participants in the process, one an agent, *farmer* and the other a patient, *duckling*. Even if we were to change the linear arrangement, the three words presented in association would serve to indicate the same process and the same roles of the participants:

farmer duckling kill
duckling farmer kill
kill duckling farmer

In all these cases, our knowledge of what these words mean in English and the very general context of our world knowledge would lead us to suppose that in all cases the farmer is the agent and the duckling the participant or entity at the receiving end of the action: the farmer does the killing and the duckling gets killed.

But let us now alter the lexis somewhat and consider the following three words in association:

hunter kill lion

We have the same process here, but now we cannot distinguish between the participant roles of *hunter* and *lion*. In the familiar world in which we live, ducklings are not known for their propensity for attacking farmers; they are classed among the victims of the killing process. But lions are a different matter. Hunters might seek to kill them, but they are quite capable of turning the tables and acting out the agent role. There is nothing outlandish in the idea of lions killing hunters. So here the relationship between the lexical concepts has to be marked in some way to make up for the inadequacy of the words to indicate what part of the general context of knowledge is to be engaged. There are two possible states of affairs here, not just one. A common marking device used in English for such cases is word order. Since the mere association of words will not unambiguously point to meaning, the words need to be set down in a particular arrangement. Thus the sequence:

hunter kill lion

signifies one thing: hunter agent, lion patient, while

lion kill hunter

signifies the opposite: the lion as agent, the killer; the hunter the patient, the victim.

Word order is not the only conceivable grammatical device for enhancing the indexical precision of lexical items. One might use morphological rather than syntactic means. Many languages do. We might propose, for example, that the participant roles in our case might be marked by different suffixes: *o*, let us say, for the agent role, *om* for the patient. Word order would then not be needed for this particular purpose of role assignment. There would be *equivalence* of meaning with *different* word orders, as in:

huntero kill lionom
lionom kill huntero

And, conversely, of course, *contrast* of meaning with the *same* word order:

huntero kill lionom
hunterom kill liono

Since word order is not now needed for signalling an increased specificity of conceptual meaning, it can be put to other purposes, as we shall see presently.

But let us for the moment look at the word that signifies the process or action itself: the word *kill*. Again, although there will be occasions when the bare lexical item will suffice to indicate meaning, when the context or the convergence of knowledge of those concerned will provide the specificity required, it will generally need to be supplemented by the addition of elements which give the word a more precise conceptual focus. We need devices for locating the process in time and for indicating its own temporal character. In other words we need some way of marking tense and aspect. In English this is done by a combination of *addition* and *alteration*. The word is *altered* to signify present and past time:

> farmer kills duckling
> farmer killed duckling

And auxiliary verbs, themselves altered as necessary, are *added* to signify aspect:

> farmer is killing duckling
> farmer was killing duckling
> farmer has killed duckling
> farmer had killed duckling

In this way, the proposition is focused a little more clearly and its dependence on contextual support decreases accordingly. Again we should note that this increase in conceptual precision can be achieved, and is achieved in other languages, without recourse to grammatical devices of this kind. Lexical items might be used instead so that the focusing effect is brought about by extra words. We might propose something like the following for English: *then* and *now* for past and present; *be* and *have* for continuous and perfective.

> *then* farmer kill duckling = farmer kill*ed* duckling
> *now* farmer kill duckling = farmer kill*s* duckling
> *then* farmer *be* kill duckling = farmer *was* kill*ing* duckling
> *then* farmer *have* kill duckling = farmer *had* kill*ed* duckling
> *now* farmer *be* kill duckling = farmer *is* kill*ing* duckling
> *now* farmer *ha*ve kill duckling = farmer *has* kill*ed* duckling

Marking for tense and aspect, then, are other communicative devices for getting features of context into focus, for providing a sharper definition of what words mean in relation to the external world. But we do not only report on events as they actually occur, we also make judgments about them, and we can call them into existence out of context. And again grammar is ready to hand to provide the required refinement of the raw lexical material:

> farmer *will kill* duckling
> farmer *must kill* duckling
> farmer *will have killed* duckling
> farmer *must have killed* duckling, and so forth

Devices are available too for giving variable prominence to one or other of the participants in the process to identify it as the topic. We noted earlier how word order can signal an assignment of participant role (agent, patient, and so on). It can also be used to indicate what is to be presented by the speaker as the topic. But then to avoid confusion we need some way of marking the participant role distinction. In English the word *by* is used for this purpose:

> hunter kill lion (hunter topic, hunter agent)
>
> hunter kill by lion (hunter topic, lion agent)

Add tense and aspect specifications in the correct combinations and we get:

> hunter killed lion
>
> hunter killed by lion
>
> hunter who killing lion
>
> hunter was killed by lion, and so forth.

The expressions we have arrived at so far still need further refinement before they are presentable as sentences of standard English. But they are gradually coming into grammatical focus. And perhaps they suffice to demonstrate, in a rudimentary way, how the arrangements and alterations of grammar provide additional specification to lexical associations so that the words can relate more precisely to features of context, including those features which are incorporated into the knowledge of the language users themselves. The greater the contribution of context in the sense of shared knowledge and experience, the less need there is for grammar to augment the association of words. The less effective the words are in identifying relevant features of context in that sense, the more dependent they become on grammatical modification of one sort or another. And of course where there can be no possibility of shared contextual knowledge, as in the case of unpredictable personal invention and interpretation, grammar provides the guarantee of individual conceptual freedom. Contrary to what Tony Lumpkin believes, speaking for all those who have been subjected to the drudgery of learning it in school, grammar is not a constraining imposition but a liberating force: it frees us from a dependency on context and the limitations of a purely lexical categorization of reality.

Grammar, then, can be seen as a resource for the adaptation of lexis. But there is no absolute distinction between the two, only a convenient distribution of semantic responsibility. Grammar is a device for indicating the most common and recurrent aspects of meaning which it would be tedious and inefficient to incorporate into separate lexical items. Thus it might be possible to have quite separate words for, say, *kills, killed, is killing*, and so on, just as we have in English separate words for *man* (male human) and *woman* (female human) or *people* (humans in the plural). But then we would have to find separate words for every action or event denoted by different lexical verbs: a mammoth and unnecessary task. So grammar simply formalizes the most widely applicable concepts, the highest common factors of experience: it provides for communicative economy. Of course, as the examples of *man*, *woman*, and *people* illustrate, one can economize in the opposite direction, as it were, from grammar to lexis. Thus, in English, the grammatical structure *the man who brings the post* can be lexically realized as *postman*; *an animal which has been killed for consumption* becomes *meat*. In this respect, the dictionary and the descriptive grammar are complementary. The dictionary shows how efficiency in the formulation of meaning can be achieved by *synthesis*; the grammar shows how it can be achieved by *analysis*. Each mutually supports the other one as a compendium of conceptual and communicative resource. Together they contribute the cultural means whereby a society organizes and acts upon its environment by the establishment of communal categories of context. Such categories naturally facilitate interaction within linguistic communities and inhibit interaction between communities to the extent that they differ in their conceptual and communicative economies. These differences might have to do with the aspects of context which are differentiated and generalized or with the distribution of responsibility for denoting these aspects within the formal resources of the language, within its lexis, morphology, and syntax.

I have suggested that it is the function of grammar to reduce the range of meaning signaled by words so as to make them more effective in the identification of features of context, thereby providing for the increased indexical potential of lexis. But of course grammatical modification cannot account for the particulars of meaning that are signaled on particular occasions. Grammar can only *denote* degrees of generality. It cannot *refer* to individual cases. Now, as will have been noticed, in all the examples I have given, one very crucial element has been missing to make the expressions grammatical as instances of standard English:

> farmer kills duckling
> hunter killed lion

We need determiners of some sort. For example:

> *The* farmer kills *a* duckling.
> *A* hunter killed *the* lion.

And so we arrive at last at the fully focused sentence. These articles, definite and indefinite, now increase the specificity of the lexical meaning of the nouns. *The* farmer, for example, narrows attention to one which is known to both speaker and hearer; *a* farmer indicates one which is not. But the hearer still has to act on this indication and find which particular farmer is thereby being referred to. All the grammar does is to signal that there is one.

Communication can only be achieved by relating language with context: grammar simply makes it easier to establish the relationship by setting, as it were, more exact coordinates. But the language user is still left with the problem of engaging the particular features of actuality which are relevant on a specific occasion. Knowing these devices for narrowing down contextual possibilities does not imply that one can judge how best to act upon such knowledge, how much can be left to be inferred from context, how much needs to be made grammatically explicit. Something must always be left unsaid, but how much? An example from history might serve to illustrate the point: another instance (to accompany the case of the operating theatre given earlier) of the possible disasters attendant on an ineffective use of grammar.

The scene is the Battle of Balaclava. On high ground, at a customary safe distance from the action, the British general Lord Raglan is directing troop movements by sending his orders by messengers on horseback. From his vantage point he sees in one part of the field the enemy trying to retreat with their artillery, and he sends a message to his brigade of light cavalry. It reads as follows: "Lord Raglan wishes the Cavalry to advance rapidly to the front, follow the enemy and try to prevent the enemy carrying away the guns." The cavalry commanders Lord Cardigan and Lord Lucan, receiving this message, recognize that the definite articles signal a particular front of battle and particular guns which both they and Lord Raglan are supposed to know about. But they are in the valley. Lord Raglan is upon the heights. The commanders cannot actually see what Lord Raglan intends to refer to. They do not in fact share the same context. The general has made an unwarranted assumption about shared knowledge. The only front that the cavalry commanders can see is right at the end of the valley where the main Russian army is massively assembled, secure behind their heavy guns. For them *this* front and *these* guns are the only possible ones indicated by the definite articles. So, since theirs is not to reason why, they attack—with disastrous consequences. And that is how the Charge of the Light Brigade, the most celebrated and glorious calamity in British military history came about: all because not of a horseshoe nail but a failure in the effective use of grammar to make an appropriate connection with context. Not all such failures, of course, are as historically momentous. But they are of very common occurrence.

But to return from history to the present. And to return also to Tony Lumpkin once more. "Grammar and nonsense and learning." What then about learning? I have presented grammar in this paper as a device for mediating between words and contexts. The device itself is very complex, and its complexity cannot be explained only by invoking communicative function (see Newmeyer, 1983). It is subject to other informing influences: the general and essential parameters of universal grammar; the particular and accidental developments of its own social history. But for language learners to learn only the intricacies of the device without knowing how to put it to use is rather like learning about the delicate mechanisms of a clock without knowing how to tell the time. What is crucial for learners to know is how grammar functions in alliance with words and contexts for the achievement of meaning.

The teaching of grammar, as traditionally practiced, does not promote such an alliance. On the contrary: it is the formal properties of the device which are commonly given prominence. Words come in only as convenient for purposes of illustration. Lexis, in other words, is put to the service of grammar. But, as I have sought to show, the function of grammar depends upon its being subservient to lexis. Teaching which gives primacy to form and uses words simply as a means of exemplification actually denies the nature of grammar as a construct for the mediation of meaning. I would suggest that a more natural and more effective approach would be to reverse this traditional pedagogic dependency, begin with words, and show how they need to be grammatically modified to be communicatively effective. But this in turn means that contexts have to be contrived to motivate this modification. Again, traditional teaching has tended to dissociate grammar from context and to deal in separate senten-ces. A pedagogy which aimed at teaching the functional potential of grammar along the lines I have tried to describe, would have to get learners to engage in problem-solving tasks which required a gradual elaboration of grammar to service an increasing precision in the identification of relevant features of context. In this way, learners would realize the communicative value of gram-mar in the very achievement of meaning.

It seems to be quite commonly supposed that what is commendable about a communicative approach to language teaching is that it does not, as a structural approach does, have to get learners to puzzle their heads with grammar. If we are looking for nonsense, this suggestion is a prime example. For if this were really the case, a communicative approach would have little or nothing to commend it. For language learning *is* essentially grammar learning, and it is a mistake to suppose otherwise. The question is how should grammar be learned so that its intrinsic communicative character is understood and acted upon. This cannot be done by restricting attention to its formal properties, the relations and regularities which make up the internal mechanism of the device. No matter how legitimate an enterprise this might be within the discipline of linguistics (and this is currently a controversial matter), it will not do for language pedagogy. Learners need to realize the *function* of the device as a way of mediating between words and contexts, as a powerful resource for the purposeful achievement of meaning. A communicative approach, properly con-ceived, does not involve the rejection of grammar. On the contrary, it involves a recognition of its central mediating role in the use and learning of language.

QUESTIONS FOR DISCUSSION

1. Widdowson's position on the relevance of linguistic theory to language pedagogy (Widdowson, 1979) was challenged earlier in the Rutherford and Sharwood Smith paper in Part II and its discussion of Chomskyan Universal Grammar. In all fairness to Widdowson, however, his valid pedagogical argument for looking at language constructs in terms not just of *product* but also of *process* is one that finds little accommodation in modern generative theory—not in Chomskyan Universal Gram-mar, at any rate. Does this mean that to accept one way of looking at language is to reject the other, or are both part of an even larger whole? Does it help here to distinguish a *linguistic* perspective from a *psycholinguistic* one?

2. Widdowson calls attention to the fact that the word order of the largest sentence constituents in English is made to serve a grammatical function—namely, the ready recognition of subject, verb, and object. Widdowson also points out, however, that languages with a much richer morphology than English do not have to rely on word order to signal these grammatical relationships. Can you explain why this is so?

3. Widdowson cites the function of grammar as one of "mediating between words and contexts" (p. 154). What do you think he means by this? Other functions as well have been ascribed to grammar. One contemporary scholar (T. Givón) refers to grammar as a "discourse-processing strategy." How do notions such as these differ from the way grammar has traditionally been talked about?

REFERENCES

Crystal, D. 1980. *A First Dictionary of Linguistics and Phonetics*. London: Andre Deutsch.

Firth, J. 1957. *Papers in Linguistics 1934–1951*. London: Oxford University Press.

Newmeyer, F. 1983. *Grammatical Theory: Its Limitations and Its Possibilities*. Chicago: University of Chicago Press.

Widdowson, H. 1979. *Explorations in Applied Linguistics*. London: Oxford University Press.

10
Notions and Functions in a Contrastive Pedagogical Grammar

Michael Sharwood Smith
Rijksuniversiteit Utrecht

When we speak of notions or functions, and of the role of contrastive analysis in a pedagogical language description, we need to tread carefully. There is a great deal of controversy surrounding these terms, and it may be claimed that they are as theoretically dubious as they are popular. Notions and functions are, broadly speaking, related to semantics and pragmatics respectively: these are complex fields much less thoroughly investigated than syntax. Contrastive analysis is an area which has turned theoretical, or rather which has tended to be applied by those whose main aim is the description and explanation of language for its own sake. This is a different type of application than the kind envisaged by the first "contrastive linguists," who had language pedagogy as their ultimate goal. No matter who did the contrastive analysis, it was aimed at providing a basis for the selection of words and structures for teaching purposes. This role has been discredited to some extent, at least in Anglo-Saxon countries. Thus, when considering what notions and functions on the one hand and contrastive analysis on the other have to offer the language teacher, we have to keep in mind the fact that if they are of use, they will have to be used judiciously and without wild promises of instant success. It is perhaps best to consider first what a pedagogical grammar should look like, what principles should underlie it and then see if, after all, contrastive analysis has a role to play and how notions and functions can be effectively dealt with. Hopefully, some of the pessimism with which the enlightened applied linguist will view

"Notions and Functions in a Contrastive Pedagogical Grammar" by Michael Sharwood Smith, in *New Linguistic Impulses in Foreign Language Teaching*, edited by A. James and P. Westney, 1981. Tübingen: Günter Narr. © 1981 by Günter Narr Verlag, Tübingen. Reprinted by permission.

contrastive grammar, and the partially formulated "communicative" approach, will be dispelled.

The necessity of defining what we mean by "pedagogical" grammar may not be immediately apparent since *pedagogical* clearly means "having to do with teaching."[1] However, it is not the strict definition that needs attention so much as the implications that people draw from the use of such a term. Introductory courses in linguistics may sometimes make a distinction between "scientific" grammars and "pedagogical" grammars and mean by this that the former type of description should be subject to the various rigorous principles that scientific method imposes upon anything that bears the name "scientific" (especially in English where the term is more restricted than its equivalents in many other European languages). The implication here is that pedagogical grammarians may ignore these principles and frame their language descriptions in a much less systematic way, paying attention only to the needs of the consumer—that is, the teacher, textbook writer, and language learner.[2] In other words pedagogical grammars may be regarded as unscientific. This is not to say there are no principles, so much as the fact that what principles *are* in fact used do not hang together within some wider theoretical perspective. It would perhaps be a little more helpful to talk about pure linguistic grammars, or *nonapplied* grammars, on the one hand and *applied* (pedagogical) grammars on the other, thus allowing the term *scientific* and its antonym to relate to a separate type of evaluation. The implication of this particular approach will become clearer as this discussion develops.

It is clear that applied grammars may or may not use a particular nonapplied description and theory as a starting point. It is highly likely, given the fragmentary state of linguistic theory at the moment, that applied descriptions are going to be based on more than one description and more than one theoretical stance. In other words, applied grammars are likely to be *eclectic*. Nevertheless, we should make a distinction between picking and choosing from what is available on a vague or semiprincipled basis, and choosing according to explicit principles that have been arrived at via theorizing and testing. A vague principle might, for example, involve simply completing a list of grammatical categories, and filling up the book with information until the list is complete. Another vague principle would be choosing insights and descriptions which *seem* comprehensible to the nonlinguist. Thus we would finish up with a pedagogical grammar which had something apparently simple to say on all of the better known categories of linguistic description. The grammarian envisaged here is more like an average, uninformed housekeeper shopping for food to fill up his or her kitchen cupboard than, say, a dietician. A basic assumption in this discussion will be that pedagogical grammarians should select notions and functions (and grammatical structures) like the dietician and not like the uninformed housekeeper.

The selection of material from nonapplied research and its presentation should follow a detailed analysis of the intended consumer—that is, those concerned with teaching, and ultimately, the learners themselves. Evidently, this has to involve principles derived from the psychology of learning and the psychology of instruction. A completely all-purpose, comprehensive grammar may have its content mainly determined on linguistic grounds whereas the presentation, ideally speaking, would be determined on psychological grounds. Grammars that are much more specialized may need to have their content restricted for psycholinguistic reasons since there may be aspects which are inherently complex for given learners, which may be left until a later stage in their learning careers. Also sociological considerations may suggest that certain aspects may be more *useful* than others in communication. For example, emphasis could be placed on such pragmatic functions as greeting and leave-taking, arguing, persuading, disagreeing, and so forth, depending on what kind of communication is valued most highly. The grammar would then only deal with complex structures to the extent that they are needed to demonstrate the chosen communicative functions and the chosen "style" (formal, informal, etc.). Thus the moment restrictions are made on content, nonapplied factors can play an important role in determining the nature of those restrictions. The factors may not only be psychological but will involve principles drawn from outside the area defined by nonapplied linguistics. The same holds for presentation—how the material is organized in the grammar—that is, the *pedagogical processing*.

From a nonapplied point of view, pedagogical descriptions may seem simplified or nonexplicit: much of the technical apparatus used by the nonapplied linguist will be absent. However, pedagogical processing may well make the descriptions less simple, or more elaborate in some other way. It may be that many existing pedagogical grammars are both technically simple from a pure linguistic point of view and also (alas) psychologically naive. Their effectiveness may be a function of the skill and imagination of the teacher who uses them (or indeed the learner). The task of the applied grammarian is surely to make certain that the pedagogical processing does not require above-average abilities on the part of the consumer. Put another way, the aim should be to formalize and apply the intuitions of the skilled practitioner in the light of appropriate theories of language and educational psychology.

Pedagogical processing may be of two different kinds: it may be *concentrated* or it may be *extended* (see Sharwood Smith, 1977b). Concentrated descriptions are those which are mainly used for purposes of reference, especially by teachers and the more advanced (older) learner. Extended descriptions are more specifically linked with a practice component. Although there is more obvious pedagogical processing where extended descriptions are concerned, concentrated descriptions should be framed in such a way as to serve as an input to extended descriptions. Another characteristic of extended descriptions is that they are framed according to very specific types of learner and teaching approaches; concentrated descriptions, on the other hand, are didactically neutral as well as being aimed at a wider audience. Explicit rule formulation is a characteristic of more cognitivist teaching approaches; therefore it might be thought that a reference grammar which includes a rule for the formation of the present tense might represent this particular teaching approach. However, this need not be the case since the teacher or textbook writer can take the information expressed in terms of a rule and "translate" it into a teaching sequence *where no mention is made of rules*. In other words, the didactic consequences of using the reference grammar (the concentrated description, that is) may just as well be a classical pattern drill. By the same token, the actual formulation of the rule may be used in a cognitivist extended description derived from the same concentrated description, or some other, simpler (or more visually attractive) version may be used. If the concentrated description is pedagogically sophisticated, it may contain alternative formulations or at least hints as to how such formulations may be developed in extended form. Thus some of the pedagogical responsibility is shifted from the teacher to the writer of the (concentrated) descriptions. We cannot ask the nonapplied linguist to frame descriptions in a pedagogically useful way, but we can ask the pedagogical grammarian to frame descriptions in such a way as to facilitate further processing in extended form for different teaching/learning situations. Thus it is not enough to fill out a list of categories and to strip the grammatical descriptions of their more technical linguistic aspects. Pedagogical processing means considerably more than that: it involves the application of principles drawn from relevant branches of psychology (instructional and learning psychology, social psychology, psycholinguistics, etc.) to the selection and processing of information about language necessary for the teacher and learner. In the first instance, such processing is applied to the problem of devising concentrated descriptions, which in their turn serve as the basis for extended presentations, which have as their direct aim mastery of language skills (rather than simply understanding either explicitly or intuitively the "facts" of the target language). This implies a new era in which a serious interdisciplinary approach to pedagogical grammar becomes generally accepted.

In view of the doubts raised in some quarters about contrastive analysis, it becomes necessary to find some justification for including contrasts and comparisons in a pedagogical language description. It is no longer possible to claim that contrasts should be enumerated in order to list aspects of the target language that are difficult to learn. However, for concentrated, comprehensive descriptions of a given target language it may be useful to draw parallels and note differences as an insightful way of presenting material to be learned, especially material that by its very complexity needs more elaborate explanation. This allows the pedagogical grammarian freedom to deal with simple aspects without referring to the native (or some other generally known) language, reserving contrastive descriptions for more complex areas, as a presentation device. The educational psychologist David Ausubel stresses the positive effects of presenting new information within the context of the old to promote what he calls *meaningful* learning (as opposed to rote learning). This involves what Jerome Bruner calls the Apostel principle (see Ausubel, 1968; Apostel, 1977; Bruner, 1978)—old learning determines new learning:

> To learn something about a domain requires that you already know something about the domain . . . there is no such thing as *ab initio* learning pure and simple. [Bruner, 1978, p. 243]

If this is reinterpreted as a teaching principle ("go from the familiar to the unfamiliar"), this means that in any given explanation concerning the target language, there is the possibility not only of drawing contrasts and parallels with previously explained facts about the *target* language but also linking up target facts with facts about a language system with which the consumer is, one way or the other, completely familiar, that is, in most cases, the mother tongue. Since this concerns concentrated descriptions, there is no implication here of bringing contrastive analysis to the classroom. This is a separate decision for those using the concentrated account to devise extended accounts (oral or written ones, that is). For some learners—notably, adults with sufficient intellectual maturity—it may be advantageous to make full use of the contrastive parts (see, e.g., Aronson Berman, 1978), but for others, young beginners for instance, the contrastive explanations may be reserved for the teacher and textbook writer who teach them: explicit reference to the native language may not help at this level. If the contrastive accounts help at all, it will be, in some indirect way, in the planning stage of the lesson or course. In conclusion, one might say that the use of contrastive analysis in pedagogical grammars in no way implies an adherence to behavioristic notions about learning difficulty; it does not imply an all-embracing approach to pedagogical grammar; it does not imply bringing contrasts and similarities to the notice of every type of language learner. What is suggested is that contrastive analysis may be a psychologically effective presentation device in explanations of certain complex areas of the target language and that these explanations may either indirectly or very directly benefit more extended accounts, depending on the type of language learner involved.

If we take concentrated language descriptions to be the source for various different extended descriptions, it is clear that the more comprehensive the source account is, the better. Comprehensiveness may be defined as covering as many facts about the *nature* and *use* of target language structure as possible. This means not only syntax and morphology but also semantic and pragmatic facts. The need for full accounts of particular languages for pedagogical purposes has been so great that pedagogical grammars have always sought to cover areas beyond those regularly covered by pure linguists, whose theoretical interests have not permitted them to cover more than fragments of languages and then more usually in the domain of syntax and morphology than elsewhere. Of course before the more rigorous approach to linguistic description was adopted, the distinction people have been making between scientific and pedagogical was blurred. Pedagogical grammarians today who are forced beyond the more well-charted areas for reasons of expediency are advised to consider how much the great comprehensive, "scholarly," grammars are still used as sources of inspiration and insight despite their generally recognized lack of rigor. Comprehensive grammars of this calibre, besides serving other interests, can also provide help in strictly nonapplied domains. However, the main point at issue is that although notional and functional aspects of language have been less thoroughly investigated by nonapplied linguists, this need not be a reason for excluding them from pedagogical descriptions today. In this respect the descriptions of English produced by Quirk, Greenbaum, Leech, and Svartvik, though not pedagogical in the sense developed here, are good examples of general purpose grammars going beyond the confines of straight-forward structural description, the most obvious example being Leech and Svartvik (1975), now in its third edition.

It is worthwhile considering notional and functional categories from a psychological point of view. Apart from the general requirement of compre-hensiveness, there are good psychological reasons for going beyond the safety of syntax. If we consider again the Apostel principle, it is clear that new syntactic information may be related to syntactic information already intro-duced (although in a concentrated description designed for reference purposes, there is the further problem of assuming the reader will read the material in the order of presentation). It can certainly be related via contrastive analysis to syntactic structures in the native language, although this will be more effective where the reader is familiar with his or her native language in a *conscious* way; otherwise remarks about native language structure may be just as novel as remarks about the structure of the target language even though the native language is so familiar in an automatized, subconscious way. It is much more likely that the user of the grammar will be fully conscious of and familiar with the semantic and pragmatic categories used by advocates of the notional/ functional approach; concepts like *requests, persuasion, politeness, tact, future time, possibility* will generally speaking be immediately familiar to the reader in a way that *aspect, determiner, notional concord, periphrastic genitive,* and other such syntactic terms may well not be. There is a motivational factor too. The professional linguist will probably find all aspects of language inherently interesting. The average language learner, and even many language teachers, will be much more interested in the extralinguistic consequences of learning the target language whether this be the reading of literature or the ability to converse with native speakers in informal environments. The communicative goals are much more clearly represented in the notional and functional catego-ries than they are in the terms relating to syntax and morphology. By leaving out notions and functions, we are depriving the teacher and learner of the most immediately attractive aspects of the language description.

To sum up what has been said about notions and functions so far, it would seem that it is worthwhile extending grammars to include them even though they have relatively little nonapplied backing at the moment. There is a good chance that sound pedagogical accounts of notions and functions may not only provide interesting material for nonapplied linguists but will also give the learner a more comprehensive and more attractive description of the target language in which it is especially easy to follow the desirable practice of going from the familiar to the unfamiliar, in this case going from facts about the world familiar to the (teacher and) learner to the means of expressing them via the target language. Moreover it is true to say that there is quite a bit of research going on now in semantic and pragmatic areas which should aid pedagogical grammarians in their efforts to enrich grammars for teachers and learners. The fact that it may not be as fully developed as that in syntax and morphology should be no deterrent. Corresponding work done in sociolinguistics as well as the writings of people interested in the philosophy of language are very relevant. In no sense is there an implication here that nonapplied linguistics has nothing to offer the pedagogical grammarian in these areas. He or she should, armed with well-motivated principles of selection, go first to the nonapplied research before attempting any new departures.

At this point in the discussion it is appropriate to represent the various approaches taken here in diagrammatic form:

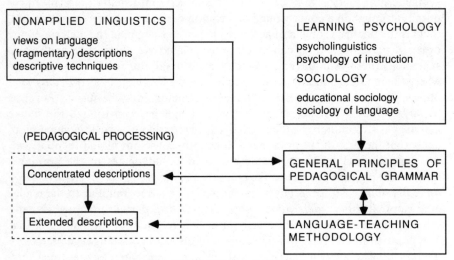

Figure 10-1 Principled selection

Figure 10-1 is fairly self-explanatory, though it is admittedly simplified. The general principles of pedagogical grammar should arguably be subsumed under language-teaching methodology. They have been separated here as a reminder that concentrated descriptions are didactically neutral and only represent a first stage in pedagogical processing whereas extended presentations will be shaped by the particular methodological approach adopted by the teacher or textbook writer.

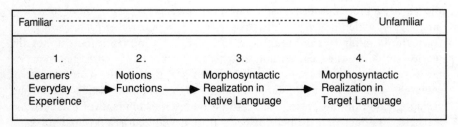

Figure 10-2 The Apostel principle in instructional terms: notions and functions

Figure 10–2 needs further discussion and illustration. The diagram re-commends a communicatively based approach to the sequencing of informa-tion in the grammar going from the learner's everyday experience to notional and functional categorizations of this for the teacher and textbook writer which are then linked up with the way these notions and functions are realized in the native language and, finally, with the way they are realized in the target language. Hence this is a sequence which is contrastive and implies a slightly less generalized concentrated description than one designed for any learner or teacher of the given target language. One thing that is not implied is that all notions and functions should be discussed fully before stage 3 is reached. Nor is the intention that stages 3 and 4 are chronologically discrete. Presumably a particular notion or function or set of notions or functions will be discussed and taken through stages 3 and 4 after which a new category or set is taken up and given the same treatment. Thus one might take from the learner's everyday experience (as prompted by sociolinguistic research) the function "greetings" and treat this in stages 2 to 4 before examining the next function. In the same way, the notion "possibility" may be discussed and illustrated in 1 and 2 and then elaborated on in stages 3 and 4 before returning to another notion.

Another apparent implication in Figure 2 which is not intended is that notions and functions are necessarily language-neutral—that the function "greetings" and the notion "possibility," for example, are the same for all languages. If that were true then the Sapir-Whorf hypothesis would be totally vacuous, which it is not. Every language does seem to impose some kind of special stamp on the native speaker's conceptualization of external reality at least in terms of what is thought to be important or worth attention. This is crucial for the contrastive pedagogical grammarian since it will be his or her job to point out to the teacher (etc.) that certain notions and functions are particularly important for the native speaker of the target language if only because the proper use of certain constructions is impossible without paying *regular* attention to these aspects of the speech situation; that is, it will often be the case that both languages have the means available for making certain notional (conceptual, semantic) distinctions but that the target language speaker regularly needs to make this distinction whereas the native speaker of the mother tongue does not as a rule bother about it so much. Thus, for example, it is possible in Dutch to make the regular, important distinction made in English between conditional *if*-clauses and temporal *when*-clauses:

indien hij komt	*op het moment dat* hij komt
	(*wanneer* hij komt)
(IF)	(WHEN)

and yet a very typical error for a Dutch speaker of English is precisely to use *when* in either case:

when he comes (*op het moment dat* . . .)
*when he comes (*indien* . . .)

This may be explained, at least partially, by the fact that Dutch speakers make regular use of the subordinating conjunction *als* which legitimately stands for both *if* and *when*. In other words, Dutch speakers do make the distinction but not regularly where no special emphasis is required. It is not a habitual distinction, generally speaking. Consequently it seems that they choose not to make a habitual distinction in English. Why they choose *when* rather than any other English subordinator may be because of the similarity of *when* with *wanneer* (and perhaps also German *wenn*): it is, so to speak, a useful all-purpose "Germanic" subordinator. Whether this is a valid speculation or not does not alter the essential point which is being illustrated—namely, that the native and target language may differ in stage 2 and that this should be carefully explained in a pedagogical grammar where the distinctions involved are found to be relevant. The differences may not only be in terms of the categories themselves: they may be even in terms of different degrees of importance of particular categories held in common, as revealed in the way native speakers make use of them. Thus two languages may differ either in that one has, say, an aspectual distinction reflected in verb usage— for example, imperfectivity versus perfectivity in Slavic verbs, which is not present in the other language described—or both languages may possess the same distinction, as illustrated by the *if/when* problem, but attach different degrees of importance to them in terms of usage. Admittedly where the two contrasted cultures involved are close, the pragmatic, functional categories will broadly speaking be very similar, differing only in the way they are subcategorized, but there may still be important differences at the semantic, notional level which need attention. The general rule can still be maintained, however, of going from the familiar to the unfamiliar since there will always be some broad functional and notional categories like *suggestions* and *time* which all languages hold in common. These will form the point of departure.

Another implication that should not be drawn from this communicative analysis of pedagogical grammar is that grammatical (morphosyntactic) structures have no independent status in the description. Any grammar should contain a systematic account of such structures in addition to how given functional and notional catgories are realized. It may be that in advanced courses, the basics of syntax and morphology are understood to have been mastered and that the major emphasis should be directed toward the notional and pragmatic aspects. This shift of focus could only be reflected in a specialized grammar for advanced learners. For intermediate learners and beginners, more focus should go on these "basics" while still retaining notions and functions deemed appropriate for this level. The whole business of playing down the systematic presentation of language structure is a difficult one. Even for advanced learners, there may be a need for revision of simpler structures as well as a proper explanation of new complex ones. The notionally and functionally based sections will bring together items that may vary greatly in syntax and morphology (and lexis) as the following list demonstrates:

Pragmatic category	Realizations
Suggestion.	How about (verb)-ing. . . ? What would you say to a(n) (noun)? Let me (verb). . . .

If the grammar is contrastive this will be extended to structures that do not occur in both languages like, for example, "conditional clauses," *si*-clauses with the verb in the (imperfect) past in French, which may express suggestions:

> Si on faisait ça plus tard?
> (How about doing that later?)

One advantage of sections that are simple with respect to the notions or functions discussed and complex with respect to the structures is that the teacher and learner will become aware of the need to acquire *repertoires* of structures to express given notions or functions. However, it will still be of value to have cross-references to other sections where the systematization follows structural rather than communicative lines since there will always be a need to check and practice command of the structures themselves as well as the *use* of those structures in communication, and structural sections will facilitate this. The teacher or textbook writer may of course choose to ignore these sections on some methodological basis having to do with the priority of communicative effectiveness over linguistic accuracy, but there may be other users of the grammar who do not share this didactic approach. The structural sections should always be useful to someone.

There are a number of practical questions facing a pedagogical grammarian with the enormous task of providing a comprehensive all-purpose description of two languages for pedagogical purposes. One of these problems is the reduplication of information. If there are to be three components (morphosyntactic/structural, semantic/notional, and pragmatic/functional), then inevitably given structures will appear two or three times in the grammar, at least. For example, *if*-clauses will appear at least once in the structural component under adverbial clauses; they will appear at least once in the notional section under conditions, and at least once in the functional section under warnings as in *If I were you, I'd come back before midnight*. This poses a problem of length. Sometimes economies may be made where there is a great deal of overlap between different components as, for example, where structural and notional categories produce similar results in the description.

Another problem relates to the use of lexical information. In the notional and pragmatic components there may logically speaking be a need to include a great deal of purely lexical information. In describing the notion "possibility," for example, one might list a number of nouns like *possibility*, *capability*, *feasibility*, and their corresponding adverbs and adjectives, all of which express the notion under consideration. In this way, the distinction between a reference grammar and a dictionary or thesaurus becomes blurred, and the grammar becomes even more voluminous than before. It is perhaps advisable to restrict lexical information to that which has clear grammatical consequences. Thus, to say that *That is possible* is a way of expressing possibility may be uninteresting and unnecessary. However, in a Dutch-English contrastive grammar, one should contrast the Dutch *Dat kan* with its unacceptable strict equivalent in English **That can*. In this context it seems more relevant to mention the acceptable English equivalent *That is possible*.

A contrastive pedagogical grammar, to continue the discussion of practical problems of design, will either be bidirectional or unidirectional. The one containing least information will presumably be the unidirectional type in which one of the languages is the target language and the other the native language. Here, less detail is necessary in the description of one of the languages being contrasted—that is, the native language. This does not mean to say that all obligatory distinctions *not* made in the target language will be ignored. An English person learning French or German or Dutch, for example, may make his English distinction between planned and unplanned future by using a present tense plus a future time adverbial only when he intends to convey the "plan" meaning (see Sharwood Smith, 1977a, for a fuller discussion), and where he does not intend it, use another verbal form corresponding to *will/shall* or *going to* plus the main verb. By the same token he may avoid using the present tense where the event or state referred to cannot possibly be planned (under normal circumstances). Thus he may tend to avoid the following (correct) structure in Dutch:

> Hij wordt binnen enkele dagen beter
> (literally: *he gets better in a few days
> or: *he is getting better in a few days).[3]

This notional distinction is obligatory in English as soon as a verb is used that requires marking for past or present. By transferring the distinction to equivalent forms in another language, the learner may end up subconsciously restricting his use of a certain target form or deliberately avoiding it in contexts where it would be perfectly permissible. Thus a unidirectional format will allow for native distinctions insofar as they are judged to affect performance in the target language. However, if economies are to be made, they will be made in the detail in which description of the native language is elaborated. A bidirectional grammar, however, will presumably have to discuss both languages in the same amount of detail, since either language can be treated as a target language—that is, the language which represents the new information to be learned and not the more familiar information to be used as a basis for learning.

To review what has been covered concerning notions and functions in a pedagogical grammar, one might say that, following the general principle of proceeding from the familiar to the unfamiliar, one should start by drawing attention to the learner's everyday experience. The next step is to go to notional and functional categories that are common to both languages and of equal importance. Those which are judged to be complex need illustration, derived from the learner's everyday experience. Once explained, the realizations of these categories should be dealt with. Similarities between the two languages need a brief mention before differences are discussed. Where learning difficulty has been detected (in terms of errors and also avoidance) more careful elaboration is required and this should include more extensive reference to the native language. It is assumed that the way that, say, a German speaker conceptualizes the world around him will be reflected in the notional and functional categories of German and that, before going on to discuss target language structures, it is necessary to introduce whatever important conceptualizations there are which can be discovered in the target language and which differ in some way from those in the native language. In other words, it is important to include in the package offered to the learner not only the structures but the spectacles with which a native speaker of the target language views what he or she talks about. This should be done by first outlining common perspectives and then drawing distinctions. It should then be possible to "motivate," for the learner, structures which are problematic because native language spectacles make the underlying notional or functional distinctions seem odd or trivial, if ever they are perceived at all (without help); once the target language spectacles are presented, exploiting similarities and differences between them and those of the native speaker, then the relevant structures can be fully discussed and thoroughly illustrated. Each structure will be cross-referenced, ideally with references to other semantic and pragmatic uses but at any rate to appropriate places in the structural sections. An illustration of the design procedure is presented below, using "time" as an example of a notion chosen for description in a unidirectional contrastive grammar.

1. What is TIME in terms of everyday experience?
2. How can TIME be subcategorized in ways that are regularly reflected in the native language (NL) and in the target language (TL) as well?
3. Give examples of all of these subcategories—realizations—in terms of NL and TL grammar, with more extensive NL illustration of the more complex ones. Always begin with subcategories that have similar realizations before going on to those that have different realizations. For example:

    FIRST: "Present Future" (see Sharwood Smith, 1977a)

    I am going to do it (NL) – Je *vais* le *faire* (TL)

    THEN: "Future Future"

    I *will do* it (NL) – Je le *ferai* (TL)

4. Are there any subcategories in the NL that do not get (regular) *grammatical* realization in the TL? For example: "Bounded time" or "temporariness" as expressed by the progressive *-ing* form in English but not in, say, German. See also the earlier discussion of *if* and *when*. Illustrate briefly the presence and lack of the (regular) distinction in the NL and TL respectively. Point out the distinction in the NL with

examples; show how the nearest grammatical TL equivalent covers
both senses and show how the distinction can be made in the TL, but
in other ways (with appropriate warning about the frequency with
which TL speakers actually bother to make the distinction).

5. Are there any subcategories in the TL that are in regular use but which
are NOT (very) relevant in the NL? Illustrate extensively giving clear
indications of the conditions of usage (see Appendixes B and C in
Sharwood Smith, 1977b; and Carpay, 1974).

Implicit in the above discussion has been the idea that notions and
functions may and should be subcategorized. As our knowledge about these
areas of language increases, the necessary systematization (in pedagogical
grammars) should become increasingly well substantiated by research in nonapplied linguistics and its sister disciplines. For the moment the pedagogical
grammarian should try as much as possible to establish systems of subcategories, following the Apostel principle; mere subdivision is not enough. Thus we
can say that as an overall concept or notion, "time" is the same in language A
and language B despite surface morphosyntactic differences in realization.
However, we can go on to say that it is not the same in the way it is
(systematically) subdivided. If I speak English, I regularly have to make a
decision, a notional or semantic decision, about whether what I am talking
about in the future is "fixed" in some way or not. This swift, automatized,
unconscious assessment of the situation determines my use of the verbal and
adverbial system in English. It is specific to English and needs to be explained
to the teacher of English as a foreign language. This makes the type of
algorithmic representation discussed elsewhere (see Landa, 1974; Carpay,
1974; Sharwood Smith, 1977b) particularly attractive since two decision procedures can be compared and contrasted—a TL one and an NL one—to show
how common superordinate decisions like "Am I talking about something in
the present or not?" are followed by language-specific decisions like "Is the
event fixed or not?" (see Sharwood Smith, 1977a and 1977b for a fuller
discussion).

It has been the aim of this discussion to demonstrate both the relevance
of notions and functions, and the useful role of contrastive analysis in a
pedagogical grammar. In terms of the approach taken here to what has been
termed *pedagogical processing*, this relevance has to be not only linguistic but
psychological as well. Following the general principle of presenting familiar
information before (and as a basis for) new information, notions and functions
stand closer to the everyday experience of the user of the grammar and
represent more directly the needs of the learner who wants to express as far as
possible familiar ideas for familiar reasons, albeit using a new code. Contrastive analysis, apart from offering useful and interesting insights into the relationships between the two languages, can help in the introduction of new,
unfamiliar ways of looking at the familiar. The pedagogical grammarian as
represented here will have problems in that what can be gleaned from nonapplied linguistics is often fragmentary or else helpful only in some global sense,

establishing right attitudes to language. A good dietician will nevertheless seek first to establish what is available and what is usable (see, e.g., Mackenzie in this volume) before attempting new solutions. The way this material is selected and presented will be according to predetermined principles, some of which will be purely linguistic and others gleaned from different disciplines. Perhaps what is wrong with the communicative approach is the paucity of well-designed communicative grammars establishing a bridge between the study of language and the practice of language teaching and language learning, and, in another sense, a bridge between linguistic structures and their use.

NOTES

1. Compare for further discussion of the principles of pedagogical grammar the papers collected in Bausch (1979).
2. A classic statement of the essential relativism of linguistic descriptions is Halliday (1964).
3. This kind of claim can be verified or falsified by people doing relevant research into language learning.

QUESTIONS FOR DISCUSSION

1. Cited in the Sharwood Smith paper is Bruner's Apostel principle—the notion that true learning can take place only within a domain in which some part of that domain is already known. Can you think of a number of different ways in which the principle may be brought to bear for consciousness raising (CR) in pedagogical grammar? In addressing this question, consider the pedagogical implications of the organization of language in its broadest sense—for example, syntax, semantics, lexicon, pragmatics, and so on—and also language universals.
2. Recall the kinds of observations that led Pienemann to formulate his Teachability Hypothesis (TH; Part II). In what way might one say that the TH exemplifies the Apostel principle, as it is discussed by Sharwood Smith? Furthermore, in what way might one say that CR and Universal Grammar exemplify the Apostel principle, as discussed in the Rutherford and Sharwood Smith paper (Part II)?
3. In what other aspects might it be the case that Pienemann and Sharwood Smith propose to address the L2 language-learning problem along similar lines? Recall Sharwood Smith's statement (p. 158) that "the task of the applied grammarian is surely to make certain that the pedagogical processing does not require above-average abilities on the part of the consumer."
4. Consider the matter of choice concerning grammatical CR. We have read of suggestions for "picking and choosing among formal statements," of criticism of this as being unprincipled eclecticism, of defense of it again if the choices are validated through classroom experience, and (in Part II) we have seen proposals that at least some choices of candidates for grammatical CR derive from principles of Universal Grammar. Do all these suggestions reflect fundamentally contradicting positions or are there ways to reconcile these various statements? Think in particular about what different connotations *pedagogical grammar* may carry for grammarian, teacher, and learner.

REFERENCES

Apostel, L. 1977. The cognitive point of view: introduction to a discussion. In M. De Mey et al. (eds.), *International Workshop on the Cognitive View*. Ghent: University of Ghent.

Aronson Berman, R. 1978. Contrastive analysis revisited: obligatory, systematic, and incidental differences between languages. *Interlanguage Studies Bulletin* 3:212–233.

Ausubel, D. 1968. *Educational Psychology: A Cognitive View*. New York: Holt, Rinehart and Winston.

Bausch, K., ed. 1979. *Beiträge zur Didaktischen Grammatik*. Königstein: Scriptor.

Bruner, J. 1978. The role of dialogue in language acquisition. In A. Sinclair, R. Jarvella, and W. Levelt (eds.), *The Child's Conception of Language*. Berlin: Springer.

Carpay, J. 1974. *Onderwijs-leerpsychologie en Leergang Ontwikkeling in het Moderne Vreemde Talenonderwijs*. Groningen: Tjeenk Willink.

Halliday, M. 1964. Syntax and the consumer. *Monograph Series on Language and Linguistics* 17:11–24.

Landa, L. 1974. *Algorithmization in Learning and Instruction*. Englewood Cliffs, N.J.: Educational Technology Publications.

Leech, G., and J. Svartvik. 1975. *A Communicative Grammar of English*. London: Longman.

Sharwood Smith, M. 1977. *Aspects of Future Reference in a Pedagogical Grammar of English*. Frankfurt/Main: Lang.

Sharwood Smith, M. 1978. Applied linguistics and the psychology of instruction: A case for transfusion? *Studies in Second Language Acquisition* 1(2):91–117. In this volume.

11

Aspects of
Pedagogical Grammar

William Rutherford
University of Southern California

INTRODUCTION

A great deal of attention is currently being devoted to the notion that in language teaching and language learning what one is striving to achieve or impart is, after all, language as an instrument of communication and not just language as the embodiment of a formal system. Virtually every student who works at learning a language does so not as a trainee for the future occupation of grammarian, phonetician, or lexicographer, but rather as a trainee for the future activity of a user of that language in either or both its spoken and written forms. Recognition of this fact has led of late to the promulgation of methodologies and to the compilation of syllabuses which give primary exposure to varieties of so-called communicative "functions" that the language may serve and which assign a subsidiary role, if indeed any at all, to systematic inspection of that language's formal properties. It has been claimed (Newmark and Reibel, 1967) that classroom attention to language form is neither a sufficient nor a necessary condition for learning to take place. In arguing for an approach to language teaching which utilizes units of communication as the points of departure, they assume that grammar will, so to speak, take care of

"Aspects of Pedagogical Grammar" by William E. Rutherford, 1980, *Applied Linguistics*, vol. 1, no. 1, pp. 60–73. Reprinted with permission of Oxford University Press.

The preparation of this paper has benefited from insightful comments by Stephen Krashen. Other helpful suggestions were provided by Jacquelyn Schachter, Herbert Seliger, Michael Sharwood Smith, Graham Thurgood, and Sheldon Wise, none of whom is responsible for whatever shortcomings are to be found herein. The original version of this paper was presented at the thirteenth annual TESOL Convention, Boston, 1979.

itself, as it does in the learning of a first language. Yet this assumption remains to be proven (Lamendella and Selinker, 1978).

It is important to understand that, even among those who argue most vehemently for a language-learning experience devoid of focus upon language form, there is nowhere the implication that form in and of itself is not a crucial part of language. In his pioneering work on notional syllabuses, for example, even Wilkins (1976) leaves the way open for some considerable attention to formal matters:

> The acquisition of the grammatical system of a language remains a most impor-
> tant element in language learning. The grammar is the means through which
> linguistic creativity is ultimately achieved and an inadequate knowledge of the
> grammar would lead to serious limitations on the capacity for communication. A
> notional syllabus, no less than a grammatical syllabus, must seek to ensure that
> the grammatical system is properly assimilated by the learner. [p. 66]

Noblitt (1972) identified the primary objective of language learning as "for the student to internalize a grammar which approximates that of a native speaker to a specifiable degree" (Noblitt 1972, p. 315). The question then is not whether to impart to the learner a knowledge of the language sytem but rather how we might go about it. This is a far more complex matter than simple decisions to say something "about" the language, or not to say something. In the remainder of this paper I would like to explore the nature of this complexity, to discuss different ways in which grammatical information can affect teaching and learning, and finally to suggest that the real potential of a "grammatical" contribution to the language-learning experience has yet to be fully realized.

The ways in which grammatical considerations have over the years been manifested in formal language learning can, I believe, be narrowed to three: the *bases* upon which pedagogical grammar may be conceived, the criteria upon which to exercise *choices* among grammatical exponents for presentation, and the *manner* in which grammatical competence is to be imparted.

BASES

The linguistic or psycholinguistic concepts that have been proposed as basic pedagogic frameworks for the introduction of grammatical material cover a rather wide field. Perhaps the best known such "applications" are those that adapt, wholly or in part, entire formal systems. We have, for example, Ann Nichols's 1965 text (*English Syntax: Advanced Composition for Non-Native Speakers*), based upon the principles of immediate constituent analysis and the earliest contributions of Chomsky (1957). *Constructing Sentences* (Rand, 1969) is a direct reflection of Lees's *Grammar of English Nominalizations* (1960), and my own *Modern English*, in its 1968 version, borrowed some of the transformational apparatus and generalizations from *Syntactic Structures* (Chomsky, 1957) and *Aspects of the Theory of Syntax* (Chomsky, 1965). There have been others. However much one may find to criticize in them, what value these texts may have is the extent to which they serve the "monitoring" capacity of students who are more predisposed to utilize this mechanism (Krashen, 1977). The place of the monitor relative to the other aspects of a person's language-learning faculty might be represented in the kind of schema proposed by Dulay and Burt (1977):

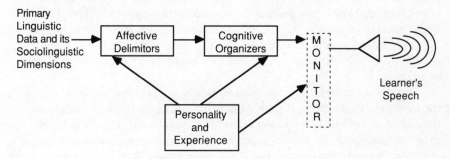

Figure 11-1   The language learning faculty

The apparent lack of success of materials like those cited earlier is therefore attributable, at least in part, to their *exclusive* catering to the monitoring capacity, the size of which varies greatly of course from learner to learner, and the effect of which may not figure at all in some of the methods for measuring communicative competence.

It is also claimed (Diller, 1975) that the aims of language pedagogy are best served by observance of the so-called "rationalist-cognitivist" theories of language, the philosophical underpinning of transformational grammar. Cited by Diller as embodiments of rationalist theory have been such pedagogical concepts, approaches, and methodologies as The Silent Way of Gattegno, the "non-silent way" of Winitz and Reeds, other versions of the Direct Method, Community Language Learning, Total Physical Response, and so on. Although they all differ strikingly in many ways, two things that they apparently have in common are, according to their own claims, (1) a high degree of success in teaching language and (2) a recognition of the importance of grammar. It is tempting here, of course, to infer the causal relationship between the two, and yet this remains to be demonstrated. It may well be that such success as these new (and not so new) approaches have enjoyed is more attributable to the extent to which they cater to all the functions of the human language-learning faculty than it is to the fact that grammar has been taken note of by them in some way.

If recognition of language as (at least in part) rule-governed behavior is one of the hallmarks of rationalist-cognitivist theory, then it would be hard to find any language-teaching methods, systems, curricula, or syllabuses that are to that extent *not* rationalist-cognitivist. Who among us would not agree that rule-governed behavior is an apt characterization of much of what happens when one says or writes something? The crucial questions for language teaching, I believe, do not devolve upon whether or not language is rule-governed behavior. Those questions, it seems to me, are rather ones like (1) What kinds of rules are we talking about? (2) Can they be adequately stated for pedagogical purposes (Krashen and Seliger, 1975)? (3) How much of what happens in language use can we account for through such rules? (4) Are any of them teachable? (5) Could teaching them have any appreciable positive effect on learning? (6) What does "teaching a rule" really mean? (7) Can features of a target language system be utilized pedagogically in ways other than those with which we are currently familiar (i.e., explicit statement, sequencing determined by grammatical complexity, etc.)? To talk meaningfully about pedagogical grammar, here or elsewhere, is to address oneself to, or elaborate upon, these questions.

I have a persistent feeling, with some empirical corroboration, that with the mention of grammatical rules what is usually in the back of one's mind are the rules, so to speak, of low-level syntax; that is, rules having to do, for example, with subject-verb agreement, plural markers, possessive markers, questions, tense formation, and so forth; in other words, rules whose terms are the overt markers of surface syntax or the morphological elements that are typically observed in studies of language acquisition. Yet these rules, precisely because their makeup may easily be observed at the level of surface syntax, require little or no explicit pedagogical formulation. Wilga Rivers, for example, has argued for paying less attention to such rules which, as we know, are continually broken even by advanced learners who can use the rest of the language quite correctly. Rivers urges that more emphasis be put instead on the ways in which the target language conceptualizes reality and the grammatical realization of those concepts. Sharwood Smith (1976) proposes teaching the English present perfect tense "within the framework of a more comprehensible notional system dealing with time reference in general" (Sharwood Smith, 1976, p. 4). Other suggestions are to be found in Wilkins (1976) and Chu (1978). If French were the target language, for example, it would not mean teaching the mechanics of gender agreement so much as inculcating a thought pattern in which the whole *concept* of gender agreement becomes dominant. If English is the target language, it means not so much teaching the intricate rule system for deployment of definite and indefinite articles (one ESL text—Robinson 1967—lists 44 separate rules); it means rather engendering an inclination to match certain features of the determiner system with notions of presupposition and raising to consciousness.

If at least some of the rules of low-level syntax are, so to speak, to be left to take care of themselves, then proposals for basing the arrangement of language content upon the findings of research in error analysis (e.g., Diller, 1975) need to be re-examined, for most of this research has been concerned with precisely that area of syntax. George (1972), for example, in his pioneering work *Common Errors in Language Learning*, attributes to perception of redundancy some errors involving the presence or absence of such items as the comparative morpheme, personal pronouns, the copula, existential *there*, question words, and so on. Information of this kind seemed at the time to have some usefulness for the design of pedagogical syllabuses, and in fact this was proposed by George and later echoed by Diller (1975). Valdman (1974) takes an even stronger position in stating that:

> [S]ince errors reflect the way in which learners acquire linguistic competence, they *must* [italics added] serve as a basis for the ordering of grammatical features, and, beyond that, for the establishment of objectives and aims of instruction. [Valdman 1974, p. 23]

More recently, however, there have come suggestions (Hakuta, 1979; Huebner, 1978; Schachter and Rutherford, 1978) that the characterization of what can be called a learner error may be a considerably more complex matter than heretofore imagined. Preoccupation by researchers with the distributional arrangement of surface syntax ought not to conflict with the need to look carefully at other less obvious possible sources for learner errors: for example, transfer of first language discourse features, influence of broad first language typological characteristics, "pressure" from first language abstract organization, and so on. This kind of scrutiny has already led to the discovery (Schachter and Rutherford, 1978) that at least one kind of "error," long identified as a malformed passive (e.g., *Chicken have cooked already*), is in fact an attempt to impose upon English the basic topic-comment form of Chinese (*Chicken, we have cooked it already*). Another researcher (Huebner, 1978) has traced errors in the English determiner system to influence from a learner's "topic-prominent" first language (Li and Thompson, 1976). Clearly, it is not rash to assume that much more may be going on in the production of learner errors than we can presently understand. And it is just as clear that caution and restraint are called for in any temptation to let current error analysis research findings influence the shape of pedagogical grammars. Warnings of this kind have already been issued. See, for instance, Tarone, Swain, and Fathman (1976) and Schachter and Celce-Murcia (1977).

One more suggestion for the basic makeup of pedagogical grammar, and one which is not necessarily inconsistent with the foregoing proposals, comes from Allen and Widdowson (1978)[1]:

> The applied linguist must pick and choose among formal statements in the light of his experience as a teacher, and decide what are pedagogically the more appropriate ways of arranging the linguistic information that he derives from linguistic grammars. [pp. 67–68]

This position has since been attacked by Sharwood Smith (1978), who at AILA Montreal said that "eclecticism as such is only a stop-gap . . . in the absence of guidelines from other disciplines" (Sharwood Smith, 1978, p. 2). If it is "unprincipled eclecticism" that Allen and Widdowson are advocating, then this criticism would seem to be well directed. However, Allen and Widdowson, if I understand them correctly, are simply saying that whatever the applied linguist borrows from theoretical linguistics to serve the needs of pedagogy must be validated "in the light of his experience as a teacher." The applied linguist's "picking and choosing" may therefore be seen as no less principled than any other means of assembling a theoretical base from which to derive the grammatical exponents appropriate for pedagogy.

CHOICES

We turn now to the subject of what criteria we might bring to bear in exercising choice among grammatical elements. It is important at the outset to realize that establishment of pedagogical grammar bases does not automatically prescribe the precise selection of grammatical features for pedagogical use. Such choices may be influenced by other considerations, some of which I will touch upon here.

With the current attention being paid to notions of syllabuses with a semantic as opposed to a grammatical orientation, the matter of choosing among structural elements is often constrained by prior semantic and functional choices. Since communication is established as an immediate goal very early in the instructional plan, what the student needs right away in order to engage in such communication is judged to be not so much mastery of units of language structure as mastery of units, so to speak, of communication. (For the dangers inherent in a view of language use that derives from a communicative taxonomy, see Widdowson, 1978.) Can the concept of "grammatical choice" have any meaning then within the syllabus which takes organized communication as its point of departure? The answer to this is far from certain. Grammatical considerations seem to affect all functionally based pedagogical materials, whether or not the effect is acknowledged by the author, in at least one of two ways: (1) an implicit, mainly intuitive criterion of simplification is invoked, such that the normal frequency of appearance of certain designated structures is artificially lowered, thereby automatically increasing the frequency of appearance of other structures; and (2) marked off in the materials are periodic specified gathering points for sets of previously practiced language elements which, collectively, illustrate the formal properties of a construction, extend the co-occurrence range of an already familiar structure, or display a completed structural paradigm. Nevertheless, form in all these instances, no matter what the nature and strength of its influence, clearly plays a subordinate role to that of what has come to be called language function.

Grammatical considerations thus have generally entered meaningfully into the planning of existing functional materials only to a very limited extent. Is this indicative of a basic incompatibility of structural and functional criteria? It is probably not yet possible to answer this with any kind of assurance, simply because not a great deal of research has been undertaken to study the relation between the two, pioneering efforts like those of Munby (1978) and Wilkins (1976) notwithstanding. It might yet be demonstrated, for example, that corresponding to a certain small number of language functions (perhaps as they are defined in Van Ek, 1975) are a small range of favored syntactic forms. This is what Fink claims (1976) is the case for syntax vis-à-vis semantics. Although there is no one-to-one syntax-semantics match-up, there are favored syntactic forms for the semantic categories "location," "experiencer," "agent," "benefactive," "instrument," and so on. Drawing on the work of Tesnière and Fillmore, Fink suggests that the nature of this relationship can be exploited pedagogically through focus on the lexico-semantic properties of verbs, which he claims will facilitate "sentence retention and reproduction" for the learner. Nevertheless, the usefulness for pedagogy of all this, it must be admitted, is still a matter for some experimentation.

Choices among grammatical exponents can also be discussed with respect to their places of introduction relative to each other—that is, sequencing. A number of studies in recent years have demonstrated that certain lists of English structures are acquired by foreign learners in the same order irrespective of teaching methods, syllabus design, or mother tongue (Krashen, Madden, and Bailey, 1975; see also a summary of such research in Corder, 1978). Others have shown that not only are the acquisition orders fixed for second language learning and for first language learning, but the orders in second language learning are the same, both for child learners (Burt and Dulay, 1974; Fathman, 1975) and adult learners (Krashen et al., 1976). Thus, we know in what order a specified class of morphemes is acquired by all second language learners, and we know that in the construction of pedagogical grammars we also want to arrange the presentation of such morphemes in some order. Here, it would seem then, is a prime example of research findings whose pedagogical applications are obvious. Krashen et al. (1975) put it this way:

> The typical learner will have a certain difficulty order regardless of what syllabus is used, and it is plausible that using a sequence identical to that difficulty order will be more comfortable and efficient, that is, learning might proceed more rapidly and with less frustration on the part of the student and teacher. [p. 46]

Yet, the "application" here may be premature. One must realize that language acquisition research has focused to date upon a very small part of the total language system (Tarone, Swain, and Fathman, 1976). I would stress, furthermore, that limitations of research technique have thus far confined empirical investigation largely to the one language area that is most amenable to itemization—namely, the morphological elements of low-level syntax. Without denying the value of morphological acquisition studies for gaining insight into the cognitive processes involved in language learning, one would still wish to question the wisdom of applying directly to language pedagogy knowledge about the sequential appearance of discrete low-level linguistic units at a time when focus in designing curricula has moved toward greater appreciation and understanding of the importance of discourse and the specific ways that discourse is encoded into grammar for different purposes.[2] As I pointed out earlier, applications of research to pedagogy at the morphological level have other dangers that only now are beginning to be noted and investigated. These have to do with the influence of first language discourse features upon second language syntactic form, resulting in unique interlanguage characteristics which traditional research methods have thus far been unable to account for (Huebner, 1978; Schachter and Rutherford, 1978; Schmidt, 1978). Again, there is clearly much more to be known about how languages are learned before we would want to take serious note of such findings in choosing what grammatical material to make pedagogical light of and where and when to do it.

Having discussed at some length the conceptual bases for pedagogical grammar and the matter of choosing among grammatical exponents, I would like now to consider the question of how grammatical information is imparted within the pedagogical setting.

MANNER

I think it is fair to say at the outset that all efforts to convey grammatical information to the learner are in effect efforts to influence learning strategies. Where this information is in any way drawn attention to—by overt arrangement, sequencing, spiraling, simplification, attenuation, explanation, or what have you—then the effort to influence is a conscious one. The conscious efforts to influence which have been recognized and identified as such often involve tampering with the well-formedness of sentences. This is done in either one of two ways. One is an attempt to anticipate stages in the development of the learner's interlanguage by incorporating these stages into the language of his input; the other is an attempt at direct guidance of the learner's hypothesis-testing capacity through exposure to selected ungrammatical language for the purpose of inducing correct generalizations. I will briefly discuss these two kinds of tampering in the order just cited.

One of the earliest mentions of interlanguage replication for pedagogy occurred in Jakobovits's *Foreign Language Learning* (1970), where he speculated upon the possibility of shaping the development of the learner's competence by exposing him "to utterances which are grammatically progressive at each stage but which fall short of having the full c mplexity of well-formed sentences" (p. 23). Somewhat later Nickel (1973) suggested that "language teaching materials should reflect the sequence of approximative systems of the learner to the point of actually teaching 'incorrect forms.'"[3] Valdman (1974) also considers this approach. At about the same time Schumann (1974) hypothesized that the learner's successive approximative systems are similar to the widely documented language developmental sequence of pidginization followed by creolization. If this is so, then it is a very short step to suggesting that in ESL/EFL classes one should actually teach a pidginized form of English, and over a stretch of learning time gradually bring it into alignment with standard English. Widdowson (in a talk at USC in 1978) is one researcher who has made this suggestion.[4] As with any other serious proposal, however, the notion of "pedagogical pidginization" needs to be thought through to all its possible consequences and ramifications. In particular, this would entail the resolution of a paradox: that whereas the communicative thrust of language-teaching objectives now tends more and more toward direct consideration of the learner's early need to express his personal feelings, pidginization is a process of simplification suited to the communication not of feelings but of information (see Schumann, 1974, and references cited therein). In other words, on the one hand assessment of language-learning *objectives* might point to early exposure of the learner to the language redundancies (i.e., morphological inflection, grammatical complexity, etc.) required for "integrative" and "expressive" function (Smith, 1972), while on the other hand assessment of language-learning *strategies* would point to a curriculum design deriving from the pidginization process, where morphological inflection and grammatical complexity are delayed until "creolization." This contradiction between objectives and strategies, would clearly need to be resolved before undertaking to make pedagogical use of pidginization.

The prime advocate of the use of ungrammaticality as a direct aid to the learner's hypothesis-testing capacity is Robin Lakoff, with actual application of this technique to be found in Rutherford (1975, 1977). Lakoff put the matter this way:

> The teacher must give the learner a boost to making his own generalizations, to learning how the native speaker understands and intuitively uses . . . sentences. This necessarily implies that it is essential to give the learner ungrammatical sentences, so that he can study these along with the grammatical ones to decide for himself what the difference is. [Lakoff 1969, pp. 125–126]
>
> The text will be rationalistically oriented—it will encourage students to ask themselves why sentences are good and bad. [p. 117]

Not all students will be predisposed, of course, to working with language in this way, since what constitutes a bad sentence will often be one thing for the linguist and quite something else for the language learner: for example, a sentence whose propositional content is false, illogical, or even unpleasant. Furthermore, it may seem counterproductive to call much attention to isolated sentences devoid of context or relevance at a time when there is increasing interest in the teaching of language as communication. This, then, is another contradiction whose resolution would be a prerequisite to the presentation of selected ungrammaticality for the inductive learning of structural generalizations.

Throughout this discussion of pedagogical grammar I have been citing the parallel need to consider the relationship between grammar and discourse. This was touched on in discussion about the teaching of conceptual systems, about the transfer of first language function, about lexico-semantic properties, and so on. Left unspecified, however, and only implied, is how the features of the grammatical system and of the realm of discourse might be learned *relative to each other*—that is, sequencing again, but at the very highest level of language organization. Others have turned this implication into an assertion— that language learning in terms of the acquisition of structures makes sense only within the framework of discourse, wherein the structures are seen as serving a communicative function. Hatch (1978) states the premise as follows:

> In second language learning . . . it is assumed that one first learns how to manipulate structures, that one gradually builds up a repertoire of structures and then, somehow, learns how to put the structures to use in discourse. We would like to consider the possibility that just the reverse happens. One learns how to interact verbally, and out of this interaction syntactic structures are developed. [pp. 403–404]

If in fact language learning proceeds in this way (and of course this has yet to be demonstrated), then for language teaching to pursue methods that project a view of language which runs counter to what the learner already knows intuitively would seem not to be sound pedagogy. The conclusion to be drawn here then is that presentation of syntax should derive, wherever possible, from the organization of discourse. All well and good. But the extent to which we are able to accomplish this on a principled basis will be a direct reflection of our understanding of how grammar encodes discourse for communication, an area of language research which is as yet little understood. Hakuta and Cansino (1977), for example, suggest that "tracing the development of the linguistic forms that the learner uses for the expression of a (pragmatic) function might well reveal orderly and lawful patterns" (p. 310), a line of investigation which they regret has not yet been pursued.

CONCLUSION

I would like to finish this paper by returning to some earlier issues that require more elaboration. There is no question that, whatever else the use of language represents, some part of that use is rule-governed behavior. No one would deny that. But what we do not agree upon is what pedagogical use is to be made of these "rules." It is a question, in other words, of how we go about making language systems serve the needs of language learning. Part of the problem is to be found in what we perceive to be a language system; part of it is to be found in what we do with that perception.

A fairly typical view of what our language is made up of and how it is put together can be obtained from inspection of most English-teaching materials, both first and second language. Although no two sets of materials will be based upon the same inventory of language categories, what most of these materials do have in common is the utilization of language categories themselves as units of learning. The role of grammar in particular has been viewed in this way. It is tempting to conceive of grammar as a language system composed of discrete units, and it is then but a short pedagogical step to let such units constitute something which is to be, so to speak, "mastered." Lending itself especially well to this notion of formal elements translating into learnable elements is surface syntax (see also Noblitt, 1972). Yet the justification for this translation still awaits empirical validation. The forms of surface grammar are, for example, not even co-extensive with functions which they seem to encode and which represent a new kind of "learnable" unit in recent EFL syllabuses. But notwithstanding the pedagogical status of surface syntax, if considerations of this kind are taken to be the extent of the grammatical contribution to pedagogy, then I would have to say that grammar has been given short shrift.

The grammatical system of English, or any other language, is still very far indeed from being fully understood. What we do know, however, is that grammatical organization exists on deeper levels than have been recognized by most pedagogical research and that the ways in which this deep organization bears on language learning is as yet little known. The kind of deep English grammar I am referring to is exemplified by the fundamental principle that word order is used almost exclusively to signal grammatical relationships and not—as in, for example Russian, Chinese, and to some extent Spanish—to signal pragmatic relationships (Thompson, 1978). Again, the kind of deep grammar I am referring to is further exemplified by the fact that basic to the English sentence is the notion "subject" and not "topic," as in, say, Chinese, or both subject and topic, as in, say, Japanese (Li and Thompson, 1976). Thompson (1978) points out that it is from these principles that English derives the need for certain kinds of grammatical features (e.g., articles: to mark subjects that are not at the same time topics) and rules (e.g., movement rules: to keep subject position filled).

It is all too obvious that the (presumably unconscious) grasp by the learner of such principles as subject prominence and grammatical word order is affected by the corresponding organizational principles of the learner's mother tongue. This fact is most clearly demonstrated by the simple act of correcting the surface errors, both "local" and "global" (Burt and Kiparsky, 1974), in a piece of written English produced by any foreign learner. When everything correctable has been corrected, what is usually left is a stretch of English that not only still tells us that it was written by a nonnative speaker but also still leaves clues as to that speaker's mother tongue. If the writer were Japanese, for example, we would be interested to know in what ways, subtle or not, that stretch of English could have been affected by typological characteristics of Japanese such as topic and subject prominence and the fact that it is left branching and rigidly verb final. This of course presupposes that we already have the corresponding typological information for English. But it is precisely this kind of grammatical knowledge, I would like to stress once more, that should be examined for its pedagogical usefulness and significance.

We are all aware of the advances that have been made in recent years in the understanding of the language-learning process. We are nowadays accustomed, in routine fashion, to formulating theories, conducting experiments, testing hypotheses, and so on. And we have witnessed methodological breakthroughs, innovative classroom techniques, and principled syllabus design. Yet, pedagogical grammar of late seems to some extent to have been left at the starting gate. The grammatical contribution to pedagogy seldom ventures beyond an inventory of constructions and sentence types that are considered to be of high frequency and representative of the language and which await incorporation into the syllabus at designated points, from there on to be practiced and hopefully mastered. This is as true for syllabuses with a functional orientation as for those with a grammatical orientation. But neglected so far have been the crucial questions of deep grammatical organization, of the discourse function of grammatical rules, and of what kinds of "meanings" are conveyed by grammatical forms themselves. Thus, despite real evidence of some serious attention, pedagogical grammar has a potential which is yet to be fulfilled.

The fulfillment of this potential will depend heavily upon the extent to which we can start thinking of grammar in broader terms. This does not mean that the already complex grammatical statements to be found in most text-books should be further complicated through the addition of more and more facts. That is not what is needed, however insightful the facts may turn out to be. On the contrary, one indeed might easily question the very assumption that the only way grammatical information can be utilized pedagogically is through overt factual presentation in teachable units, so to speak. It has yet to be proven that grammar has of necessity to call attention to itself in order to be pedagogically useful, and with the curricular goals of language for communica-tion the deeper grammatical organization of the syllabus might well be ac-complished in such a way as to be invisible to the untrained eye. Grammar in this more sweeping sense would thus play a different kind of role in the language-learning experience, and one that is more consistent with the concept of language as a vehicle for communication. The kind of role I am speaking of would be one which focuses as much attention upon what we use a grammati-cal construction for as upon how that construction is put together. Such a role would bring to consciousness the necessity for choosing among grammatical alternatives in satisfying the basic principles of information arrangement within discourse. Such a role would take serious note of the formal characteris-tics that distinguish the English language typologically from other languages, characteristics like the central position of the notion "subject" as distinct from "topic" and the use of word order to reflect grammatical relationships. And such a role would serve to support a way of looking at and thinking about language, for teacher and student alike. It is by moving in these directions, I believe, that pedagogical grammar is most likely to realize its unfulfilled potential and to facilitate learning how to communicate in a foreign language.

NOTES

1. Noblitt (1972) holds a similar view.
2. Krashen (personal communication) has since modified his position to a considera-tion that what might be best for sequencing is grammatical input that the learner understands. Candlin (1978) suggests sequencing of discourse patterns.
3. This quote on Nickel's suggestion is taken from Corder (1978, p. 72).
4. See also his paper "Pidgin and Babu" in Widdowson (1979).

QUESTIONS FOR DISCUSSION

1. The Rutherford paper suggests that pedagogical aids to learning (again, the function of pedagogical grammar according to Corder) need not always be in the form of actual descriptions and that "the deeper grammatical organization of the syllabus might well be accomplished in such a way as to be invisible to the untrained eye." What do you think this really means? What kinds of grammatical information might better be imparted to the learner without recourse to descriptive statements, and how might this be done? Compare the implications of this question with those of question 6 for the Corder selection.

2. Rutherford argues for a concept of grammar that ranges beyond the conventional view of language as an assemblage of discrete grammatical constructs, and Widdowson, in his paper, characterized the role of grammar in language as "mediating between words and contexts." Do these views represent notions of grammar that are different from what is to be seen in general linguistic research? Can you expound on this a little?

3. The Bialystok paper in Part II discusses the learner's progress in terms of movement from "nonanalyzed" (syntactic) knowledge to "analyzed" knowledge whose capacity for intercombination with the rest of language is that much greater. Rutherford, in this paper, scores the traditional pedagogical preoccupation with "low-level syntax" and argues instead for thinking of grammar in broader terms—for example, typological characteristics. Are these two claims compatible? For example, can the learner of English who initially hypothesizes topic-comment and over time changes his or her perception to subject-predicate be thought of in any way as acquiring more "analyzed" knowledge?

4. Many people apparently assume that language is assembled in hierarchical fashion from building blocks—phonology at the bottom, discourse at the top—and that the bottom-to-top route is also the one that learning (and teaching) should take. Others, as in the quote from Hatch, believe differently: "One learns how to interact verbally, and out of this interaction syntactic structures are developed" (p. 180). Is one of these concepts wrong and the other right, or are they both right/wrong, and/or are there still other (and better) ways of looking at language?

REFERENCES

Allen, J., and H. Widdowson. 1978. Teaching the communicative use of English. In R. Mackay and A. Mountford (eds.), *English for Specific Purposes*. London: Longman, Chapter 4.

Burt, M., and H. Dulay. 1974. Natural sequences in child second language acquisition. *Language Learning* 24:37–54.

Burt, M., and K. Kiparsky. 1974. Global and local mistakes. In J. Schumann and N. Stenson (eds.), *New Frontiers in Second Language Learning*. Rowley, Mass.: Newbury House.

Candlin, C. 1978. Discoursal patterning and the equalizing of interpretive opportunity. Paper presented at Conference on English as an International and Auxiliary Language, University of Hawaii, April 1–5.

Chomsky, N. 1957. *Syntactic Structures*. The Hague: Mouton.

Chomsky, N. 1965. *Aspects of the Theory of Syntax*. Cambridge, Mass.: MIT Press.

Chu, C. 1978. A semantico-syntactic approach to contrastive analysis—some "be" and "have" sentences in English and Chinese. *IRAL* 16:273–296.

Corder, S. 1978. Error analysis, interlanguage, and second language acquisition. In V. Kinsella (ed.), *Language Teaching and Linguistics: Surveys*. Cambridge: Cambridge University Press.

Diller, K. 1975. Some new trends for applied linguistics and foreign language teaching in the United States. *TESOL Quarterly* **9**:65–74.

Dulay, H., and M. Burt. 1977. Remarks on creativity in language acquisition. In M. Burt et al. (eds.), *Viewpoints on English as a Second Language*. New York: Regents.

Fathman, A. 1975. Language background, age, and the order of acquisition of English structures. In M. Burt and H. Dulay (eds.), *On TESOL '75*. Washington, D.C.: TESOL.

Fink, S. 1976. Semantic-pragmatic aspects in foreign language pedagogy based on case grammar and valence theory. *Linguistische Berichte* **41**:77–87.

George, H. 1972. *Common Errors in Language Learning*. Rowley, Mass.: Newbury House.

Hakuta, K. 1979. Some common goals for first and second language acquisition research. Paper presented at TESOL Convention, Boston.

Hakuta, K., and H. Cansino. 1977. Trends in second language acquisition research. *Harvard Educational Review* **47**.

Hatch, E. 1978. Discourse analysis and second language acquisition. In E. Hatch (ed.), *Second Language Acquisition*. Rowley, Mass.: Newbury House.

Huebner, T. 1978. Order-of-acquisition vs. dynamic paradigm: a comparison of method in interlanguage research. Paper presented at TESOL Convention, Mexico City.

Jakobovits, L. 1970. *Foreign Language Learning*. Rowley, Mass.: Newbury House.

Krashen, S. 1977. The monitor model for adult second language performance. In M. Burt et al. (eds.), *Viewpoints on English as a Second Language*. New York: Regents.

Krashen, S., C. Madden, and N. Bailey. 1975. Theoretical aspects of grammatical sequencing. In M. Burt and H. Dulay (eds.), *On TESOL '75*. Washington, D.C.: TESOL.

Krashen, S., and H. Seliger. 1975. The essential contribution of formal instruction in adult second language learning. *TESOL Quarterly* **9**:173–184.

Krashen, S., V. Sferlazza, L. Feldman, and A. Fathman. 1976. Adult performance on the SLOPE test: more evidence for a natural sequence in adult second language acquisition. *Language Learning* **26**:145–152.

Lakoff, R. 1969. Transformational grammar and language teaching. *Language Learning* **19**:117–140.

Lamendella, J., and L. Selinker. 1978. Two perspectives on fossilization in interlanguage learning. *Interlanguage Studies Bulletin* **3**:143–191.

Lees, R. 1960. *The Grammar of English Nominalizations*. *IJAL* vol. 26, no. 3 (part II).

Li, C., and S. Thompson. 1976. Subject and topic: a new typology of language. In C. Li (ed.), *Subject and Topic*. New York: Academic Press.

Munby, J. 1978. *Communicative Syllabus Design*. Cambridge: Cambridge University Press.

Newmark, L., and D. Reibel. 1967. Necessity and sufficiency in language learning. In M. Lester (ed.), *Readings in Applied Transformational Grammar*. New York: Holt, Rinehart and Winston.

Nichols, A. 1965. *Advanced Composition for Non-Native Speakers*. New York: Holt, Rinehart and Winston.

Nickel, G. 1973. Aspects of error analysis and grading. In J. Svartvik (ed.), *Errata: Papers in Error Analysis*. Lund: Gleerup.

Noblitt, J. 1972. Pedagogical grammar: towards a theory of foreign language materials preparation. *IRAL* **10**:313–331.

Rand, E. 1969. *Constructing Sentences.* New York: Holt, Rinehart & Winston.

Robinson, L. 1967. *Guided Writing and Free Writing.* New York: Harper and Row.

Rutherford, W. 1968. *Modern English.* New York: Harcourt, Brace and World.

Rutherford, W. 1975, 1977. *Modern English,* 2nd ed., Vols. 1 and 2. New York: Harcourt Brace Jovanovich.

Schachter, J., and M. Celce-Murcia. 1977. Some reservations concerning error analysis. *TESOL Quarterly* **11**:441–451.

Schachter, J., and W. Rutherford. 1978. Discourse function and language transfer. Paper presented at AILA Congress, Montreal, August.

Schmidt, M. 1978. Coordinate structures and deletion in learner English. Master's thesis, University of Washington.

Schumann, J. 1974. Implications of pidginization and creolization for the study of adult second language acquisition. In J. Schumann and N. Stenson (eds.), *New Frontiers in Second Language Learning.* Rowley, Mass.: Newbury House.

Schumann, J., and N. Stenson, eds. 1974. *New Frontiers in Second Language Learning.* Rowley, Mass.: Newbury House.

Sharwood Smith, M. 1976. Pedagogical grammars and the semantics of time reference in English. Linguistic Agency, University of Trier. Series B, paper 17.

Sharwood Smith, M. 1978. On the future of pedagogical grammar. Paper presented at AILA Congress, Montreal, August.

Smith, D. 1972. Some implications for the social status of pidgin languages. In D. Smith and R. Shuy (eds.), *Sociolinguistics and Cross-Cultural Analysis.* Washington, D.C.: Georgetown University Press.

Tarone, E., M. Swain, and A. Fathman. 1976. Some limitations to the classroom applications of current second language acquisition research. *TESOL Quarterly* **10**:19–32.

Thompson, S. 1978. Modern English from a typological point of view: some implications of the function of word order. *Linguistische Berichte* **54**:19–35.

Valdman, A. 1974. Error analysis and pedagogical ordering. Linguistic Agency, University of Trier. Series B, paper 11.

Van Ek, J. 1975. *The Theshold Level.* Strasbourg: Council of Europe.

Widdowson, H. 1978. Notional syllabuses, part 4. In C. Blatchford and J. Schachter (eds.), *On TESOL '78.* Washington, D.C.: TESOL.

Widdowson, H. 1979. *Explorations in Applied Linguistics.* Oxford: Oxford University Press.

Wilkins, D. 1976. *Notional Syllabuses.* London: Oxford University Press.

Activities for part Two

1. The rubric for this section asks what pedagogical grammar is. Having now read the four papers included here, what kind of answer would you provide to this question?
2. Collect one or more fragments of pedagogical grammar and submit them to a critical analysis in terms of each of the papers in part two:
   a. Try to guess what particular principles lie behind the pedagogical processing (the selection and presentation) of the grammatical information in the fragments you have chosen.
   b. Take the five questions on time at the end of the Sharwood Smith paper and try to answer them with reference to a particular pair of languages of your choice.
3. Take two claims made in part two and make proposals for testing them out in a context with which you are familiar.

three

THE REALIZATION OF PEDAGOGICAL GRAMMAR

In an ideal world, the theory and the design principles relating to pedagogical grammar would be settled first and then materials would be written accordingly. In the real world, however, the practical cart usually comes before the theoretical horse. Learners cannot be expected to wait until teachers and textbook writers have a clear idea of what is required and of how to structure their approach to the teaching of grammar. In the ordering of the theory/practice relationship, then, reality usually supersedes "ideality."

In this book, however, we have opted for the ideal-world order; that is, the realizations follow the theory. This section presents then some more concrete examples of how grammar may be presented in a manner that has some foundation in research—that is, presentation proposals based on something other than teaching experience and intuition alone. Mackenzie discusses and demonstrates the applicability of an approach that incorporates notions of case grammar as reflected in the work of Fillmore and Anderson. Since the time of writing, case theory has assumed an important role in Chomskyan generative grammar, though this does not really alter the most essential points that Mackenzie makes. His contribution, like the others in this section, provides a useful basis for investigating techniques of facilitation in pedagogical grammar.

Sharwood Smith's first paper in this section illustrates how the presentation of information about the target language can follow from proposals put forth by scholars in the field of instructional psychology. This idea implies that the term *applied linguistics* is in some sense a misnomer and that, as most scholars would now agree, *applied psychology* would be equally appropriate—in this case, applied *cognitive* psychology. Sharwood Smith provides a number of examples of how instructional psychologists might want to facilitate the acquisition of certain areas of target language semantics.

In another study of Sharwood Smith's, this time based on an analysis of errors made by Polish learners of English, the focus is on semantic distinctions associated with aspect and tense viewed from the point of view of how these distinctions are reflected in discourse. An exercise is suggested that requires the learner to create discourse with the help of mnemonic devices that signal the relevant discourse functions.

Finally, the Rutherford paper provides a series of concrete examples to illustrate his concern, voiced in part three, that the pedagogical domain *grammar* should include *deep* grammar. He argues that learners can be given information, one way or another, about how the target language is structured with regard to its gross canonical form and the effect that such form has on the proper organization of grammar at the level of discourse.

It is obviously fitting that this final section of the book should include some practical examples of how pedagogical grammar may actually be realized. And the realizations that have been proposed are fairly consistent with current research findings on the nature of language and of its acquisition. Nevertheless, it is important to stress that the procedures described here still need to be subjected to rigorous empirical investigation—something that has almost always been absent where serious pronouncements about formal instruction are concerned. It is only in this way, we believe, that significant progress is ultimately to be made in getting the practical cart back behind the theoretical horse, where it belongs.

12
Pedagogically Relevant
Aspects of
Case Grammar

J. Lachlan Mackenzie
Free University of Amsterdam

INTRODUCTION

Case grammar emerged in the late sixties as an alternative to standard transformational-generative grammar, and has since established itself as one of the
most revealing theories of language currently available. There is as yet no
unified theory of case grammar: readers of Fillmore (1966, 1968, 1971, 1977),
Cook (1973), and Anderson (1971, 1977), for example, will observe that many
fundamental questions remain unanswered and that the theory is continually
being adapted to tackle new problems and state new generalizations. I shall,
however, attempt to give a broad definition of case grammar, one which will
both be relevant for a wide range of language-types and also do justice to the
various (partial) models that have been proposed. Thus, let us call a case
grammar any theory of language whereby noun phrases are classified according to the following three criteria:

1. which (if any) case-marking prefixes, suffixes, and infixes (henceforth
   "(case-)affixes") and/or prepositions, postpositions, and "ambiposi-
   tions" (henceforth "adpositions") are associated with the head noun of
   each noun phrase (NP);
2. the function of each NP in the (surface-)syntactic structure of the
   clause: subject, object (in some languages, subdivisible into direct,

"Pedagogically Relevant Aspects of Case Grammar" by J. Lachlan Mackenzie, in *New Linguistic
Impulses in Foreign Language Teaching*, edited by A. James and P. Westney, 1981. Tübingen:
Günter Narr. © 1981 by Günter Narr Verlag, Tübingen. Reprinted by permission.

indirect, prepositional, etc.); complement (also potentially subdivisible); "functionless NPs" (e.g., NPs in circumstantial adverbials);
3. the type of meaning relationship holding between each NP and the main verb of the clause in which the NP occurs in underlying structure.

The levels at which each of these criteria are relevant I shall refer to as the morphological, syntactic, and semantic levels respectively.

It is uncontroversial that the number of possibilities at the morphological and syntactic levels, although differing considerably from language to language, is in each language limited; case grammar makes the added claim that the set of semantic relationships (so-called case relations, CRs) that may be contracted by a main verb and its associated NPs is also limited, although, as will be discussed below, the precise number of CRs that must be posited continues to be the object of dispute. Case grammar further claims that the set of CRs, in the "best theory," is the same for all languages: CRs are "universals."

It can easily be demonstrated that the three levels are, to a large extent, autonomous. Zimmermann (1972, p. 167) exaggerates somewhat, however, in claiming *daß es keine festen Beziehungen zwischen den drei Ebenen gibt* since, in many languages (e.g., Latin), nominative affixes are found exclusively on NPs, fulfilling the syntactic functions of subject and subject-complement, and adpositions are associated only with NPs, not fulfilling these (and other) functions; and, in other languages (e.g., Japanese), all NPs co-occur with a postposition, but subject and object are characterized by postpositions that are formally different from those marking other functions. The extent to which there are correspondences between the occurrence of particular case-affixes and adpositions and the CR contracted by the NP to which these are attached is a matter of some disagreement among "case-grammarians"; recent research, as will be discussed below, suggests that the relationship between the morphological and semantic levels is not entirely arbitrary: preference is given to those accounts which analyze particular morphemes as "naturally" realizing certain case relations.

Case grammar has, in my view, a dual contribution to make to language pedagogy. First, it offers a descriptive framework which is particularly suitable for research in contrastive analysis, that branch of linguistics which seeks to identify similarities and differences between languages.[1] The findings of contrastive analysis may be used to determine which aspects of one language will be found most unfamiliar and, therefore, it is assumed, most difficult to acquire by the speaker of another language. This information is regarded by many as a vital prerequisite for the improvement of language teaching, as regards both course materials and the general background of the individual teacher. The particular advantage of the incorporation of case grammar into contrastive analysis is that the semantic level may be used as a *tertium comparationis*. Rather than directly comparing the syntactic and morphological aspects of translationally equivalent sentences, the linguist, through reference to the shared, explicitly representable semantic level, can now pinpoint how the different languages grammaticalize the same configuration of semantic structure.[2] This makes it possible to predict recurring correspondences between entire sets of translationally equivalent sentences: should these predictions be confirmed, then a regularity has been established that can be duly incorporated into language teaching; should they be disconfirmed, further work will be needed to discover more abstruse regularities. Even if, ultimately, no satisfying regularities can be found, this conclusion can also be exploited in practical teaching in the form of a warning against the uninhibited formation of analogies.

A perhaps even more important contribution of case grammar is that it offers the language teacher a set of labels and, indeed, a general descriptive framework which have indubitable intuitive appeal.[3] A standard inventory of CRs, such as that offered by Fillmore (1971), is in my experience easily assimilated and applied by tertiary-level students of English; this tends not to be the case for the major syntactic functions, which are found much more difficult to identify. Appeal may be made to case grammar, or to a framework derived from theoretical writings on case grammar, not only in the presentation of grammar but also in the study of lexis; it is to this latter aspect that I shall devote the bulk of this paper.

The direct applicability of transformational-generative grammar (TGG) (in the sense of the "Standard Theory") to language teaching has often, and justly, been questioned (cf. Arndt, 1972). Many of the topical unresolved issues of TGG (complementation, pronominalization, NP movement) relate to questions that are of marginal concern to noninitiate students of language, even at the highest levels of learning: they tend to be self-evidently problematic only to native speakers who have a good grasp of the theory within which they have problematic status. Case grammar, on the other hand, is centrally preoccupied with what are unquestionably two of the core problems of language learning: (1) the "valency" of the verb in the clause and (2) the occurrence of case-affixes and adpositions.

THREE TYPES OF VALENCY

The valency of a verb is frequently defined as the number of NPs with which it co-occurs in a well-formed clause. Thus intransitive verbs such as EMERGE have a valency of 1, monotransitive verbs such as DIGEST have a valency of 2, and ditransitive verbs such as OFFER and complex-transitive verbs such as APPOINT have a valency of 3. Following Lyons, I shall extend the notion of valency

> [T]o account for differences in the membership of the sets of expressions that may be combined with different verbs. For example, "give" and "put," in their most common uses, both have a valency of 3, but they differ with respect to one of the three expressions which (in the extended sense of "government") they may be said to govern: "give" governs a subject, a direct object, and an indirect object; and "put" governs a subject, a direct object, and a directional locative. [1977, p. 486]

A full specification of valency will therefore indicate not only the number of NPs but also details of their function. To the type of valency referred to by Lyons I shall give the more specific name of "syntactic valency." I shall, however, also have occasion to invoke the notions of "situational valency" and "semantic valency." By situational valency, I mean the number and type of participants in a recognizable "situation" (a term that covers states, events, processes, and actions—cf. Lyons, 1977, p. 483).[4] For example, in the "bartering situation,"[5] there is a minimum of five participants: the buyer, the seller, the beneficiary, the goods, and the money; further participants are not ruled out (e.g., middlemen, brokers, etc.). Note that one individual may embody more than one participant: the buyer may (or may not) coincide with the beneficiary; similarly, when you sell yourself, you are both seller and goods. By semantic valency, on the other hand, I mean the maximum number and type of NPs required by a specific verb, the type being specified in terms of CRs. What counts as "required" is of course established on the basis of syntactic criteria which will differ from language to language. In English, an NP will be said to be required by a verb if it may occur in "close cohesion" with that verb—that is, as subject, object (direct, indirect, or prepositional), or prepositional complement. Thus BUY requires an Agent (which may function as subject, cf. (1)), a Patient (which may function as direct object, cf. (1)), a Beneficiary (which may function as indirect object, cf. (1)), a Source (which may function as prepositional object, cf. (1)), and an Instrument (which may function as subject, cf. (2)):

(1) I bought her a bunch of roses from the old flower seller.
(2) Twenty dollars will buy you a good meal for two.

With many verbs, the number of NPs required will correspond exactly with the minimum number of "situational participants." BUY is such a verb: as we have seen, it has a semantic valency of 5, and bartering situations, as mentioned, are characterized by at least five participants. With other verbs, however, the number of required NPs is fewer than that of partipants in the situation denoted. An example is RETORT, which has a semantic valency of 2, namely Agent and Patient, although the "retorting situation" involves a minimum of three participants (the "retorter," the addressee, and the retort); cf. (3) and (4):

(3) 'I did nothing of the kind!' he retorted.
(4) *'I did nothing of the kind!' he retorted to me/my accusation.

Whereas participants in situations are potentially unlimited in number and their appellation is largely arbitrary, case grammar makes the specific claim that the denotation of situations in language involves the classification of situational participants under a limited number of headings according to the role they play in the situation. Thus the seller in a bartering situation and the giver in a giving situation, although distinct at the situational level, are identical at the semantic level (at least as regards case relations): both may be identified as Agent.[6] It may also occur that one and the same situation will be differently classified at the semantic level: for intance, the bartering situation may be denoted by such "buying verbs" as BUY and PURCHASE (Valency: Agent, Patient, Source, Instrument, and Beneficiary), by such "selling verbs" as SELL and FLOG (Valency: Agent, Patient, Goal, and Instrument), by such "charging verbs" as CHARGE and ASK (Valency: Agent, Patient, Source, and Purpose), or by such "paying verbs" as PAY and SPEND (Valency: Agent, Patient, Goal, and Purpose). With "buying" and "selling" verbs, the money is Instrument and the goods Patient; with "charging" and "paying" verbs, the money is Patient and the goods Purpose; with "buying" and "paying" verbs, the buyer is Agent; with "selling" and "charging" verbs, the seller is Agent. Thus the ability to use verbs correctly, in the sense of integrating them properly into sentence structure, involves an understanding on the learner's part of how situational valency interacts with semantic valency.

To a large extent, the learner of a foreign language will, by virtue of his experience of the world, already know the valency of each situation he wishes to evoke. His teacher, however, should not ignore those cultural differences which cause speakers of the target language to structure their experiences into situations in a way unfamiliar to the learner. It frequently occurs that situations which are comparable to situations in the learner's own culture, particularly when of a ritual nature, will differ as to the number of participants involved. Such cultural differences are interesting in their own right; they deserve the linguist's attention when differences in situational valency are carried over to semantic and/or syntactic valency. Where both mother tongue and target language are classifiable as "Standard Average European" (in the sense of Whorf, 1956), linguistically relevant differences in situational valency are liable to be relatively few. One example worth consideration, perhaps, is the situation of "confession," which typically has a valency of 3: the person confessing, the person to whom the confession is addressed, and the "sins" being confessed to. Learners of a language used by Roman Catholics, if they do not recognize formal confession to a priest as a separate situation, must of course familiarize themselves with the details of this situation, and also with its linguistic reflexes. Learners of English, for instance, must realize that, of the verbs that may be used to denote the situation of confession (CONFESS, OWN, ADMIT, ACKNOWLEDGE, RECOGNIZE, etc.), only CONFESS is appropriate to denote the more particular situation of religious confession; that CONFESS, whether in the general or the particular sense, has a semantic valency of either 3 (Agent, Patient, Goal), corresponding directly with the minimum situational valency (cf. (5) below), or of 2 (Agent, Patient) (cf. (6) and (7) below); and that, as regards syntactic valency, either Patient or Goal, or both, are omissible (cf. (8) to (10) below), Indirect Object Formation is illicit (cf. (11) below), and finally, only in the religious use of CONFESS, the Goal may function as subject, and the Agent as object, with obligatory deletion of the object (cf. (12) and (13)):

(5) The sinner confessed his misdeeds to the priest.
(6) The sinner confessed to his misdeeds.
(7) *The sinner confessed to his misdeeds to the priest.
(8) The sinner confessed his misdeeds.
(9) The sinner confessed to the priest.
(10) The sinner confessed.
(11) *The sinner confessed the priest his misdeeds.
(12) The priest confessed the sinner.
(13) *The priest confessed the sinner to his misdeeds.

CONFESS is an example of the many verbs that have variable semantic valency. Consider, as a further example, the pair ASK and INQUIRE, which in almost all environments have a semantic valency of 3 (Agent, Patient, Source). However, where inquiries are being made as to the general welfare of the entity denoted by the Patient, it is marked by *after*, and both ASK and INQUIRE are necessarily bivalent (Agent, Patient):

(14) He asked me about my mother.
(15) He inquired of me about my mother.
(16) He asked after my mother.
(17) He inquired after my mother.
(18) He asked me after my mother (not well formed in the desired interpretation).
(19) *He inquired of me after my mother.

Students can be encouraged to make "discoveries" about the relationship between situational and semantic valency in tutorial: given the lack of information about these matters in existing textbooks, this type of exercise must take place under the direct guidance of the tutor. The fact that they are in effect conducting "original research" will be welcomed by students disillusioned with the passive role they typically find themselves playing in language learning. Interest is focused on a particular situation (which may arise naturally from other work, should a "situational approach" be being followed) and, with critical reference to thesauri and "dictionaries of synonyms," an attempt made to produce a list of the verbs, either one-word or phrasal, that are available to denote the situation chosen. The purpose is to determine the situational valency and to compare it with the semantic valency of each of the verbs under examination. In this way, students may learn how lexical choices of verb affect the way in which a situation can be described. Without this information, the students will remain unsure about using the synonyms they find in dictionaries. Consider, for example, the situation of the "transfer of goods without payment." This may be termed either the *giving* situation or the *receiving* situation: the choice of name implies a particular perspective, a fact which in itself can be exploited for expository purposes. In either case, however, the situational valency is minimally 3: the goods, the source, and the goal. Among the verbs of receiving are RECEIVE, GET, ACQUIRE, COME INTO THE

POSSESSION OF, COME BY. Experiment with the construction of sentences will show that the first three have a semantic valency of 3 (Goal, Patient, Source):

(20) The child received/got/acquired a teddy-bear from his grand mother.

whereas COME INTO THE POSSESSION OF and COME BY have a valency of 2 (Agent, Patient):

(21) The criminal came by/into the possession of a diamond tiara.

Further experiment will show that an interpretation of the subject of ACQUIRE as an Agent will tend to reduce its valency to 2. Indeed, it may be hypothesized that, in general, the more agentivity is associated with the Goal of a verb of receiving, the more difficult it becomes to include Source among the required CRs. This hypothesis can be further tested and, I would suggest, confirmed, by constructing parallel sentences with OBTAIN, SECURE, GET HOLD OF, and so on. It should be stressed that this type of exercise can be accomplished quite satisfactorily without the use of much case-grammar jargon: such terms as *situation*, *role*, *agent*, *patient*, *source*, *goal*, and so on are quickly grasped by students, and are confidently used within a remarkably short time.

The ability to use a verb correctly involves not only an understanding of the relationship between situational and semantic valency but also knowledge about the interaction of semantic and syntactic valency. It frequently occurs that verbs closely related in meaning[7] and identical in semantic valency differ unpredictably with respect to syntactic valency. Consider, for example, BUY and PURCHASE. Whereas the former permits the Beneficiary NP as indirect object, the latter does not:

(22)   I bought a bunch of roses for Mary.
(23)   I bought Mary a bunch of roses.
(24)   I purchased a bunch of roses for Mary.
(25)   *I purchased Mary a bunch of roses.

Similarly, ASK and INQUIRE, although near-synonyms and identical in semantic valency (3: Agent, Patient, Source), differ in that the former may take an indirect object, but the latter may not:

(26)   I asked the way of the passer-by.
(27)   I asked the passer-by the way.
(28)   I inquired the way of the passer-by.
(29)   *I inquired the passer-by the way.

Likewise, GIVE and DONATE[8]:

(30) He gave all his money to the Salvation Army.
(31) He gave the Salvation Army all his money.
(32) He donated all his money to the Salvation Army.
(33) *He donated the Salvation Army all his money.

To consider another problem of syntactic valency, note that GET (in the desired sense) and RECEIVE have the same semantic valency, but differ in that passive sentences with the latter tend to sound much more natural:

(34) They got a lot of contributions.
(35) ?A lot of contributions were got.
(36) They received a lot of contributions.
(37) A lot of contributions were received.

ASK and BEG, with the same semantic valency, similarly differ in the relative acceptability of the passive voice:

(38) They asked me to make a speech.
(39) I was asked to make a speech.
(40) They begged me to make a speech.
(41) ?I was begged to make a speech.

Furthermore, verbs with the same semantic valency may also differ with respect to the possibility of omitting (deleting) participants. Consider, for instance, CONFESS and OWN:

(42) He confessed to his sins.
(43) He confessed.
(44) He owned to his sins.
(45) *He owned.

or ADMIT and ACKNOWLEDGE (in the sense of "confess"):

(46) He admitted his sins to me.
(47) He admitted his sins.
(48) He admitted.
(49) He acknowledged his sins to me.
(50) He acknowledged his sins.
(51) *He acknowledged.

Finally, consider an example where the application of a rule (Indirect Object Formation) is obligatory. The verbs DENY, REFUSE, and BEGRUDGE are all semantically related ("be unwilling to give") and all share the semantic valency of 3 (Agent, Patient, Goal), yet each differs from the others with respect to syntactic valency:

(52)   He denied the most fundamental rights to his children.
(53)   ??He refused the most fundamental rights to his children.
(54)   *He begrudged the most fundamental rights to his children.
(55)   He denied his children the most fundamental rights.
(56)   He refused his children the most fundamental rights.
(57)   He begrudged his children the most fundamental rights.

The facts that emerge from (52) to (57)—namely, that DENY has two syntactic valencies, BEGRUDGE one, and REFUSE two only under restricted circumstances—should not, in my view, be presented as separate pieces of information about these verbs, as idiosyncratic or inexplicable; rather they should be grouped in presentation, as should each of the pairs of verbs discussed previously, and the syntactic potential of each explicitly gone into, again in the type of tutorial experiment alluded to previously. There will of course never be time to discuss each verb in the lexis as extensively as is ideally desirable. Discussion of a selected few will, however, stimulate the student to be dissatisfied with the mere acquisition of synonyms and to seek information about how the choice of any one of the synonyms determines the range of syntactic structures to which he is thereby restricted.

It was mentioned earlier that one by-product of a case-grammar approach is that certain similarities between situations—for example, the giving and the selling situations—may be made explicit. This is particularly true of the "localist" variant of case grammar, especially associated with the works of Anderson (1971, 1977).[9] Adherents of localism, "the hypothesis that spatial expressions are more basic, semantically and grammatically, than various kinds of nonspatial expressions" (Lyons, 1977, p. 718), claim that no more CRs need to be recognized than are required for the generation of sentences denoting location (and movement) in space. Anderson (1977, p. 119), for example, maintains that only three CRs need to be distinguished (Absolutive, Locative, and Ablative), whereas other scholars, working outwith a localist framework, have proposed larger, and in some instances much larger, inventories.[10] Localist case grammar thus throws light on the parallelisms in expression between sentences denoting nonspatial situations and sentences denoting spatial situations, and thereby on parallelisms between the situations themselves. Anderson (1971, p. 100), for instance, considers the simlarity, initially none too obvious, between "containing" and "knowing," pointing to the shared syntactic characteristics of CONTAIN and KNOW. It emerges from Anderson's analysis that homo loquens regards cognition merely as a special kind of containing, in one's head, of ideas, beliefs, and so on. The advantage of this insight is that a larger number of idiomatic expressions concerned with the possession and acquisition of knowledge become susceptible of systematic analysis:

(58) I'll keep you in mind.
(59) Who put that into his head?
(60) Did that idea come out of his head?
(61) Keep that under your hat!

If (58) is glossed as, say, "I'll cause my head to contain the idea of you," (59) as "Who caused that idea to be contained in his head?," and (61) as "Continue to contain that idea in your head"—(60) is sufficiently explicit to require no gloss—then the semantic interaction of these, and many further idioms, may be explained naturally.

In more general terms, localism has a vital contribution to make to the study of idiomatics in being able to offer a principled account of what Meier (1975, p. 163), in recognition of the contribution of Smith (1925) to our understanding of idiomatics, has dubbed "Smith's Law," which states that the two typical nuclei of (English) idioms are a "purely kinaesthetic verb" (COME, GET, GIVE, GO, LAY, LOOK, PUT, RUN, STAND, TAKE, TURN, etc.) and "somatic imagery" (ARM, BONE, EAR, EYE, FOOT, HAND, HEAD, LIP, MOUTH, NOSE, TONGUE, TOOTH, etc.). To the localist, the difference between REMEMBER and KEEP IN MIND is that the (let us suppose) shared underlying representation, expressed entirely in terms of spatial notions, is obscured by lexicalization in REMEMBER, but remains relatively transparent in KEEP IN MIND. The "purely kinaesthetic verbs" are indeed all[11] verbs of location and direction, and the body parts (the somatic imagery) are all concrete entities with specific locational properties (cf. Friedrich, 1970; Lehrer, 1974, pp. 116–119). Thus, idioms such as KEEP IN MIND have a form which is relatively directly translatable into localist underlying representations. Note, interestingly, that the adoption of a framework based on localist case grammar will result in a rather different viewpoint on idiomatics than is perhaps usual: a large class of idioms, particularly those obeying Smith's Law, will be regarded not as exceptional, problematic, epiphenomenal, but rather as "more basic" than their one-word, "abstract" counterparts, in that they reflect more directly the semantic representation with which they are associated. There are clear pedagogical implications: if localist representations of meaning have claims to "universality," if human language is indeed constructed on principles that hold first and foremost for the generation of sentences denoting relations of location and direction, then it may well be that those items in the vocabulary of nonspatial situations which manifest forms more typically associated with the denotation of spatial situations are acquired and manipulated more readily by learners than forms which have no spatial function. Should such a hypothesis be borne out by experimental investigation, the repercussions on the study of lexis and (more particularly) the status of idiomatics as a component element of lexis would be considerable.

ADPOSITIONS

The localist version of case grammar has had the added merit of paving the way towards a more revealing account of adpositional meaning than has hitherto been available. This is again of particular interest to the language teacher if for no other reason than that the meaning and "usage" of the adposition has long been recognized as one of the most formidable stumbling blocks for the learner of a foreign language. The difficulties he encounters may,

in my view, be ascribed to three factors. The first is his lack of familiarity with
the idiosyncratic way in which the language he is seeking to acquire analyzes
external reality and, in particular, recognizes spatial relations between objects
and temporal relations between situations. The structural principles underlying
the adpositional system of the foreign language often cannot be readily corre-
lated with those of his own tongue. The second is the purely mnemonic
difficulty involved in recalling which adposition is required by each member of
the extensive sets of verbs, adjectives, and nouns in the target language that
may be linked to a dependent NP by one specific adposition only, where the
"right choice," which can usually be motivated diachronically, must often
appear quite arbitrary to the learner of the contemporary language: compare,
in German, the use of *um* in *Er lief um sein Leben* as against *Er kam ums
Leben.* The third is the multiple meaning, or polysemy, of most adpositions—
that is, the fact that several different meanings, some intuitively relatable to
one another, others without any apparent connection, may be expressed by
one and the same preposition. I believe that the insights which case grammar
has to offer are of benefit to the teacher anxious to pilot his pupils through the
reefs of adpositional usage.

Case grammar analyzes adpositions as "case-markers"—that is, as indicating, more or less directly, the CR holding between the head noun of the
adpositional phrase and the main verb. The general thrust of case grammar,
particularly those versions which posit a highly restricted inventory of CRs, is to
seek maximal generalization by assuming minimal adpositional polysemy. Bennett (1975), many of whose proposals are not incompatible with certain versions
of case grammar, has argued persuasively that the identification of a limited
number of "sememes" (locative, goal, interior, surface, etc.) is sufficient to
clarify most of the major facts about adpositional meaning, facts which tend not
to emerge clearly from those descriptions of adpositional usage which ascribe
myriads of subtly differentiated interpretations to each adposition (cf. especially
Lindkvist, 1950, 1976). It indeed emerges from Bennett's discussion that the
great majority of English prepositions may be given a unitary componential
analysis, and that the very few which may not can be accounted for in terms of a
highly restricted set of analyses. Similarly, it is one ambition of localist case
grammar to provide representations which are "lexically natural," that is:

> *ceteris paribus*, accounts which assign a unitary source to a particular lexical
> form will be preferred to those which require homonymy. [Anderson, 1977, p. 64]

Anderson seeks, for example, to link the agentive, instrumental and
comitative senses of *with* (1977, pp. 122–124); Ikegami (1976, p. 34) attempts
to link the goal and purpose senses of *for*; Prinz (1977) shows how the various
meanings of the Slavic preposition *za* may be linked. The ultimate aim of such
scholars is the achievement of a grammar which will assign as few semantic
representations to each adposition as is compatible with the facts. I believe that
it is on the basis of such efforts that the adpositional systems of different
languages will be best contrasted and made accessible to learners.

One problem to which case grammar may offer an initial answer is that of the marking of agency and instrumentality. Brown (1971) has considered the rivalry of *de, par*, and *avec* in French as markers of these CRs, and concludes that the regularities underlying the use of these prepositions are best stated in terms of case grammar. Whereas the Agent is necessarily marked by *par*, Instrument may select any of the three: *de* occurs before abstract, but *par* or *avec* before concrete nouns, with the difference that the latter implies the existence of an unspecified Agent—note that this last contrast is particularly naturally expressible in case-grammar terms. A further complication observed by Brown, and which also lends itself to a case-grammar analysis, is that Instrument may be marked by *de* even if the noun denotes a concrete entity, provided that the verb denotes a change of state and includes a Dative in its valency:

(62) *Il a brisé la fenêtre d'une branche.
(63) Paul a blessé Jean d'une flèche.

Mackenzie (1977) considers the semantically equivalent prepositions in German, *von, durch*, and *mit*, and claims that, whereas *von* and *mit*, in their relevant uses, clearly mark agentivity and instrumentality respectively, *durch* combines both the "originativity" of *von* and the "mediativity" of *mit*. In such a sentence as (64):

(64) Durch ihren Freund lernt Karola außer Mao und Marcuse auch die Liebe und etwas Mäßigung kennen.

the *durch*-phrase is characterized both as an originator of action and also as a mediator. It is claimed that this is the fundamental abstract use of *durch*, one which may be linked naturally to its spatial use, and that the preposition spreads out from this core meaning to become, in many instances, an alternative to either *mit* or *von*. It is clear that the type of information offered by such studies may be usefully incorporated into more large-scale projects in contrastive analysis, or indeed be directly exploited by the language teacher.

What Heringer (1970) has dubbed "translative" adopositions present particularly hard problems to the learner. These are the typically meaningless[12] "function words" which link verbs, adjectives and nouns to dependent noun phrases. The difficulties experienced by the learner are twofold. First, there is often no apparent connection between the environment of a translative preposition and the environments in whch the same preposition is used with spatial meaning: consider that *different* may, in the speech of many people, be linked to a dependent NP either by *from* or *to* (or indeed *than*), despite the fact that *from* and *to* are diametrically opposed in their spatial meanings. Second, the standard, translational relationships between adopositions of different languages are hopelessly and, it appears, haphazardly violated in the case of translative adopositions: consider Dutch *gevoelig voor* 'sensitive for,' but English *sensitive to*, Dutch *reactie op* 'reaction on,' but English *reaction to*, or, more confusingly, Dutch *discrimineren* φ (i.e., with direct object), but English *discriminate against*. The grammarian anxious to systematize the chaos of translative adpositional usage will be disappointed in TGG which takes such items to be inserted automatically: Jacobs and Rosenbaum (1968), for instance, in their textbook presentation, have translative *of* developed from a feature on *approve*, but no explanation is offered why it should indeed be *of* and not some other preposition. Traditional grammar seeks, at best, a historically oriented explanation for the occurrence of particular prepositions as "fossils" of previously productive usage. The case grammar of Fillmore (1968) similarly treats such adpositions as "idiosyncratic," "marked": according to his proposals, the unmarked marker of Dative is, in English, *to*, but, for example, where the main verb is *blame*, *to* will be replaced by *on*. A case grammar which strives to achieve "lexical naturalness" cannot, however, be fully satisfied with such an account. It may remain ultimately impossible to capture all the quirks of translative adpositions, but an extended case grammar of the type adumbrated above, one which considers aspects of the situations denoted as relevant to an understanding of linguistic phenomena, can, I believe, make some contribution to providing explanations for the occurrence of at least some translative adpositions that will be of benefit to both student and teacher. Consider, for example, the verbs PUT UP, FALL IN, AGREE, FIGHT, all of which take prepositional objects introduced by *with*; by drawing attention to the situations denoted by these verbs, the teacher will be able to point to a general notion of concomitance which is common to all the situations and which motivates the occurrence of *with*; from this, he can proceed to a discussion of such points as the ambiguity of *fight with*, 'fight against,' and 'fight alongside.'[13] Or consider COMPLAIN, DIE, BE GLAD, BE JEALOUS, BE TIRED, all of which take prepositional objects introduced by *of*; here there is a general notion of causation which can, if so desired, be linked with the historically ablative sense of *of*. Vague and ungeneralizable as such an approach may seem, it is at least a first attempt to remove the problem of translative adpositions from the realm of the totally idiosyncratic.

CONCLUSIONS

The purpose of this paper has been to show that various recent developments in the theory of case grammar are potentially of great interest to the practicing teacher and to those who provide the theoretical background to his work. This is, I have suggested, because two of the most intractable problems in language learning, verb valency and adpositional usage, are also of prime concern to the case grammarian; moreover, what the case grammarian has to say about these matters can, as it happens, contribute to lightening the burden of the language learner. It is, however, worth emphasizing that case grammar, just as every other theory of language currently enjoying the attention of linguists, has not been developed with a view to facilitating language acquisition. Although the goals and motivations of theoretical linguistic work are established independently of the interests of those who seek to benefit from the output of that work, the language teacher can still derive enormous profit from familiarizing himself with theoretical writings. The teacher who dips into studies on case grammar will find there much that will stimulate him: some aspects he will feel able to translate directly into practice; others will need major adaptation before they can be put to service; others will be assimilated into his store of knowledge about language to be integrated more subtly, perhaps barely consciously, into his exposition. What I hope to have shown here is that case grammar is a theory of language which is particularly worthy of his attention.   *

NOTES

1. Compare especially Rohdenburg (1969) and Fink (1977).
2. This approach presupposes, of course, that semantic structure is indeed identical for all languages (as is assumed by, for instance, Nilsen, 1971, p. 298); the discussion following assumes only that the set of case relations, the formation rules for semantic structure, and the operations by which these are mapped into surface structures are universal.
3. Compare Roulet's comment (1976, p. 204): "Peu importe . . . que, du point de vue de la science linguistique, la grammaire de cas soit encore loin de répondre aux exigences d'explicitation et de falsification, si elle constitue un instrument heuristique utile pour le pédagogue."
4. Compare in this connection Fillmore's (1977) notion of a "scene": ". . . when I say that meanings are relativized to scenes, what I mean is that we choose and understand expressions by having or activating in our minds scenes or images or memories or describing or classifying functions" (p. 74). Exactly what constitutes a situation or scene will depend on the conceptual framework and the immediate communicative intentions of the speaker.
5. Fillmore (1977, p. 72) also discusses this situation, terming it a *commercial event*; he recognizes only four participants, the buyer, the seller, the money, and the goods. Consider also Lakoff's (1977, pp. 259–262) analysis of Fillmore's commercial event as coded into a "conceptual gestalt," which in turn is mapped into a "linguistic gestalt."
6. Here, as elsewhere in this paper, my assignment of particular CRs to NPs should not be regarded as my final word on the matters at hand. In this instance, the issue whether such an NP should be assigned two CRs, as is proposed by Anderson (1971, p. 130), will not be examined. My point is that both NPs must be assigned the *same* case node, whether it indicates one or more CRs.
7. Note that all distinctions between verbs not relating to "cognitive meaning" (e.g., register, frequency, currency, collocation, etc.) are disregarded here in the interests of simplicity.
8. The conditions governing Indirect Object Formation (particularly as regards benefactive indirect objects) have been meticulously examined by Allerton (1978). Storm's (1977) claim that Indirect Object Formation is possible provided (a) that the verb is not a manner-of-speaking verb (*mutter, screech*, etc.) and (b) that the verb stem is monomorphemic is unfortunately descriptively inadequate; *purchase* and *inquire* are surely monomorphemic, yet neither permits an indirect object; both *return* and *refuse* have the same morphemic structure, yet the first disallows Indirect Object Formation and the second all but requires it.

9. Compare also Ikegami (1976) and the "Theorie des sprachlichen Bildes" of Prinz (1977).
10. For a bibliography of proposals and counterproposals, see Anderson (1977, p. 281, fn. 12).
11. For an analysis of the apparent exception LOOK on the basis of which it may be regarded as a verb of direction, see Gruber (1967).
12. It has been suggested by Engelen (1975, p. 112) that translative adpositions are not merely meaningless function words: ". . . in Fällen mit einem Unsinnswort wie *klumborgen* wie z.B. *Man hat mich darum klumborgt, ihm meinen Vortrag zu leihen. Wir haben sorgfältig über diesen Sachverhalt klumborgt. Das hat mich von der Teilnahme an dieser Sitzung klumborgt.* Wird man nicht umhin können, der Präposition—es muß hinzugefügt werden: im Rahmen der jeweiligen Konstruktion—einen semantischen Wert zuzugestehen, auch wenn dieser nicht leicht zu fassen ist und auch nicht unabhängig von der jeweiligen Umgebung ist."
13. Compare Vestergaard (1977, pp. 182–184).

QUESTIONS FOR DISCUSSION

1. Mackenzie makes a strong case for the relevance to pedagogical grammar (PG) of case grammar in the sense of Fillmore. Identified in particular as of great importance to learning are the case-grammar attributes of adposition and verb valency. Do these claims square with your experience as a language teacher? Are there aspects of PG that you consider to be of more importance? If so, can you justify them?

2. A distinction is drawn by Mackenzie among three kinds of "valency"—situational, semantic, and syntactic. One would be exemplified in terms of the number of NPs with which, say, the verb *confess* co-occurs and their structural relation (such as subject, object, etc.); another would be exemplified in terms of the relationships (such as agent, patient, instrument, etc.) that the NP bears to the verb; and the other would be exemplified in terms of the notion of "confessing" and who does what to whom and so on. Which is which, and why is it necessary to make any kind of distinction at all? Why not just a single concept of "valency"?

3. How might the notion of valency be turned into an example of the Apostel principle (cf. Sharwood Smith's paper in Part II) for language learning? Which of the three kinds of valency is most crucial to invocation of the Apostel principle?

4. Mackenzie reminds us that case grammar analyzes adpositions as case markers. What does he mean by this? What other syntactic category (the only other) also assigns case? Some languages (e.g., Turkish, Russian, Mohawk) do not have adpositions, or at least very few. Can you guess how these languages realize the marking of case? Since all languages seem to mark case in some fashion, case would appear to be extremely important. Why should this be? Is it possible that we could do without it? Why not?

5. Many people find Mackenzie's arguments for paying serious pedagogical attention to the notion of adposition very persuasive. From your experience would you say that adposition information has thus far been neglected in language pedagogy? How has adposition been handled in the various pedagogical materials with which you are familiar, and how different is this from Mackenzie's approach?

6. Learners of a foreign language typically make extensive use of bilingual dictionaries, usually small ones that they can carry around with them. While such dictionaries are certainly helpful in some respects, they can also pose problems for the learner. With reference to the kinds of language features discussed in the Mackenzie paper, what would you say are the shortcomings of small bilingual dictionaries? Are these problems absent in monolingual dictionaries? Are the problems addressed in some of the recent English dictionaries compiled specifically for learners of English, and if so, how?

REFERENCES

Allerton, D. 1978. Generating indirect objects in English. *Journal of Linguistics* **14**:21–34.

Anderson, J. 1971. *The Grammar of Case: Towards a Localistic Theory*. London: Cambridge University Press.

Anderson, J. 1977. *On Case Grammar: Prolegomena to a Theory of Grammatical Relations*. London: Croom Helm.

Arndt, H. 1972. Tendenzen der transformationallen Schulgrammatik in Deutschland. *Linguistik und Didaktik* **12**:247–265.

Bennett, D. 1975. *The Spatial and Temporal Uses of Prepositions in English*. London: Longman.

Brown, T. 1971. Pedagogical implications of a case grammar of French. *IRAL* **9**:229–244.

Cook, W. 1973. A set of postulates for case grammar analysis. *Working Papers in Languages and Linguistics* **4**:35–49.

Engelen, B. 1975. *Untersuchungen zu Satzbauplan und Wortfeld in der Geschriebenen Deutschen Sprache der Gegenwart*. Munich: Hueber.

Fillmore, C. 1966. A proposal concerning English prepositions. *Monograph Series on Language and Linguistics, Georgetown University* **19**:19–33.

Fillmore, C. 1968. The case for case. In E. Bach and R. Harms (eds.), *Universals in Linguistic Theory*. New York: Holt, Rinehart and Winston.

Fillmore, C. 1971. Some problems for case grammar. *Monograph Series on Language and Linguistics* **24**:35–56.

Fillmore, C. 1977. The case for case reopened. In P. Cole and J. Sadock (eds.), *Syntax and Semantics 8: Grammatical Relations*. New York: Academic Press.

Fink, S. 1977. *Aspects of a Pedagogical Grammar Based on Case Grammar and Valence Theory*. Tübingen: Niemeyer.

Friedrich, P. 1970. Shape in grammar. *Language* **46**:379–407.

Gruber, J. 1967. Look and see. *Language* **43**:937–947.

Heringer, H. 1970. *Theorie der Deutschen Syntax*. Munich: Heuber.

Ikegami, Y. 1976. Syntactic structure and the underlying semantic patterns: a "localistic hypothesis." *Linguistics* **170**:31–44.

Jacobs, R., and P. Rosenbaum. 1968. *English Transformational Grammar*. Waltham, Mass.: Ginn and Co.

Lakoff, G. 1977. Linguistic gestalts. *CLS* **13**:236–287.

Lehrer, A. 1974. *Semantic Fields and Lexical Structure*. Amsterdam: North-Holland.

Lindkvist, K. 1950. *Studies on the Local Sense of the Prepositions IN, AT, ON and TO in Modern English*. Lund and Copenhagen: Munksgaard.

Lindkvist, K. 1976. *A Comprehensive Study of Conceptions of Locality in Which English Prepositions Occur*. Stockholm: Almqvist and Wiksell.

Lyons, J. 1977. *Semantics*. Cambridge: Cambridge University Press.

Mackenzie, J. 1977. The marking of agents and instruments in contemporary standard German. *Work in Progress* (University of Edinburgh) **10**:116–128.

Meier, H. 1975. The state of idiomatics. *Dutch Quarterly Review* **5**:163–179.

Nilsen, D. 1971. The use of case grammar in teaching English as a foreign language. *TESOL Quarterly* **5**:293–299.

Prinz, J. 1977. Die theorie des sprachlichen bildes und die syntax slavischer präpositionen. *Folia Linguistica* **10**:35–84.

Rohdenburg, G. 1969. Kasusgrammatik und kontrastive analyse. *PAKS-Arbeitsbericht* **2**:35–58. Uni Kiel.

Roulet, E. 1976. Théories grammaticales et pédagogie les langues. *Language Teaching and Linguistics: Abstracts* **9**:197–211.

Smith, L. 1925. English idioms. In *Words and Idioms*. London: Constable.

Storm, P. 1977. Predicting the applicability of dative movement. In S. Fox, W. Beach, and S. Philosoph (eds.), *CLS Book of Squibs*. Chicago: Chicago Linguistic Society.

Vestergaard, T. 1977. *Prepositional Phrases and Prepositional Verbs: A Study in Grammatical Function*. The Hague: Mouton.

Whorf, B. 1956. *Language, Thought and Reality: Selected Writings of Benjamin Lee Whorf*. New York: John Wiley & Sons.

Zimmerman, R. 1972. Die Kasusgrammatik in der angewandten und kontrastiven Linguistik. *IRAL* **10**:167–178.

13

Applied Linguistics
and the Psychology
of Instruction:
A Case for Transfusion?

Michael Sharwood Smith
Rijksuniversiteit, Utrecht

It has become increasingly evident in recent years that what is by convention termed *applied linguistics*, in that it has to do with foreign language learning and instruction, should be as much applied *psychology* as applied linguistics to say nothing of other possible types of applications. Still, it is by no means unfortunate that linguistics has established itself as the primary discipline since it is, after all, *language* that is being taught and learned. It is admittedly symptomatic of this, dare one say, historical bias in applied linguistics that a good theory of language applied with a minimal knowledge of psychological theory (plus, one hopes, a large amount of common sense) is probably more generally regarded as acceptable than a way of working based on a sound knowledge of psychology and only a brief acquaintance with linguistics. However, it would be extremely unwise to presume that, by applying just linguistics to problems of second language instruction or learning, one had all that one needed as far as sources (content and techniques) are concerned. This would be to ignore all past and present theorizing and experimentation within the field of instructional and learning psychology. The bias needs to be corrected.

The full acceptance by everyone of psychology as a source discipline alongside linguistics does not of course solve all our problems; in fact, it increases them. It means that applied linguists not only have to be linguists, they have to be good psychologists as well (a problem that will be mentioned

"Applied Linguistics and the Psychology of Instruction: A Case for Transfusion?" by M. Sharwood Smith, 1978, *Studies in Second Language Acquisition*, vol. 1, no. 2, pp. 91–115. Reprinted with permission of Indiana University Linguistics Club.

again in the conclusion). The dangers of misinterpretations and misapplications of theory are doubled. One may find, apparently, unfortunate examples of this in other fields already (see, e.g., the critique of the artificial intelligence theories of Winograd, Minsky, and Schank in Dresher and Hornstein, 1976). There is some reason to suppose that the same may happen when psychological insights and techniques are used in applied linguistics. However, to look on the bright side, there is testing of various ideas and techniques where conditions exist for deciding via experimentation about the relative *effectiveness* of one idea over another. S. Papert's assertion (at the Ghent conference *Communication and Cognition: The Cognitive Viewpoint*, March 1977) that what matters in science is not what is *true* but what *works* may be highly dubious as it stands but may, nevertheless, have a certain amount of validity for work carried out in this "preparadigmatic" (to use a Kuhnian term) stage of our field of inquiry. Starting from this point of view, this paper will proceed to investigate some aspects of psychology, particularly the psychology of instruction, and show how they have been, or may be applied within the field of applied linguistics together with insights from linguistics proper. Special reference will be paid to the problem of framing the facts of language for pedagogical presentation. Pedagogical description will be dealt with first in terms of *concentrated* and then *extended* descriptions (see also the discussion in Corder, 1974). First, a general viewpoint will be suggested and then, second, a number of ways of formulating and presenting language descriptions to learners will be discussed.

A GENERAL VIEWPOINT

With the growing rejection of a purely behaviorist ideology in foreign language methodology (and a recognition that it has seldom, if ever, been totally adopted in practice), more emphasis has been placed on *cognitive* orientation, which admits of and in fact focuses on internal processes in the human mind that are not directly accessible to empirical observation (e.g., Carroll, 1965; Chastain, 1971). Apart from the fact that the cognitive viewpoint seems to be implicit in most of contemporary linguistic theory, it also represents the orientation of a large number of prominent psychologists who have busied themselves with problems of human learning and instruction and who are by no means to be labelled as belonging to the same school (e.g., Bruner, Piaget, Vygotsky, Gal'perin, Landa, etc.). Of particular interest, in the context of this paper, are two basic principles that are broadly accepted by cognitivists of whatever persuasion. The first is that *new* knowledge is to a greater or lesser degree acquired via *old* knowledge. The second is that knowledge is not uniquely or even primarily *assertional* in nature, but often *procedural*—that is, knowing *how* as opposed to knowing *what*. To use a cybernetic analogy (one that needs careful handling, admittedly) much of what we know is in the form of programs, or plans (Miller, Galanter, and Pribam, 1960), designed to solve various types of problems. Grammatical knowledge or "competence" viewed in psychological terms may be a good example of this; we do not simply store *lists* of all possible words and combinations of units but rather programs for enabling us to solve the myriads of problems involved in encoding and decoding utterances in a given language. The first principle implies that all instruction should, in a systematic manner, build on what has been established one way or another as old information (i.e., already properly learned). The second principle implies that instruction should be especially concerned with teaching ways of solving problems rather than with a mere provision of "facts." If we look for reflections of this in everyday teaching, we may find the first principle underlying phrases that teachers use such as *laying the foundations* and *building up from* and the second principle in expressions such as *rules of thumb*. The job of the applied linguists is of course to apply or indicate how to apply such principles in a conscious and systematic manner. There is where insights and techniques have to be sought in the psychology of education.

With regard to the framing of information within a framework of previously acquired knowledge, David Ausubel (1968, e.g.) makes two important general distinctions. First, he distinguishes between *reception learning* and *discovery learning*. Reception learning involves having all the relevant information available in its final form; discovery learning, on the other hand, involves the learner's having to discover the principle content of what he is to learn before he can learn it.[1] The second distinction, which cuts across the first, is between *rote learning* and *meaningful learning*. Rote learning involves the internalization of concepts in a purely arbitrary, verbatim fashion. This may take place because the learning task is composed of purely arbitrary associations or because the learner chooses to internalize the material in this manner, or again because he is forced to do so because he lacks the prior knowledge necessary for making it "meaningful." One can easily see how vocabulary lists may be learned rotely. An example of rote *discovery* learning would be the rote memorization of mathematical formulae or sequences of operations for solving a problem without the awareness of the underlying concepts involved.

Meaningful learning is precisely the learning of material in a nonarbitrary, nonverbatim manner by relating it to knowledge already established in cognitive structure. There have been a fair number of experiments (see Ausubel, 1968, e.g.) to show that knowledge acquired meaningfully is definitely more stable— that is, is retained longer in cognitive structure—than knowledge acquired via rote learning. It is consequently the proper goal in language pedagogy to facilitate meaningful (whether it be reception or discovery) learning.[2]

If we further consider the problem of rote versus meaningful learning, we may observe that in language there seem to be a very large number of arbitrary associations, particularly as seen from the viewpoint of the linguistically naive language learner. If it is the primary aim of language pedagogy to promote meaningful learning, it is obviously the task of the applied linguist to render the facts of the language in such a way that it reduces as much as possible the apparent arbitrariness of so much of it. It is for this reason, for example, that he would be unwise to ignore linguistic insights based on deep-structures-based theory (orthodox Chomskyan or otherwise) since grammatical descriptions based on the deep-surface type of distinction contain a large number of far-reaching interrelations that help to decrease the arbitrary appearance of many of the associations. The point is, of course, not a matter of arbitrariness per se[3] but of the presence or absence of comprehensible systems that can make the smaller local associations in utterances seem part of a larger whole (or wholes). In short, the more system you can reveal to the learner the better. There is, however, more to be said on this. Systems in themselves, although they provide possibilities for meaningful learning, are more or less effective to the extent that they can be tied in with concepts that are already familiar to the learner— that is, well established in cognitive structure. This may shed some light on the current debate concerning notional versus structural grammar and notional versus structural syllabuses (Wilkins, 1972 etc.). There are clearly very good cognitivist reasons for supporting a notional dimension to language descriptions and syllabuses in that it provides us with a very large number of possibilities of relating the new facts of the target language to the world that is familiar to the learner via his native language and his everyday experience. In presenting rule-governed linguistic systems to the learner, we should exploit as much as possible the fact that they serve to express meanings that are relatable to the conceptual systems already anchored in the learner's cognitive structure. Moreover, the kinds of meanings we are talking about here are much more part of the learner's *conscious knowledge* than the kind of knowledge we now call grammatical competence (however it is stored). That is to say, for those who favor more or less *explicit* presentations of the patterns to be learned (Carpay, 1976), and there seems to be experimental evidence to support this general approach, it makes sense to link up units and patterns of a purely linguistic nature to aspects of experience that are readily appreciated by the average learner—that is, emotions, time relations, persuasion, and so on (to be linked up in a psychologically and sociologically sophisticated way, however, see Cook, 1977). This need not mean rejecting "the pedagogic benefits of using a language's formal regularities in the organisation of teaching" (Wilkins, 1972, p. 19). It means that there are strong psychological reasons besides that of motivation to go beyond these kinds of regularities of which the average learner is only dimly aware. Accordingly, the more system that linguists may discover in semantic and pragmatic aspects of language, the greater is the potential, in applied linguistics, of producing pedagogically effective descriptions (Sharwood Smith, 1974, 1976).

"PSYCHOLOGICALLY RESPECTABLE" CONCENTRATED DESCRIPTIONS

It would seem appropriate at this juncture to give two small examples of pedagogical descriptions, one lexical, the other (morpho)syntactic, that might be psychologically respectable—that is, accord with the general viewpoint expressed earlier. By "concentrated" description is meant the type of source description that teachers, textbook writers, and the more advanced student consults.

This is opposed here to "extended" descriptions, which are fragmentary and supposed to bring about complete (receptive or productive) mastery within a given language-teaching program. Concentrated descriptions, if they are to be granted the name "pedagogical," must also be formulated in such a way as to facilitate learning, though in a less *conclusive* manner: they must at least be framed with a view to serving as input to extended descriptions (Sharwood Smith, 1974, 1976). Both types of descriptions should provide the maximum amount of relevant information; extended descriptions, however, are programmed into a course with a practice component, and the selection and sequencing of information are geared to particular types of learners in particular types of learning situations.

The first example, chosen to illustrate (within the modest scope of this paper) the integration of linguistic analysis and psychological requirements, relates to the *decomposition* of lexical units. It is certainly true that even if two given languages seem to express the same conceptual reality (in Sapir-Whorfian terms), there will never be a total one-to-one correspondence between individual lexical items and their equivalents in the other language as regards the "subconcepts" that go to make up that larger reality. Different languages, and this is perhaps now a truism, cut up reality in different ways. The language learner has, as an important part of his learning task, to master the resulting conceptual distinctions that are unfamiliar to him. A linguistic analysis that decomposes the semantic content of separate lexical items into smaller conceptual units that underlie *both* (or all) languages clearly offers a psychological advantage that is not possessed by other types of analyses that do not view things in terms of *shared* concepts—namely, the advantage of proceeding from the familiar to the unfamiliar. The familiar in this case is the sum of subconcepts (semantic features, if you like); the unfamiliar is the way subconcepts are *combined* to form the semantic content of lexical items, or patterns of lexical items. If we take a very concrete example, Di Pietro's Koya example (Di Pietro, 1971, p. 111) of the word *mancu* (meaning *fog, dew,* and *ice*), we should quickly appreciate that, for the Koya speaker, *dew, fog,* and *ice* are all manifestations of *mancu*; for the English speaker *mancu* represents a superordinate concept that is not linguistically expressed in his language. If we now focus on the problems of the hypothetical Koya learner of English, to continue our simple example, it ought not to be any problem to demonstrate the meanings of *fog, dew,* and *ice* ($mancu_1$, $mancu_2$, and $mancu_3$ for him). Any competent teacher could do this. However, if he is to incorporate the necessary distinctions into his automatic control of the target language, English, it will surely be especially effective to provide him, in addition to a standard demonstration, with an explicit means of categorizing the three English words/concepts in conceptual terms familiar to him. The decomposition of lexical items (as demonstrated by Di Pietro using other examples) affords us this possibility; psychological principles provide us with certain criteria for choosing from among possible alternative analyses.[4] For example, *frozen* and *vapor* might be acceptable as crucial distinguishing features provided these could be expressed in a way commensurate with the everyday experience of the average Koya learner. Thus, from the following grid:

	FROZEN	VAPOR
DEW	−	−
FOG	−	+
ICE	+	−

we get "not frozen and not vapor" for *dew*, "not frozen but vapor" for *fog* and "frozen and not vapor" for *ice*. A technique analogous to the application of redundancy rules will be discussed in the next section. Suffice it to say here that such a description is obviously not exhaustive and would have to be supplemented if the items were not introduced *contrastively* (here, in terms of *mancu*). It may in fact be difficult for speakers of languages like English with the threefold distinction to fully appreciate that there *is* a learning problem in this type of situation. The difficulties may become clearer if we consider similar problems discussed in the literature but of a more *abstract* nature—for example, English *walk* and *go* versus Dutch *gaan* and German *gehen*, and so on (Dirven, 1976) and also groups like *persuade* and *convince, beyond* and *behind*, and *purpose*, which have only one Russian equivalent.[5] A relatively simple example of a morpho-syntactic problem encountered by Polish university students of English was discussed by the present writer (1976) together with a suggested pedagogical solution based on cognitive principles. It concerned the choice of the so-called progressive aspect (Adamczewski, 1974, and others), in this case in combination with past tense forms, to refer to actions in the past. Errors and spontaneous self-diagnosis seemed to indicate a mistaken equivalence posited as existing between the English progressive/nonprogressive distinction and the Polish (Slavic) imperfective/perfective distinction. That is to say, these Polish learners seemed to confirm, that for them, the continuous forms in English ("continuous" was the label they were most familiar with, rather than "progressive") were semantically equivalent to corresponding *im*perfective forms in Polish.[6] In the absence of a thorough semantically oriented contrastive analysis, the present writer saw fit to take a readily comprehensible rhetorical distinction as a basis for explaining and practicing the use of the past progressive forms in English. This distinction was between "moving the story on" and "describing the scene at one chronological point in the narrative"—that is, between what was termed the *narrative* function of a verb and the *descriptive* function. The distinction can be represented pictorially by means of cartoon strips. Actions that need a *separate picture* are represented by the narrative form (nonprogressive) on the basis that separate pictures usually represent separate steps in the narrative. The same actions represented together in *one* picture illustrate the descriptive function associated with the progressive form. Thus single pictures are often used to elicit descriptions of what is/was going on at the time. It may then be shown that, where English employs this aspectual difference to distinguish between these two functions, Polish does not. This may be illustrated (Sharwood Smith, 1976, p. 87) as follows:

IMPERFECTIVE

Przez pierwsze trzy kilometry SZEDŁ

(For the first three kilometers he │ walked
                                    │ *was walking

IMPERFECTIVE

a przez nastepne dwa BIEGŁ.

and for the next two he │ ran   )
                         │ *was running

The Polish learner of English tends to choose (in a free writing situation) the lower, normally unacceptable versions of the English verb apparently on the basis that where emphasis seems to be placed on the *durative* nature of the event the conditions for choosing the "continuous" form exist.[7] These conditions are those that elicit the imperfective verb forms in Polish. The narrative/ descriptive distinction was chosen as a necessary preliminary for explaining this (particular) use of the progressive not only because it was felt to have some validity within a limited context from a linguistic point of view but also because it is a distinction readily explainable to anyone familiar with story-telling—that is, obeys the principle of moving from the familiar to the unfamiliar. In a concentrated pedagogical description it would need to be adapted to a more general description of verbs, time, and so forth.

"PSYCHOLOGICALLY RESPECTABLE" EXTENDED DESCRIPTIONS

If, in pedagogical descriptions of the concentrated type, we present the facts of the target language in a condensed form, presentation may be extended through time to promote mastery. The description has to be processed to maximize meaningful learning. The necessary practice element may be realized in any number of ways, memorizing lists and conversations, doing translations, and working through pattern drills being obvious examples. Most practical language teaching as it is carried out at the classroom level shows either a very indirect adherence to psychological theory or none at all. At their best, teachers and textbooks show enormous amounts of intuition and common sense, but to what extent should a given learner count on getting by chance the right teacher and the right textbook when there are so many other types around? A brief survey of existing textbook material will show at least as much ignorance of, or lip service to, relevant ideas in educational psychology as direct, careful application. There are various obvious administrative and commercial reasons for this, which will not be discussed here. Still, one may reasonably ask whether there *are* insights and techniques available within the field of psychology for use in the extended description of target languages. To the extent that behavioristic ideas have filtered through with unimpressive results to the classroom, one might well take a pessimistic view of the prospects. The question here is really whether cognitively oriented research has anything to offer yet, beyond general principles. What follows later will be an attempt to show briefly that it does.

One of the interesting developments that may proceed from applying experimentally investigated techniques in the classroom will be the increase of specially devised (see Cole, 1976, for a warning) *visual* devices in intermediate and advanced learning and with adolescent and adult learners.[8] By "visual," both verbal and nonverbal, pictorial and nonpictorial representations and illustrations of the facts of language are meant. One gets the impression sometimes that whereas young beginners get the benefit of a strong visual component (particularly nonverbal in character) other types of learners do not. Psychological and psychologically oriented experimental research seems to indicate that for all types of learners, the maximum use of extra visual devices (over and above the words of the language per se) is necessary for unimpeded effective learning to take place. As a small pointer to what is involved here, a recent experiment by Erdelyi et al. (1976), apparently using university students as subjects, showed that a significant increase in the recall of words occurred when those words were linked with visual images. Earlier evidence indicated that recall of pictures, unlike recall of words, may increase with time and effort. This experiment showed that whereas one group that were required to memorize a certain number of words did *not* show any increase in recall over time (hypermnesia), a second group that was instructed, in addition, to form vivid mental pictures of the objects named and a third group that was given pictures only *did*. Without immediately extrapolating from this, it does seem suggestive of the fact that maximizing visual representations to accompany, illustrate, and explain linguistic items may well improve learning a great deal especially where the content is too abstract to expect the learner to resort to "visualizing strategies." Some experimentation (Carpay, 1974) has lent support to this hypothesis.

One development in psychology that holds out great promise for pedagogical descriptions of language is cognitively oriented programmed instruction. We may observe some features of this type of instruction in the Skinner and Crowder type of program but without the cognitivist dimension (Leont'ev and Gal'perin, in Stones, 1970). Those who have been especially concerned with the internal, specifically human processes that organize knowledge have been developing the notion of programmed learning much further. A good example is the use of *algorithms*, or quasi-algorithms[9] (Landa, 1970, 1975, 1976; Bung, 1973), whereby the learner is taught how to "think his way through" a problem in controlled steps following a set of instructions of an algorithmic type. The assumption behind the use of algorithms in teaching is that human problem-solving behavior is very much algorithmic in character. Landa's classic example is starting a car, which, for a beginner, is a very complex and confusing proposition but for an experienced driver is a sequence of actions which has been totally automatized and can be executed swiftly and easily. We can help the learner by giving him a set of linked instructions composed of questions (*Is the gear lever at neutral?*) and commands (*Turn the key fully to the right and immediately release.*) which he can learn and run through as he encounters the car-starting problem. A simple example of "algorithmizing" a learning task in language teaching would be the following development of the *mancu* example. The reader should speculate about how to provide algorithms for the more abstract lexical problems mentioned in the same connection, or indeed for the narrative/descriptive analysis of the English past progressive.

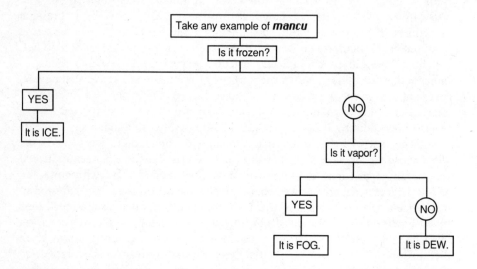

In explaining the pedagogical use of algorithms, Landa (1975) refers to the complaint by teachers that their learners "very often possess all the knowledge that is necessary in a certain subject, but they cannot solve problems" (p. 99); they know what they should do but have problems in applying their knowledge. Landa had success in testing out his methods with pupils learning geometry but found even better results when he applied it to the teaching of grammar.[10] The hypothesized reason for this was that the particular grammatical problems could be expressed in unambiguous terms whereas the geometry ones could not. This implies that algorithms should be based not only on fundamentally correct descriptions of the language but also on maximally explicit and unambiguous ones. To conclude this extremely brief survey of the use of algorithms, the following relevant points made by Landa may be mentioned:

1. Not all problems are necessarily soluble via algorithms.
2. One can never acquire *complete* control over the formation and development of all the learner's psychological processes (Oller, 1975; Bung, 1973).
3. Algorithmic procedures in themselves are noncreative: the solution to

the given problem is completely predetermined and specified (though *constructing* algorithms does call for some creativity).

To give a very brief final survey of actual experimentation in what has here been termed *extended description*, first an impression of what Keuleers calls "cognitive drills" (Keuleers, 1974a, 1974b) will be given, and then this will be followed by a short account of research done at Utrecht by Carpay, Bol, and others together with an overview of earlier research as described in Carpay (1974). This neither does justice to the above-mentioned nor covers similar research done elsewhere, but it will serve as an illustration at least.

Keuleers, at Louvain (Leuven), has developed a method whereby the practice element inherent in the standard language laboratory drill is combined with a specifically cognitive element—namely, the provision of conscious insight into rules. The aim is to have the learner master the material creatively (in the Chomskyan sense). Crucial to this method is the use of *mediators*,[11] which provide the learner with the necessary metalanguage that enables him, while doing the drills, to consciously apply the rules. These rules should be "internalised gradually into an automatic implicit skill" (Keuleers, 1974a, p. 59). These mediators may be *enclosed* within the sentences (like *since yesterday*) or they may be *constructed* in the form of additional (preferably semantic) information stated concisely in a manner that immediately evokes the relevant meaning, and *annexed* (Keuleers, 1974b) to the text (see appendix). The learners, students, are presented with a number of standardized models which they have to convert into correct utterances. The models are mixed up so as to prevent the development of a mechanical pattern of response. Here is one example of a model and the required response:

STIMULUS

(he can't walk) Sam *fall* down the staircase. Yes.
How this time?/ probably while sliding down the banister rail;
general
    often.

CORRECT RESPONSE (the slash above indicates a pause while student
                waits for feedback.)
Sam has fallen down the stairs, hasn't he? Yes, he has. How did he fall down it this time? He probably fell while sliding down the banister rail; he often falls down when doing that.

Carpay (1974)[12] discusses the use of schemas against the background of the Soviet psychologist Gal'perin's theory of stage-by-stage formation of mental operations (Talysina, 1973; Landa, 1975, pp. 102–103), and the following excerpt of the account he gives of the empirical research conducted by Bragina (1972), Gol'din (1970), Kabanova (1971), Keuleers (1974a), and Zimmerman (1969, 1971) may shed some light on the issues involved. The problems dealt with were as follows (Carpay, 1974, pp. 132–133):

1. Choice of the correct case in Russian (Gol'din)
2. Choice of the correct tense form (Bragina, Keuleers, and Zimmerman)
3. Use of the passive in German (Kabanova)
4. Use of the modal auxiliaries in English (Keuleers).

Differences and similarities were summarized as follows:

1. Keuleers and Zimmerman use signal words rather than visual schemas and/or superordinate notions. Bragina uses both spatial (visual) schemas and superordinate notions, also picture symbols and verbal labels like *past* and *nonpast* in contradiction of Engels (1970) who required that didactic schemas should make abstraction and generalization possible. Keuleers also uses verbal label (see above).
2. Unlike Keuleers and Zimerman, Bragina, Gol'din, and Kabanova made a definite break with the stage-by-stage procedure by introducing a series of lessons giving the *whole system* first to provide initial orientation.[13] They also start work with algorithmic procedures prior to work with schemas. They make sure that the learners acquire these procedures. Keuleers and Zimmerman lack this guidance element; they do give verbal instructions but leave it to the learner's autonomous development as to how to acquire the schemas.
3. Bragina, Gol'din, and Kabanova, using "identification" algorithms (Landa, 1970), first present reality seen through target language spectacles, in the *native* language (following Gal'perin), whereas Keuleers and Zimmerman start directly with the target language. They also pay attention to frequent and infrequent usage following Gal'perin's structures on presenting the total system first.

Together with Bol, Carpay set up an experimental three-hour program designed to teach Russian aspect (the semantics of) to first- and second-year psychology students in two sessions. This was done in groups of a maximum of twelve students. It was teacher-free, although at given moments the learners were required to work in dyads (interacting pairs). The students were voluntary participants. The results of the final test reported in (for example) Carpay (1974, p. 149) were most encouraging: the students were highly motivated.[14] Ten out of twelve reached the 80% criteria; there was a .001 correlation between performance at schema drawing (in the test they had to draw the appropriate visual schemas indicating the aspect of a target verb) and performance at verbal identification. Briefly, the learners were presented with pictures with Dutch captions (the Russian terms were used as a metalanguage) focussing on the relevant features for choice of aspect. A number of visual models (see appendix)—for example, shaded and unshaded squares representing perfective and imperfective aspects respectively with the vertical sides continuous or dotted showing whether the temporal limitation of the action was defined or left unspecified respectively—were used first separately, and then later they were brought directly into an algorithmic procedure. As the learners progressed, certain features of the visual schemas were missed out, and the possibility arose for the learners to take shortcuts in the algorithm. All in all, considering the difficulty learners of Russian seem to have with the semantics of aspect, the short period that was necessary for them to master it in this program is impressive.

CONCLUSION

There does seem to be considerable evidence for the desirability of a sizeable transfusion from psychology. Not only do we need the study of actual teaching (Allwright, 1972; Corder, 1974) but we need, in applied linguistics, experimental application of psychological theory together with lingustic analysis; in other words, we need to work from both ends. From a practical administrative point of view, this seems to point towards *group research* with at least one trained psychologist, one trained linguist/applied linguist, and someone with substantial practical experience of classroom teaching.[15] For the pedagogical grammarian and lexicographer, this means choosing theoretical linguistic insights and formulations according to principles that have stood the test of experimentation and which proceed from theoretical psychology and, second, forming those insights in such a way as to facilitate rather than impede the later formulation of extended descriptions. For example, this might mean, it has been suggested here, an increase in the principled use of visual devices, schemas, and pictorial representations, which may eventually be developed into the kind of cognitively oriented programming that has been briefly touched upon in the previous section. There are definite indications that the psychology of instruction has something to offer.

APPENDIX: FURTHER ILLUSTRATIONS OF INSTRUCTIONAL DEVICES

A. Mediators for cognitive drills (Keuleers, 1974a): Constructed mediators (excerpt).
B. Visual schemas for the Carpay and Bol Russian Aspect experiment (Carpay, 1974) (excerpt).
C. An introductory (expository) algorithm based on Sharwood Smith (1974, 1977).

A.   *fool! I P* = *it would be foolish to do so and I do not permit (P) you:*
       not   *must not.*
  annoy/irrita = *It annoys/irritates me that he should keep . . . . : might.*
    m
  general P = *general permission, not referring to one particular and actually given permission: could.*
   P done = *actually given permission: was allowed to.*
   they P = *permission given by someone else: can, is allowed to.*
  You P? = *do you permit me (explicitly, formally)?: may*

Note: These were taken from one model (model I), as in, for example, fool! I P

Bill not must keep Guinea in our cellar, must he (Keuleers, 1974a, p. 76). By such texts, the mediators for a given series of exercises are introduced. The source description in this case is Leech, *Meaning and the English Verb*, London: Longmans, 1971.

B. These schemas, and others, were introduced into the three algorithmic trees in the course of the 12-step program:

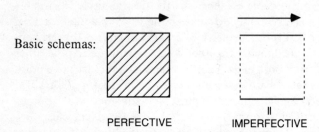

Basic schemas:

I
PERFECTIVE

II
IMPERFECTIVE

Arrows represent the time axis; shading represents perfectiveness; boxes represent actions; vertical lines indicate beginning and end of action; a dotted line means that the action does/did not reach its natural conclusion and that the end is not clearly specified.

V. Consecutive actions (*he drank up his beer and left*)

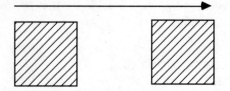

VI. Completely simultaneous actions [*Ivanov watched (to see) how Simrnov was working/worked*]

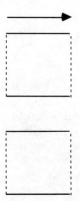

VII. Partially simultaneous actions (*when Olga came in, Piotr was reading Pravda*)

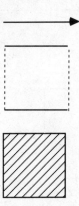

C. ALGORITHMIC PROCEDURE FOR EXPRESSING FUTURE REFERENCE IN SIMPLE DECLARATIVE SENTENCES

Overview: In English future reference, you have the choice between linking the future state or event (STATE/EVENT) with PRESENT time or not. In other words there may be indications or you may have knowledge of certain facts which make the future state or event more predictable. You must decide whether to communicate this or not. You have the choice.

Assumptions: You know how to form the Present Simple and Present Progressive. You can use *going to* + INFIN. and the modals *will* and *shall*, as far as their form and position in the sentence are concerned.

You do not want to use *if* or *unless* etc., i.e., you want a simple sentence.

You do not wish to use modals other than *will* and *shall*.

You wish to make a statement.

PRACTICE

1. Take any Dutch sentence and see what English versions are possible via the algorithmic procedure on the following page.
2. For someone to say, in English, *He dies tomorrow* or *They arrive on Tuesday*, they must have made the following sequence of decisions (or path): 1-2-4-7. If you take Dutch versions with the main verb in the present tense—that is, formal equivalents—could you say that the same sequence of decisions must *necessarily* have been made?
3. In terms of the above algorithmic procedure, why is *it rains tomorrow* odd? What would we have to assume in order to regard it as an acceptable English sentence?

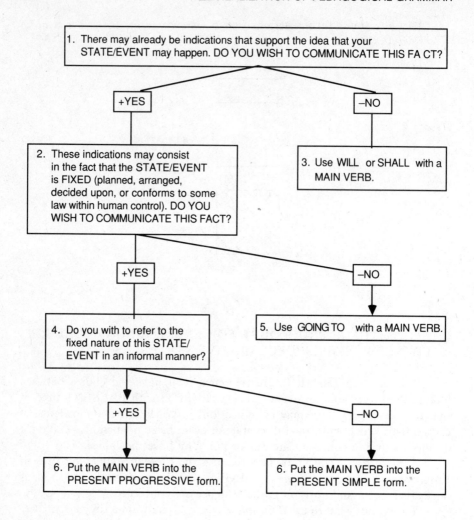

NOTES

1. Discovery learning typically precedes a stage which is basically one of reception learning—that is, when the relevant content has been discovered (Ausubel, 1968, p. 22).
2. This is not to say that rote learning has absolutely no role to play.
3. The fundamental fact of the arbitrariness of language as expressed by de Saussure still stands, of course.
4. Linguistic (semantic) considerations also operate in that one would like to use features that could be employed in the description of other meteorological phenomena.
5. These were mentioned to me and my colleagues by Professor Landa during a guest lecture on the subject of algorithms in language teaching.
6. This by no means implies *necessary* interference from Polish and other Slavic languages (Kellerman, 1976).

7. Meaningful learning of course may take place without didactic help. Polish learners may be either making a (heuristic) equivalence between NL and TL systems or they may be interpreting the term *continuous* wrongly irrespective of any features of their native linguistic code, or both. In any case the result is that they learn a pattern that does not conform to target norms on the basis of prior knowledge.
8. Teachers and materials writers may be inhibited from using too much nonverbal symbolism, particularly of the pictorial kind, because they or the learners feel it is childish. This would be a pity.
9. The term *quasi* is introduced because algorithms for humans, as opposed to algorithms for machines, do not have every last "bit" of information specified: they are expressed in *natural* language.
10. In the geometry test the 25% of problems solved was raised in the posttest to 87%.
11. The concept of mediators is discussed critically in Spoelders (1974).
12. Comments by Carpay (1974, p. 132) and Spoelders (1977, p. 124) suggest that there may be a number of problems with metalanguage where learners have followed a different system prior to the experiment. Beginners typically do better than nonbeginners; but this should not be an insoluble problem.
13. This would accord with Ausubel's notion of providing "advance expository organisers" to create the basis for future meaningful learning (Ausubel, 1968, p. 149).
14. We have to consider the Hawthorne effect here, of course.
15. We might more usefully speak here of roles rather than people; that is, we might have one person fulfilling more than one role. It is quite reasonable to suppose that one person might, for example, be the linguist and the applied linguist, or the applied linguist and the classroom teacher, and so on.

QUESTIONS FOR DISCUSSION

1. This Sharwood Smith paper argues for a cognitive approach to grammatical consciousness raising (CR) that is infused with principles drawn from instructional psychology. What is the relationship between this kind of approach and the nature of second language acquisition that is reflected in the papers from Part II? For example, the use of algorithms in grammatical CR might well mesh with the problem-solving characteristics of L2 learning claimed by Bley-Vroman. Are there other examples of this kind?
2. Discuss the possibility that some areas of language can be taught using techniques to promote meaningful learning whereas others exist for which rote learning seems the only solution.
3. Discuss the practical problems associated with using techniques proposed in this paper, assuming for the moment that they are, in principle, worth trying out.

REFERENCES

Adamczewski, H. 1974. Be + ing revisited. In S. Corder and E. Roulet (eds.), *Linguistic Insights in Applied Linguistics*. Brussels: AIMAV.

Allwright, R. 1974. Prescription and description in the training of language teachers. In J. Qvistgaard, H. Schwarz, and H. Spang-Hanssen (eds.), *Proceedings of the Third AILA Congress 1972*, Vol. 3. Heidelberg: Groos.

Ausubel, D. 1968. *Educational Psychology: A Cognitive View*. New York: Holt, Rinehart and Winston.

Bragina, T. 1972. *Nekotorye Psychologiceskije Uslovija Formizovanija Reci na Innos-trannom Jazijke.* Moskva: Avtoreferat.

Bung, K. 1973. *Towards a Theory of Programmed Language Instruction.* The Hague: Mouton.

Carpay, J. 1974. *Onderwijs-Leerpsychologie en Leergang-Ontwikkeling in het Moderne Vreemde Talenonderwijs.* Groningen: Tjeenk-Willink.

Carpay, J. 1976. Impliciete en expliciete grammatika. Paper presented at the ANELA-ABELA Conference, Tilburg, November.

Carroll, J. 1965. The contributions of psychological theory and educational research to the teaching of foreign languages. *Modern Language Journal* **49**:273-281.

Chastain, K. 1971. *The Development of Modern Language Skills: Theory to Practice.* Chicago: Rand McNally.

Cole, L. 1976. Picture-language relationships. *International Review of Applied Linguistics* **14**:339-350.

Cook, V. 1977. Cognitive processes in foreign language learning. *International Review of Applied Linguistics* **15**:1-21.

Corder, S. 1974. Pedagogical grammar or the pedagogy of grammar? In S. Corder and E. Roulet (eds.), *Linguistic Insights in Applied Linguistics.* Brussels: AIMAV.

Di Pietro, R. 1971. *Language Structure in Contrast.* Rowley, Mass.: Newbury House.

Dirven, R. 1976. A redefinition of contrastive linguistics. *International Review of Applied Linguistics* **14**:1-14.

Dresher, B., and N. Hornstein. 1976. On some supposed contributions of artificial intelligence to the scientific study of language. *Cognition* **4**:321-398.

Engels, L. 1970. The function of grammar in the teaching of English as a foreign language. *ITL* **10**:11-12.

Erdelyi, M., S. Finkelstein, N. Herrell, B. Miller, and J. Thomas. 1976. Coding modality versus input modality in hypermnesia: Is a rose a rose a rose? *Cognition* **4**:311-321.

Fisiak, J., ed. 1976. *Papers and Studies in Contrastive Linguistics.* Poznań: Adam Mickiewicz University.

Gal'perin, P. 1970. An experimental study in the formation of mental actions. In E. Stones (ed.), *Readings in Educational Psychology.* London: Methuen.

Gol'din, Z. 1970. *Metodika Obucenija Inostrancev Russkomy Skloneniju.* Moskva: Avtoreferat.

Kabanova, O. 1971. *Formorovanije Grammaticeskoj Struktury Vyskasivanija.* Moskva: Avtoreferat.

Kellerman, E. 1976. Elicitation, lateralization, and error analysis. *Interlanguage Studies Bulletin* **1**:79-115.

Keuleers, A. 1974a. The use of mediators in "cognitive drills." *ITL* **23**:57-83.

Keuleers, A. 1974b. Insight, automatization and creativity in foreign language learning. Ph.D. dissertation, Katolieke Universiteit, Leuven.

Landa, L. 1970. Algoritmen en heuristiken in het onderwijs en het programmeren van de denkaktiviteiten van leerlingen (trans. by A. Carpay). *Pedagogischen Studien* **47**:293-307.

Landa, L. 1975. Some problems of algorithmization and heuristics. *Instructional Science* **4**:99-112.

Landa, L. 1976. Algorithms in foreign language teaching. Paper presented at Department of English, University of Utrecht, December.

Mey, M. de, R. Pinxton, M. Poriac, and F. Vandamme, eds. 1977. *A Cognitive Viewpoint.* Ghent: University of Ghent.

Miller, G., E. Galanter, and K. Pribam. 1960. *Plans and the Structure of Behavior*. New York: Holt, Rinehart and Winston.

Oller, J. 1975. An evaluation of steps toward a theory of programmed language instruction (review of Bung, 1973). *Foundations of Language* 13:449–456.

Papert, S. 1977. Untitled paper on the structure of knowledge presented at the Ghent Conference on Communication and Cognition, University of Ghent, April.

Qvistgaard, J., H. Schwarz, and H. Spang-Hanssen, eds. 1974. *Proceedings of Third AILA Congress 1972*, Vol. 3. Heidelberg: Groos.

Sharwood Smith, M. 1974. Aspects of future reference in a pedagogical grammar of English. Ph.D. dissertation, Adam Mickiewicz University, Poznań.

Sharwood Smith, M. 1976. Imperfective versus perfective: problems and pedagogical solutions. In J. Fisiak (ed.), *Papers and Studies in Contrastive Linguistics*. Posnań: Adam Mickiewicz University.

Spoelders, M. 1972. Reflexions on mediators. *ITL* 17:1–15.

Spoelders, M. 1977. On cognitive foreign language learning theory and its applications. In M. de Mey et al. (eds.), *A Cognitive Viewpoint*. Ghent: University of Ghent.

Stones, E., ed. 1970. *Readings in Educational Psychology*. London: Methuen.

Talysina, N. 1970. The stage theory in the formation of mental operations. In E. Stones (ed.), *Readings in Educational Psychology*. London: Methuen.

Wilkins, D. 1972. *Linguistics in Language Teaching*. London: Edward Arnold.

Zimmermann, G. 1969. Integrierung und Transfer im neusprachlichen Unterricht. *Praxis des Neusprachlichen Unterrichts* 16:145–160.

Zimmermann, G. 1971. Teacher's Manual for *Passport to English* (Junior Course, German ed.). Wiesbaden: Hueber-Dicher.

14

Imperfective versus Progressive: An Exercise in Contrastive Pedagogical Linguistics

Michael Sharwood Smith
Rijksuniversiteit, Utrecht

The present paper is concerned with one particular problem in relating English and Polish which arises out of error analysis and which is best discussed at a level above that of the sentence. The reason for starting from actual recorded errors rather than from a purely theoretical model is a subject for discussion in itself. Suffice it to say here that, as the aim is primarily pedagogical the starting point is a pedagogical requirement, namely, to correct a misinterpretation on the part of Polish students of English regarding the use of the English Past Progressive (or Past Continuous as it is often called) Tense. The hypothesis is that there is interference from Polish and in particular from its Perfective/ Imperfective system. Apart from the pedagogical framework in which this contrastive paper is undertaken, there is a practical reason for starting from recorded errors: contrasting two languages is a task of such enormity, especially if one takes into consideration the limitations of time and resources, that error analysis is a very useful basis for choosing which areas of the two languages one should concentrate on. It certainly does not rule out theoretical models since the detection and analysis of language errors presupposes some kind of linguistic theory. Even more to the point, it presupposes a theory of acquisition, but at least at the time of writing, there was no well-developed model to suit the purpose in hand.

"Imperfective Versus Progressive: An Exercise in Contrastive Pedagogical Linguistics" by Michael Sharwood Smith, 1975, in *Papers and Studies in Contrastive Linguistics*, vol. 3, edited by Jacek Fisiak, pp. 85–90. Washington, D.C.: Center for Applied Linguistics. Reprinted with permission of the Center for Applied Linguistics.

The reason for dealing with the present problem on the level of *text*, that is, interrelated sentences, will become apparent later. One might, however, reflect how much text as a level of analysis is profitable if not vital to contrastive analysis. This is especially true of a Polish-English contrastive project where the article necessarily figures as a major problem. Features such as the article, comparatives, demonstratives, and pronominals need to be examined as features of text, that is, as phenomena occurring suprasententially. A sentence-based grammar is inadequate to cope with this type of problem unless it goes beyond sentence embedding to units of text where *sentence* is a subunit. However, the discussion here will not deal with the technicalities of text grammar but rather informally, with the problem as it confronts Polish students of English and a suggestion will be made for presenting this particular difference between the two languages in a readily comprehensible way.

The perfective/imperfective distinction in Polish is summed up in general terms in the well-known beginner's course *Mówimy po polsku*, thus:

> Almost all Polish verbs make their appearance in two forms (so-called imperfective and perfective form). A distinction should be made between their meanings. Imperfective verbs express the fact of the duration of an action as well as the fact of its incompleteness. Perfective verbs, on the contrary, express the completeness of an action. [Bisko et al., 1966, p. 271]

Certainly some kind of link may be made between the meaning expressed by imperfective verbs in Polish and English verbs in their Progressive forms. The *Grammar of Contemporary English* (Quirk et al., 1972) describes the features of the progressive aspect as first, temporariness, as in:

1. *John is playing the banjo.*

Then it lists as "overtones," limited duration as in:

2. *The professor is typing his own letters* (these days).

Incompletion as in:

3. *I was reading a book that evening.*

Simultaneity, vividness of description, and emotional coloring and emphasis, an example of the last overtone being:

4. *He was always getting his hands dirty* (my example).

Certain features held in common might induce the Polish learner of English to relate English progressive forms with imperfective verbs generalizing the meaning of incompleteness and a certain duration to form an ad hoc equivalence in spite of the different formal realizations in the two languages. This at least seems feasible when we deal with past tenses. Thus:

5. *Czytałem list wczoraj.*

may be translated as:

6. *I was reading the letter yesterday* (but did not finish it).

and:

7. *Przeczytałem list wczoraj.*

is equivalent to:

8. *I read the letter yesterday* (to the end).

If we move upwards to the unit text we may cite an example which also seems to offer no problem:

9. *He opened his eyes. The sun was shining. He sat up. He looked through the window. The children were playing in the garden.*

The Polish equivalent would read as follows:

10. *Otworzył oczy. Słońce świeciło. Usiadł. Wyjrzał przez okno. Dzieci bawiły się w ogrodzie.*

Here the verbs expressing completed nondurative events are perfective in Polish and nonprogressive in English. The verbs expressing durative (i.e., lasting) events are imperfective in Polish and progressive in English. Thus:

Completed	Incomplete
opened/otworzył	was shining/*świeciło*
sat up/usiadł	*were playing/bawiły się*
looked/wyjrzał	

Such examples confirm the ad hoc rule of equivalence. However, if we now take example 11, we come to the snag:

11. (*Biedny Jan*), *przez pierwsze trzy kilometry szedł a przez następne dwa biegł.*

Here the durative character of the walking and running is signalled through the use of the imperfective verbs *szedł* and *biegł*. First there was a long period of walking and then there was a long period of running. The Polish learner of English would be tempted as often seems to be the case to translate this as follows:

12. **For the first three kilometers he was walking and for the next two he was running.*

This is an erroneous translation. It is just feasible that a native speaker might assign some kind of dramatic descriptive interpretation to it, but the normal equivalent would be as follows:

13. *For the first three kilometers he walked and for the next two he ran.*

The use of the nonprogressive Past Simple Tense does not in any way obliterate the idea that the two events seemed to last a long time, and we could certainly begin the sentence with some such expression as *poor old Jan* to make this clearer. What does seem to matter here is that the event signalled by the nonprogressive verb moves the narrative on one step, chronologically speaking. That the event seemed to "have duration" is not important. The fact is, it is a completed action and one step in the narrative. This does not hold true for Polish where you can separate two imperfective verbs with a time expression like *potem*.

The English nonprogressive Simple Past, then, performs a certain function in a narrative text. Three instances grouped side by side represent three steps in the narration as, for example, in Caesar's famous statement:

14. *I came. I saw. I conquered. (Veni. Vidi. Vici.)*

If, on the other hand, we group three instances of the progressive form of the verb side by side, then it is clear that the events described are to some degree simultaneous as in:

15. *His legs were shaking. His hands were trembling and his left cheek was twitching uncontrollably.*

These two facts can also be illustrated within one sentence as in the following two examples:

16. *When they arrived on the beach, they leapt ashore and ran towards the islanders.*
17. *When I was laughing, John was shouting and Mary was crying.*

We may say that the English nonprogressive tense fulfils a *narrative function* moving the action on chronologically. The progressive tense, on the other hand, fulfills a *descriptive function* describing "what was going on" at a given point in time. Interestingly enough, the progressive form depends on this point in time being given by the context (linguistic or situational) usually in the form of a time adverbial like *yesterday at 5 p.m.*, or by a nearby nonprogressive verb. In a simple narrative text the nonprogressive verbs form the basic framework on which the progressive verbs, rather like bound morphemes, depend for their existence. Although both *I went home* and *I was going home* demand some context to explicate the full meaning, *I was going home* somehow impels the listener or reader immediately to search for some specific time or some action with which to relate it directly. It is describing or filling out a point in the narrative without which it is meaningless. If we take a text with a string of progressive verbs, all the states or actions described by these verbs relate to a part of the narrative establishing a point in time. This is often a nonprogressive verb which lies adjacent to the progressive verbs. It may come before them as in:

18. I drew *the curtains apart. The sun* was shining. *The children* were playing *in the yard. Some women* were hanging *clothes on the washing lines.*

or it may come afterwards as in:

19. *The coach was* coming *round the bend. Its wheels* were bumping *against the side of the road. The driver* was shouting. *Hoss Cartwright* drew *his gun.*

In both cases the actions described progressively are understood to be more or less simultaneous and taking place during the event described by the nearest nonprogressive verb *drew*. This is obviously not a characteristic of the Polish imperfective verb which can appear next to another imperfective verb and signal a move in the narrative on to the next step as is exemplified in 11 (*Biedny Jan*, etc.). In other words, Polish imperfective verbs seem just as capable of performing what has been called the narrative function as perfective verbs. Yet in a text like the following:

20. *I took the child to the clinic. The doctor examined him for a long time very carefully. Finally he pronounced him healthy.*

many Polish learners would be tempted to write or say *was examining* and would be surprised to learn that the result sounds very odd to the native speaker of English.

As far as pedagogical solutions are concerned, there is obviously a remedial problem here to counteract Polish interference and, as far as university students are concerned and sophisticated adult learners as a whole, there is no reason why the problem should not be explained in notional terms in much the same manner as has been done here, as a small sample of contrastive pedagogical grammar. In an experimental written English exercise devised in Poznań to remedy the problem, the symbol (N) was used to represent the narrative function and the symbol (D) to represent the descriptive function. Students are asked to write short texts based on a sequence of these symbols together with a corresponding sequence of suggested verbs. At first simple sequences of (N) are required, for example, (N.N.N.) using, say, the verbs, *run*, *climb*, and *jump*. A realization of this pattern would be as follows:

> **21.** *The prisoner* ran *to the wall.* He climbed *to the top and* jumped *down to the other side.*

Then the required pattern can be varied and dependent (D) verbs brought in. For example, one pattern is (N.D.D.) with all the Ds of course dependent on the N. Using the same verbs as before we might arrive at the following small text:

> **22.** *The prison guard* ran *to the wall. Two convicts* were climbing *to the top. Another* was *already* jumping *down to the other side.*

A freer section gives a pattern but, instead of verbs, just a general situation such as "A prison escape" or "A teacher collapses in class."

Pedagogical solutions need not contain such overtly contrastive statements as the exercises here suggest. Adult learners probably appreciate this cognitive approach to materials construction. However, a more concealed planning of materials of the pattern drill type might profit from contrastive insights. Ideally, teaching exercises should be text based, especially in the case of exercises teaching the English Past Progressive and Simple Past to Polish learners. Learners should be forced overtly or covertly to look for the function of verbs within the text rather than rely on a vague feeling for the independent meanings of particular tenses. In learning a second language, the presence of the native language must play some role. The teacher and materials writer cannot afford to overlook this.

QUESTIONS FOR DISCUSSION

1. In the Sharwood Smith paper from Part II we read of the possibilities for color coding word endings that signal tense distinctions. His second paper in this section describes a contrastive pedagogical grammar (Polish/English) designed to help the learner sort out the intricacies of the imperfective/progressive distinction. How might the color-coding procedure be of use here?

2. Sharwood Smith suggested in an earlier paper (Part II) that learners can learn from their own output. Suggest some ways in which a teacher might promote this kind of self-learning for the kinds of grammatical problems described in the present paper.

3. Discuss the relationship between (1) particular teaching techniques such as demonstrated in this paper with regard to English and Polish and (2) learner characteristics such as age, maturity, level of proficiency, and so forth.

REFERENCES

Bisko, W., S. Karolak, S. Wasilewska, and D. Kryński. 1966. *Mówimy po polsku.* Warsaw: P W, "Wiedza Powszechna."

Quirk, R., S. Greenbaum, G. Leech, and J. Svartvik. 1972. *A Grammar of Contemporary English.* London: Longman.

15
Functions of Grammar in a Language-Teaching Syllabus

William Rutherford
University of Southern California

Much has been said over the years about the nature of the grammatical contribution to the second-language-learning experience. Discussion of this kind shows that various degrees of weight have been proposed for grammatical matter relative to functional matter. These possible grammar-function ratios group roughly into four. It seems that any formal language-learning experience would have to be one of the following: (1) grammar-based and without functional focus, (2) grammar-based but with functional focus, (3) function-based but with grammatical focus, and (4) function-based and without grammatical focus. Commercially produced materials that exemplify the four categories will no doubt be familiar to the general reader.

Empirical evidence bearing on these categories is another matter. For the effectiveness of a grammar-based experience with no functional focus there seems to be no supporting evidence. This is also true of the function-based experience with no grammatical focus, although vigorous arguments have been offered in support of this position (Newmark, 1970; Newmark and Reibel, 1970). What reliable evidence there is in this general area applies to the possibilities for tandem grammar/function focus (categories (2) and (3)). A useful summary of this research is provided by Canale and Swain (1980), which leads them to the opinion that although "focus on grammatical competence in the classroom is not a sufficient condition for the development of communica-

"Functions of Grammar in a Language-Teaching Syllabus" by William E. Rutherford, 1982, *Language Learning and Communication*, vol. 1, pp. 21–36. © 1982 by John Wiley & Sons, Inc. Reprinted with permission of John Wiley & Sons, Inc.

tive competence, it would be inappropriate . . . to conclude . . . that the development of grammatical competence is irrelevant to or unnecessary for the development of communicative competence" (p. 13). Other related conclusions drawn by Canale and Swain, based upon scansion of this same body of research, are that there should be emphasis on both grammatical accuracy and meaningful communication from the onset of second language study, that early meaningful verbal communication is not possible without some grammatical knowledge, and that if the goal of language learning is communicative competence, then the language-teaching syllabus must integrate aspects of both grammar and function. Following from all this could be, one might say, a general conclusion that in the second-language-learning experience, language as a formal system must be taken note of in some way. On the face of it, this would not appear to be a very startling affirmation, given that language, whatever else it may be, is certainly also the embodiment of a formal system and that any use to which language may be put entails the activation of that system. The real issue, however, is how knowledge of the system is to be imparted to the learner. In other words, what does it mean to "focus" on grammar? What are the ways by which one may "take note" of language system in syllabus planning? It is to these broad questions that I wish to address this paper. In the sections that follow we will first examine the various roles which grammatical consciousness can assume in the planning stages of a language-teaching syllabus, followed by examples of learning activities that can engender unconscious awareness of crucial aspects of language organization. We will then consider what modification these roles might undergo in the course of future research.

Grammatical consciousness in pedagogy is closely bound up with the answers to two basic questions: "What is it that is to be brought to consciousness?" and "How is it to be done?" The "what" question is the pedagogical extension of "What do we know about how language is organized and how it serves communication?" The "how" question is the pedagogical extension of "What do we know about how language learning takes place?"

It will be suggested here that what it is of language system that is available for pedagogical consideration is a richer resource than is customarily recognized, if cursory inspection of current commercial language-teaching materials is an accurate indication.

Pedagogical attention to language form is rooted in a conception of language whose formalism is directly manifested in discrete entities such as the familiar bound morphemes, parts of speech, verb tense, clausal units, sentence types, and so forth. It is therefore a relatively easy matter to let such entities constitute points of focus in the teaching syllabus, or units to be mastered, so to speak (Rutherford, 1980). Underlying this approach is usually the tacit assumption that successful language learning is equivalent in large part to the cumulative mastery of sequentially introduced such units. And more recently, of course, the "unit-accumulation" approach has been extended to include varieties of so-called language functions (for discussion of this, see Widdowson, 1978; Rutherford, 1978). That language system should be conceived for pedagogical purposes as a structural taxonomy is not surprising, however, given (1) that language pedagogy is still under the influence of the pretransformational linguistic paradigm (Kuhn, 1970) in which *language system* is defined exclusively as the hierarchical distribution of language constituents, and (2) that what is most readily available in language system for immediate conscious inspection, by teacher and learner alike, are these same constituents of surface syntax, morphology, and phonology. Largely absent then from the thinking that goes into language pedagogy are the notions (1) that there are unobservable properties of language system that are crucial to its implementation, and (2) that pedagogical attention to language system need not of necessity lead automatically to classroom attention. Long characteristic of language pedagogy has been the conversion of observable discrete language entities into observable discrete language-learning material, and I would like to suggest that such practices even at best reveal an impoverished view of what language system really is, at least to the extent that we can presently know it.

What, then, are some of these properties with respect to English? The nonnative learner who has acquired the ability to communicate in English must "know" in at least some passive, tacit, intuitive sense the following salient characteristics of the English language (Thompson, 1978):

1. that the category "subject," as distinct from "topic," is basic to canonical sentence form;
2. that (preverbal) subject position must always be filled;
3. that the obligatory filling of subject position and stable SVO constituent order require that there be an extensive battery of movement rules (i.e., structure-p reserving transformations; Emonds, 1976) for maintaining these positional relationships;
4. that it is common, contrary to what is possible in many other languages, to have rhematic material (i.e., bearing a heavy information load) in subject position;
5. that if a noun phrase immediately preceding a verb is not the grammatical subject of that verb then the verb must be marked (e.g., as an infinitival: persuade NP *to go*);
6. that in order to maintain the subject before the lexical verb in question a rule of *do*-support is invoked.

The net effect of these characteristics, as Thompson points out, is to make of English a language in which word order functions almost exclusively to signal grammatical rather than pragmatic relationships. And these word-order requirements produce a surface constituent order that is often very different from the order of elements within the corresponding propositional content. Hawkins (1980) states that:

English speakers have, in effect, more work to do in extracting meaning from form. They must systematically exclude contextually inappropriate interpretations from ambiguous and semantically diverse surface structures; they must reconstruct semantic argument-predicate relations over often large syntactic domains; and they must infer semantically relevant material which is not present in surface form. [p. 46]

Also crucial to the effective use of language but not necessarily observable at the surface would be the question of through what means the target language conceptualizes reality. For example, temporal reference in English is encoded into an elaborate system that is notoriously resistant to the "item-unit" approach for learning purposes. For the system to take hold it needs to be perceived as a system. This cannot be achieved in piecemeal fashion simply because temporal reference is not an entity built up out of subconstituents but rather a code network that realizes through language one important area of cognition—namely, the perception of time. (See Sharwood Smith, 1978, for a particularly good illustration of this. See also Clark, 1973, for a cognitive accounting of temporal and spatial deixis.)

An even better example of the mistake of trying to impart the whole through a set of contrived constituent parts is what is usually done in language pedagogy with the English determiner system, separate "rules" for which tally close to 50 in one particular language-teaching text. Entry into the system for the learner will not be through sets of rules, sequenced or not, but rather through cognitive correlates of the determiner system such as presupposition and raising-to-consciousness (Rutherford, 1980). Again, the conceptualization of reality through language is not amenable to an item-unit approach in language pedagogy.

One final principle of language organization that is crucial to language use but cannot be accommodated within the item-unit pedagogic paradigm is that of "relationship." A simple two-sentence passage will serve here as an illustration of the kinds of relationships that obtain both intra- and extralinguistically in any piece of text (Munby, 1978; Halliday and Hasan, 1976) and that must be grasped if communication is to take place: "One characteristic of wars in general is that often nobody wins. Somebody did, however, in the American Revolution, but even this conflagration is said to have taken a heavy toll on both sides." The comprehension of this passage entails, among other things, that the following relationships be perceived: (1) of hyponymy, as between "war" and "American Revolution"; (2) of anaphora, as between "American Revolution" and "conflagration" and between "conflagration" and "its"; (3) of contrast, as signaled by "but"; (4) of contradiction, as conveyed by "somebody did"; and (5) of major category to surrogate, as between "win" and "do." Moreover, "conflagration" must be seen to be in a subject relationship to "take," what is "said" in the passive must be understood as something like "This conflagration took a heavy toll," and "heavy toll" must be perceived as in an object relationship to "take." Even more, of course, could be pointed out, such as the relation between semantic concept and syntactic realization mentioned earlier. The inculcation of an awareness of such relationships is of great importance for successful language learning, but once again they represent aspects of language organization that are not amenable to pedagogical itemization.

Consideration of how grammatical knowledge is to be imparted addresses the second of the two questions posed above, and once again I will suggest that the available means for attempting this outnumber those that actually find their way into published material.

Perception of language system as a taxonomy of discrete units can, as we have said, lead quite understandably to conversion of such language units into teaching units. One obvious assumption underlying this sort of conversion is that the grammar must be visible, so to speak, in order for it to be effectively mastered. But visibility, in turn, is all the more easily accomplished given a view of language that can conveniently isolate its putative constituents. Thus the item/unit conception of language system and the notion that language system needs to call attention to itself for pedagogical purposes go hand in hand, as it were.

One result of this relationship has been the development of a rather elaborate set of heuristics for the teaching of grammatical content. For convenience, we can plot these on a kind of grid, along whose vertical side are listed the language forms or structures included in the syllabus (e.g., the comparative, subject relative clause, embedded question, etc.) and whose horizontal side is given over to the specification of four parameters: *method*, *approach*, *procedure*, and *technique*. Taking as an example the possible treatments of the English passive, one would consider whether the passive should be shown (1) as a derivative of something else—that is, the active (a *process*); (2) as related to something—for example, the active (a *relationship*); (3) as the result of a special co-occurrence—for example, that a noun phrase marked "object" occupy subject position if no other noun phrase is available (a *condition*); or (4) as a sequence of certain items pertaining to specific word classes, with a list of items belonging to the governing class—that is, that of the verb (a *pattern* with an optional *list*). Under *technique* one would consider whether the selected procedure should be imparted by means of a labeled box, a modified case frame, a phrase structure tree, a certain bracketing convention, a contrast with a related structure or with selected ungrammaticality, natural examples, or verbal description. By *method* it is suggested that the entire treatment can be effected by *induction* or *deduction*, or a combination thereof. The plotting of all these parameters can be represented graphically (see Fig. 15–1).

STRUCTURE	METHOD	APPROACH	PROCEDURE	TECHNIQUE
	induction	formation	relationship	PS tree
	deduction	use	process	labeled box
			condition	case frame
			pattern/list	bracketing
				contrast
				examples
				description

Figure 15-1 Heuristics for the teaching of grammatical content

Without necessarily denying the usefulness of calling pedagogical attention to itemizable features of language as noted, it is important, I think, to recognize that the general set of heuristics that we share in this endeavor has been shaped largely by our beliefs, conscious or unconscious, about what language actually is and how it is put together.

Now the important language attributes cited above are considerably less amenable to the kind of treatment schematized in Figure 1. Processes, concepts, systems, and relationships are not entities. They cannot conveniently or sensibly be singled out, identified, exemplified, labeled, and described. Attempts to do so can produce a kind of language-system focus for pedagogical purposes that is either self-defeating (e.g., the reduction of the English determiner system to a vast catalogue of rules) or meaningless (e.g., "Sentences are formed from words." Samuelson, 1976, p. 40), or both. But if these aspects of language organization cannot profitably be brought into the open, as it were, then what place do they have in the language-teaching syllabus? If you can't fit it into the presentation-explication-exploitation frame, then what else is there to say about it? I would like to suggest that not only are there ways of focusing on language-organizational principles such as these without actually calling direct attention to them but also that it is often perhaps better to bypass such attention.

Language-teaching research has for some time been questioning the wisdom of teaching grammatical formulations for their own sake—be they rules, diagrams, formulas, or what have you. Just as important as how a certain construction is put together, if not more so, is what we use it for, or why we choose to employ this construction in a particular context and not some other syntactically different but supposedly semantically equivalent one. (See Bolinger, 1977, for a scathing indictment of the notion that a semantic constant can be realized through syntactic alternatives.) Chafe (1976) refers to the realization of meaning in syntactic form as "packaging." Now although the form in which propositional content is packaged may be influenced by a number of factors, one very important factor is certainly the discourse requirements for the distribution of "given" and "new" information (Halliday, 1967). The given/new "contract" (Clark and Haviland, 1977) is not limited to complex language, nor is it a language principle that can be grasped only after some prerequisite amount of language learning has taken place. As a basic organizing principle, the given/new contract is in force for all of the language, from the very simple to the very complex. Therefore, if it makes more sense in language acquisition, as some have claimed (Givon, 1979; Hatch, 1978), to conceive of the mastery of syntax as deriving from the use of discourse rather than the other way round, then it would also make sense in language pedagogy to promote understanding of syntactic rules as one means to achieving textual cohesion (Halliday and Hasan, 1976), or as manifestations of choices made at the level of discourse, and to do this from the very beginning of instruction.

How might one go about this? Keeping in mind a fundamental requirement of "subject-prominent" English (Li and Thompson, 1976) that subject position in full clauses be occupied, and that the choice of what should fill subject position is determined by principles of discourse coherence, it is not difficult to devise a basically simple practice in which the student exercises precisely this kind of choice (Rutherford, 1976). The semantic content of the practice material (which for demonstration purposes can be of a scientific nature) might be laid out in this fashion:

(a) be—natural numbers—symbols for cardinal numbers
(b) allow—natural number system—two binary operations
(c) call—addition and multiplication—operations

Such an arrangement, which is somewhat reminiscent of case-grammar representation (Fillmore, 1968), puts the verb root on the left and strings out its associated noun phrases (minus their determiners) in random order to the right. Through this kind of display one can avoid the bias of pre-selected sentence word-order, since, after all, word-order choices—which activate so much of the grammatical machinery of English—are what we want to get the student to make.

The student therefore selects a noun phrase to be moved into subject position (e.g., *natural numbers* in 1 (a)), chooses for all noun phrases determiners that are compatible with the given/new contract (e.g., "zero" for generic in 1 (a)), decides on an appropriate verb tense (e.g., present), and applies the necessary rules of concord, thus producing 2 (a) *Natural numbers are symbols for cardinal numbers.*

In 1 (b), the given/new contract constrains the choice of subject to *natural number system* plus the definite article (or a deictic element like *this*) and the verb tense is still present: 2 (b) *The natural number system allows two binary operations.*

In 1 (c), however, where the choice of subject is limited by the given/new contract to *operations* (plus the definite article or a deictic element like *these*), the subject-verb relationship is such that the verb has of course to occur in the passive: 2 (c) *These operations are called addition and multiplication.*

If there is no noun phrase available for subjecthood—for example, where *be* is the verb and only one noun phrase is associated with it (e.g., *be—another solution to the problem*)—the student learns that the filling of subject position is still so strong that a "dummy" (i.e., *there*) has to occupy that position (*There is another solution to the problem*). If the noun phrase has a relative clause attached (e.g., *the problem that we just discussed*), it can be represented in full underlying sentence form (*the problem*[*We just discussed the problem*]). And if the noun phrase to be selected happens to dominate a sentence (*necessary—* [*One finds a solution to the problem*]), the student can learn not just the rule of extraposition but the principle of "end weight" (Quirk et al., 1972) which the rule of extraposition serves (*It is necessary to find a solution to the problem*). If we add adverbial clauses to the propositional strings and supply the necessary transitional cohesion markers (e.g., *therefore, however, and, but, so,* etc.), we come close to being able informally to represent any propositional content in a display that allows the student to exercise the crucial discourse-determined syntactic choices. The following example shows one paragraph source (Adler, 1959, p. 27) and its suggested schematized rendition:

3. (a) 1 Arabic numerals displaced all others because of their great convenience.
     2 They are most convenient to use because they give us a way of writing an indefinite amount of numbers while using only a small number of symbols called digits.
     3 This feat is accomplished by attaching different meanings to the same digit.
     4 In the number 111, three ones are used, and
     5 each has a different meaning.
     6 The 1 on the extreme right stands for the number one.
     7 The 1 in the second column from the right stands for the number ten, and
     8 the 1 in the third column stands for the number one hundred.
     9 The symbol stands for the sum of one, ten, and one hundred.
    10 Because the meaning of a digit depends on its position in the written numeral, we say the Arabic system of numerals is a *place value* system.

 (b) 1 displace — all others — Arabic numerals — because of their great convenience
     2 convenient to use — they — because they give us a way of writing an indefinite amount of numbers while using only a small number of symbols called digits
     3 accomplish — [One attaches different meanings — this feat to the same digit]
     4 use — three ones — number 111 and
     5 have — each — different meaning
     6 stand for — number *one* — 1 on the extreme right
     7 stand for — number *ten* — 1 in the second column from the right and
     8 stand for — number *one hundred* — 1 in the third column
     9 stand for — symbol — sum of one, ten, and one hundred
    10 say — we — because the meaning — [be — Arabic — place of a digit depends   system   value on its position in   system] the written numeral

Appropriate syntactic choices need not of course always be realized as in 3 (a). In 3 (b) 4, for example, the author of the original passage triggered the passive by putting *three ones* in subject position, thus leaving (*in*) *number 111* as a locative, but then fronted the locative itself, since "three ones" is given information—that is, an example of the same digit from the previous sentence. Alternatively, *number 111* could have been selected as the subject, with no further movement, thus producing *The number 111 uses three ones*. What is important for a learner to grasp, however, is the basic principle that any preverbal noun phrase in English that is not the subject of the adjacent verb must be marked as such. Hence the retention, or not, of *in* when *the number 111* occurs preverbally: as a subject *the number 111* occurs without *in*; as a fronted locative it occurs with *in*. In the exercise as a whole it is the constant promotion of noun phrases to subjecthood that strengthens the learner's sense of the obligatoriness of filling subject position, without the necessity of extracting the principle itself for special focus and/or explanation.

It is possible to devise other classroom activities that depend upon successful invocation of the given/new contract. One of these is a variation of the well-known strip story activity (Gibson, 1975), in which each student is handed a single sentence of a little written narrative and then has to contribute to the reconstruction of the story by determining, through verbal communication with his classmates, where his own sentence occurs in the narrative sequence. This same problem-solving activity can be utilized in the teaching, say, of English for science and technology, with the order of propositional content across the individual sentences now being determined not by the logical sequence of events but rather by the given/new contract exclusively. In other words, students would collectively reconstruct the original passage through consideration (probably unconsciously) of presuppositions and what has been raised to consciousness, as this is reflected through the selection of determiners and the use of anaphora. A passage such as 3 (a) would serve very well for this kind of activity.

There are still other classroom activities for imparting a knowledge of grammatical machinery by means of discourse principles that the machinery is designed to serve. One of these will suffice here, a technique first suggested in Gleason (1965) and further developed in Rutherford (1977). Students are asked to choose among alternative syntactic arrangements that realize essentially the same propositional content—a choice, in other words, among sentence versions that place the same semantic content in different positions. But what determines the appropriate position is what has been expressed immediately preceding. A certain discourse context is established through one or two sentences that open a stretch of text and then each succeeding sentence is laid out as a set of options where the information content has been arranged in several possible orders and the necessary grammatical operations invoked (i.e., movement rules) in order to realize these alternative arrangements as full, roughly "equal" grammatical sentences. The student has only to trace a path through these successive sets of alternatives—letting the discourse requirements for the placement of new and given information lead the way—until he reaches the end of the text. An example of such an activity would be the following: the information content taken from Brandwein et al. (1968):

4. Weathering and erosion of rock exposed to the atmosphere constantly remove particles from the rock.

(a)	(b)	(c)
1 These rock particles are called sediment.	Sediment is what these rock particles are called.	What these rock particles are called is sediment.

(a)	(b)
2 The upper layers press down on the lower ones as sediments accumulate.	As sediments accumulate, the upper layers press down on the lower ones

(a)	(b)
3 Sediments that stick together form sedimentary rocks.	Sedimentary rocks are formed by sediments that stick together.

(a)	(b)
4 Such rocks have been able to survive the test of time only in this way.	Only in this way have such rocks been able to survive the test of time.

These activities are intended to make several contributions to the learning of English, especially written English:

- sharpen learner perceptions of crucial principles of language arrangement,
- engender an understanding of the use of grammatical rules as the
  syntactic means for realizing discoursal objectives,
- demonstrate the overriding importance of the use of word order to
  signal grammatical relationships,
- foster awareness of the tight "syntactization" (Givon, 1979) that distinguishes planned from unplanned language use.

Although the language activities just outlined involve the application of
syntactic rules and the manipulation of syntactic rules and the manipulation of
syntactic structures, these events are not the real purpose of the activity. The
purpose, of course, is to apply principles of discourse in the selection and
ordering of semantic content, that content being thereby assigned the required
syntactic form. But if syntactic realization falls short while all else is satisfac-
tory, the effort might still be considered a successful one, for it is the discourse
criteria which must first be met. In other words, in choosing between a textual
arrangement that correctly implemented the given/new contract but contained
malformed syntactic constructions, and an arrangement that repeatedly violated the given/new contract but otherwise was a paragon of well-formedness,
one would value the former more highly than the latter. This is so because
communication is less likely to suffer in the former instance than in the latter.
It must be admitted, however, that reflections upon this kind of pedagogical
role for grammar are of only very recent origin, and we will presently consider
what directions such investigations might take in the near future.

I think it would be fair to say that all attempts to let attention to language
form influence, to whatever extent, the shape of the language syllabus are,

in effect, attempts (either conscious or unconscious) to influence language-learning strategies. Although the strategies that a learner employs in his language learning experience can of course only be inferred from his behavior, still a number of them have been adduced through research and experimentation. These include the so-called strategies of transfer (both positive and negative), avoidance, overgeneralization, simplification, prefabricated patterns, and others, a useful summary of which can be found in Brown (1980).

Let us consider the matter of transfer. Until very recently it was customary to suppose that mother tongue transfer was in force whenever the learner's "interlanguage" (Selinker, 1972) manifested a form (1) that was similar to a surface form in his native tongue and (2) that was not present, or present to a much lesser degree, in the interlanguage of learners with other native languages. More recently, however, it has been shown that the occurrence of transfer need not be tied at all to the first of these two conditions where acquisition of L2 interlanguage form has been influenced by L1 discourse features that do not show up in a one-to-one syntactic cross-language comparison (Huebner, 1978; Schmidt, 1978; Schachter and Rutherford, 1979). Is it reasonable then to expect that there might be other instances of transfer that are not inferrable from inspection of cross-language surface characteristics—other instances of transfer across language typological features, for example, as predicted by Hakuta (1979)? To narrow the quesetion a little more, given the fact that English represents an extreme case of a language that makes use of word order almost exclusively to signal grammatical rather than pragmatic relationships (Thompson, 1978), what sorts of characteristics might show up in the interlanguage production of learners whose mother tongues do not exhibit this typological feature (the vast majority of the languages of the world, as far as we know) and who are devising strategies for mastering it in English? Since this overriding grammatical word-order typological attribute of English necessitates that there be a large battery of rules for moving constituents around to satisfy discourse requirements while at the same time maintaining the positional relationships of subject, verb, and object, one might therefore predict that errors will occur that violate precisely these relationships. Although no research, to my knowledge, has been conducted for the purpose of testing such a hypothesis, it is interesting to look back at some of the kinds of errors that have been documented in past studies and the kinds of explanations offered for them.

One of the largest repositories of learner error types in English is *The Gooficon* (Burt and Kiparsky, 1972). The authors divide their book into six chapters each corresponding to a major area of English syntax (e.g., the auxiliary, passives, sentential complement, etc.), and they subdivide each of these chapters into specific "goof types" which for the whole book add up to 64. What is interesting is that of these 64 types no fewer than 24, or nearly 40 percent, can be analyzed (in the absence of context or any other essential information) as failure in one way or another to correctly observe the various rules, constraints, or requirements that are a direct consequence of the abstract typological organization of English discussed earlier. Although these errors were not attributed to learners with particular native languages, there are enough hints in the book to suggest that the authors do not consider many of the errors to be developmental (i.e., characteristic of learners of English in general) but rather transfer errors. However, it is what this wide range of documented errors have in common—that is, within the gross typological descriptive framework discussed earlier—that interests us here.

The range in question comprises, for example, the following groups, with labeling and sample citations carried over from the original:

1. Wrong omission of subject:
   (a) Daddy has a lot of work. Mother expects ∧ to stay at his office late.
   (b) I couldn't sleep until you got back. It worries me ∧ to stay out so late.
2. Nonfiniteness of subordinate clauses:
   (a) He will give us money before ∧ leaves.
   (b) John sleeps a lot after ∧ eats a lot.
3. Subject pronoun missing:
   (a) My father been so fortunate. ∧ Hold a big post in the government.
   (b) Abdul not enjoyed the party. ∧ Went home early.
4. Object pronoun missing:
   (a) Donald is mean so no one likes ∧ .
   (b) Do you like this dress? I made ∧ myself.
5. Surrogate subject missing: *there* and *it*:
   (a) ∧ Was a riot last night.
   (b) ∧ Is raining.
6. Verb before subject:
   (a) Walked the priest very far.
   (b) Was falling a lot of rain.
7. Subject and object permuted/Passive order but active form:
   (a) English use many countries.
   (b) Much money will get a politician.
8. Underuse (of *do*) in questions:
   (a) Paints the boy?
   (b) Go you to school?
9. Missing passives in complex sentences:
   (a) We were recommended by her to spend less money.
   (b) Mark was hoped to become a football player.
10. Snatched subject as subject of main clause:
    (a) He is unusual to have a new auto.
    (b) The door is strange to be unlocked.
11. Snatched subject as object of main clause:
    (a) A girl was decided to play the piano.
    (b) We were demanded to return the hymnbook.
12. Misordering with reverse adjectives:
    (a) You are important to come on time.
    (b) I am wonderful to see you.
13. Misordering in embedded sentences:
    (a) He admits me hard to learn quickly.
    (b) He thinks you important to hurry up.

Whatever else numbers 1 through 5 may represent, they certainly reveal defective obligatory SVO occurrence. (In fact, the first three categories, different labeling not withstanding, seem to show the same phenomenon.) It would appear that the obligatory S or O that is omitted in these examples is just that S or O which can be interpreted as topic, the learner presumably taking coreference with topic as governing deletion, as is typically the case in topic-prominent languages. In category 5, of course, empty subject position requires a dummy element for the preservation of S-V order.

The violation in categories 6 through 8 involves not defective SVO occurrence, obviously, but SVO misordering. That is, although the learner may well have already grasped the basic principle of SVO ordering, he perhaps hasn't yet learned that modifications in that ordering are governed by syntactic principles and not, as in many other languages, by pragmatic ones.

In categories 9 through 13 movement rules have been invoked and SVO order is preserved, but subject-to-subject raising has applied to verbs and adjectives that are not strictly subcategorized for this rule feature (Chomsky, 1965).

Although we do not know which, if any, of these error categories were produced by learners with particular native language backgrounds (that information not being cited in the book), it would be strange if the categories did not align themselves in this way at least to some extent. For example, one might quite reasonably suppose, consistent with what is known of language universals and language typology, (1) that learners in general would devise special strategies in order effectively to process a language (viz., English) in which there is often a not very tight fit between semantic content and the linear order of syntactic constituents, and (2) that those strategies would in turn be influenced by individual native-language typological characteristics. Substantiation of the first of these hypotheses might be borne out by a high incidence of error in precisely those areas of English that reveal syntactic "distance" from semantic content, as in the preceding enumerated categories, for example. Substantiation of the second hypothesis might be borne out by the fact that different kinds of errors are made within these same areas. A useful clue to look for—a clue, that is, to the possibility that these sorts of strategies are being brought to bear in learner production—would be errors that are in the syntactic-semantic "ill-fitting" areas of English and that are unique to learners with the same native language.

In fact, just such a clue turned up in the written production of Japanese learners of English that was analyzed in Schachter and Rutherford (1979). It was noted that Japanese speakers, alone among the learner population under scrutiny, were producing errors in which there occurred grammatically disallowed predications of certain nouns and adjectives to sentential subjects (both *that* clauses and infinitivals), which subjects were extraposed sentence-finally. For example:

5. (a) It is a tendency that such a friendly restaurants become less in big city.
   (b) It is more likeable to be in a large university so that I could choose one out of many courses.

We suspected at the time that these and many other similar examples were evidence of negative transfer from Japanese, because no other language group was producing them. Yet it clearly could not have been "transfer" in the usual sense of that term, for nothing in Japanese surface structure corresponded to the interlingual forms being produced. For example, Japanese, a rigidly verb-final SOV language, has no need for dummy place-holders for subject position, like English *it* or *there*. After close examination of this production, the most plausible explanation we could suggest was that the transfer in question was not L1 syntax to L2 syntax but rather L1 discourse to L2 syntax; that is, the English extraposition examples produced by Japanese learners were all being used to make "generic statements." Yet, this hypothesis remains to be tested.

Meanwhile, other possible explanations come to mind. It might be claimed, for example, that what this kind of error represents is the result of the interaction in a learning situation of two different language typologies, Japanese SOV and English SVO, together with accompanying important characteristics such as invariant verb finality for Japanese. In pursuit of such a claim, it is possible to demonstrate that the order of constituents in 5, excluding dummy *it*, is the "mirror image" of what it is in Japanese (Smith 1978), and that it would be worth investigating whether these sentences of the form *it is*—$\left\{ {Adj \atop N} \right\}$—(sentoid), overproduced by Japanese learners, are at least partially the product of a strategy devised to enable the learner to conceptualize from an L1 typology (viz. left-branching SOV) to a very different L2 typology (viz. right-branching SVO). If something like this does take place, then the above strategy could be regarded simply as another example of what the learner does when confronted with an "ill fit" between (the learner's conceptualized) semantic content and (the target language's) syntactic realization of it.

Another kind of English interlanguage (IL) overproduction is evident among learners whose native language is Mandarin. They tend to produce a great quantity of written sentences with nonextraposed sentential subjects. For example:

6. To choose a wife or husband is the most important thing in one's life.
7. Choosing a husband or wife in my country is quite an interesting thing.
8. How a man or woman chooses a husband or wife is also a big thing for them.

Such examples of surprisingly complex English are often to be found even at the earliest stages of learning; although the less "syntacticized" versions (i.e., where the rules of complementizer placement have not yet been applied, leaving full-sentence embedding) tend, not surprisingly, to occur more frequently at the lower levels. For example:

9. Man and woman chooses a husband or wife is very simple.

What is interesting about these data, however, is (1) that nonextraposed sentential subjects are cognitively more difficult to process, but (2) that non-movement of the subjects by extraposition is nevertheless the appropriate syntactic choice to exercise within these discourses; that is, the assigned composition topic itself having been a sentence ("How a man or woman chooses a wife or husband in your country"), many students chose to begin writing by assigning first topic mention to the unmarked topic position in English— namely, (sentence-initial) subject position. The fact that on this composition assignment only the Mandarin-speaking learners produced sentential subjects leads one to consider the topic-prominent character of Mandarin (Li and Thompson, 1976). It would appear here that L1 Mandarin topic-prominence is so strong as to bring about very early in English IL the syntacticization of complex semantic material in subject/topic position that with other learners would be extraposed, decomposed, or avoided.

The implications of these language-learning strategies for the language-teaching syllabus are very important. Future research will need to investigate to what extent it is possible, through formal instruction, to facilitate implementation of the strategies that are needed by all language users for the perception of the loose relationship in English between semantic content and its syntactic realization. If the native English speaker has subconsciously to "work hard" at doing this, as Hawkins suggests, then how much harder the task of the language learner, whose notion of such a relationship has already been shaped in a different way by the typological organization of his own mother tongue? It is recognition of this particular kind of language-learning difficulty, and of the desirability of exploring ways in which the syllabus might alleviate it, that could well be taken up in ongoing research into pedagogical grammar and its place in the language-teaching syllabus.

The past history of the language-teaching profession might lead one to want to turn any findings from the above suggested research into a new kind of language-teaching "unit," one which served to focus classroom attention upon these newly emergent language organizational principles. Needless to say, I don't think that is what is called for. As we saw earlier, language information such as this is not amenable to an item/unit approach in pedagogy, nor would even the "visibility" of this information necessarily be beneficial.

The suggestion has been made several times now throughout this paper that thoughts about the function of grammar in a language-teaching syllabus might well flow in channels other than those to which we have for so long been accustomed. Such channels would lead away from a conception of grammar as an accumulation of autonomous discrete entities (i.e., constructions and rules) and lead instead toward a conception of grammar as a means for processing language at the level of discourse (Givon, 1979). The real function of grammar thus becomes understandable only as it relates to discourse. Hurtig (1977) put it this way:

> Our general hypothesis concerning the relationship of sentence grammar, discourse grammar and the psychological processes operative in the encoding of sentences and discourses is that the sentence (clause) is the on-line perceptual unit while the discourse (*idea set*/*logical event space*) is the unit of cognitive (seman-

tic) memory. Put in other terms, the discourse is the cognitive organizational unit while the sentence (syntactic structure) is the production planning unit. [pp. 103–104]

Once again, however, the functions of pedagogical grammar which we have been discussing do not imply that classroom attention is to be drawn to them, nor should one draw that implication. What is called attention to in pedagogy should at least have the possibility that it can be remembered, although not necessarily in the same way for each learner (Seliger, 1979). And it has been shown that the use of memory in language learning is not demonstrated through the acquisition of syntax. To quote Hurtig (1977) again, "Encoding of discourse into memory operates in terms of the topical or propositional nature of the discourse rather than the surface linguistic form of the constituent sentences" (p. 96). Even less then will that encoding into memory operate in terms of the opaque yet crucial language organizational principles that we have been discussing. Paradoxically perhaps, they are too important to be turned into language lessons.

It is time to look back at what we have been saying. Past considerations of pedagogical grammar are largely deficient in one major respect: they stem from a concept of language organization that is quite naively at variance with the much richer concepts suggested by contemporary theoretical research. This impoverished pedagogical view has had two direct consequences for the design of language-teaching syllabuses: (1) the role of grammar is seen invariably as one in which the grammatical content should be made the object of classroom attention, and (2) grammatical attention is limited to that part of language organization that has definable boundaries—limited, in other words, to language constituents.

Absent for the most part from the thinking that goes into how attention to language form can most effectively serve the needs of language learning is the realization that there are language properties crucial to its use for communication that are not readily observable and that consequently do not lend themselves to exploitation within the language-teaching paradigm that we have become accustomed to. These properties include above all the extensive typological information that specifies a language's gross canonical form and the relationship between that form and the principles of discourse that the form is designed to serve. If efforts to let such properties influence language syllabus planning ultimately contribute to a reshaping of the syllabus itself, then this is as it should be. For limitations inherent in our long familiar language-instructional models must not be allowed to prevent the richest possible grammatical contribution to the language-teaching syllabus.

QUESTIONS FOR DISCUSSION

1. We have now seen suggestions, proposals, even arguments in favor of a variety of language models, linguistic schools, theoretical approaches, and so on, as sources for informed decision making and selection of material for realization in pedagogical grammar. There are, for example, case grammar (Mackenzie), Universal Grammar (Rutherford and Sharwood Smith), traditional grammar (Widdowson), and functional grammar (Rutherford). Is the proper conclusion to draw from all this that total chaos and confusion reign among pedagogical grammarians, or is this situation to be looked on as a healthy development in the field? Why are there in fact so many seemingly different approaches to pedagogical grammar?

2. Rutherford is very critical of common approaches to pedagogical grammar in which language is perceived as a buildup of items and units. To what extent are current language-teaching methodologies a reflection of this perception? What methodological implications (if any) arise from the view of language and its organizational principles that Rutherford is in favor of? Can you foresee any obstacles to overcome if one is to move in this direction?

3. In discussion of the sample exercise material displaying "propositional clusters" that are to be realized as full sentences (p. 238ff), Rutherford states that the learner's task of continually promoting noun phrases to subjecthood implicitly strengthens his awareness of the principle that subject position in English must always be filled. Could there be other effects of this kind of problem-solving activity that would relate to the features of verb valency and adposition that Mackenzie talked about in his paper?

4. What do you think Rutherford means by his statement that "paradoxically perhaps, [the opaque yet crucial language organizational principles being discussed] are too important to be turned into language lessons" (p. 246)?

REFERENCES

Adler, I. 1959. *The New Mathematics.* New York: John Day.

Blatchford, C. and J. Schachter (eds.). 1978. *On TESOL 1978.* Washington, D.C.: TESOL.

Bolinger, D. 1977. *Meaning and Form.* London: Longman.

Brandwein, P. F., R. Stollberg, and R. W. Burnett. 1968. *Matter: Its Forms and Changes.* New York: Harcourt Brace Jovanovich.

Brown, H. D. 1980. *Principles of Language Learning and Teaching.* Englewood Cliffs, N.J.: Prentice-Hall.

Burt, M., and C. Kiparsky. 1972. *The Gooficon: A Repair Manual for English.* Rowley, Mass.: Newbury House Publishers.

Canale, M., and M. Swain. 1980. Theoretical bases of communicative approaches to second language teaching and testing. *Applied Linguistics* 1:1.

Chafe, W. 1976. Givenness, contrastiveness, definiteness, subjects, topics, and point of view. In C. N. Li (ed.), *Subject and Topic.* New York: Academic Press.

Chomsky, N. 1965. *Aspects of the Theory of Syntax.* Cambridge, Mass.: MIT Press.

Clark, H. 1973. Space, time semantics, and the child. In T. Noore (ed.), *Cognitive Development and the Acquisition of Language.* New York: Academic Press.

Clark, H., and S. E. Haviland. 1977. Comprehension and the given-new contract. In R.O. Freedle (ed.), *Discourse Production and Comprehension.* Norwood, N.J.: Ablex Publishing Corporation.

Emonds, J. E. 1976. *A Transformational Approach to English Syntax: Root, Structure-Preserving, and Local Transformations.* New York: Academic Press.

Fillmore, C. 1968. The case for case. In E. Bach and R. Harms (eds.), *Universals in Linguistic Theory.* New York: Holt, Rinehart & Winston.

Freedle, R. O., ed. 1977. *Discourse Production and Comprehension.* Norwood, N.J.: Ablex Publishing Corporation.

Gibson, R. E. 1975. The strip story: a catalyst for communication. *TESOL Quarterly* 9:2.

Givon, T. 1979. *On Understanding Grammar.* New York: Academic Press.

Hakuta, K. 1979. Some common goals for first and second language acquisition research. Paper presented at TESOL Convention, Boston.

Halliday, M. A. K., and R. Hasan. 1976. *Cohesion in English.* London: Longman.

Hatch, E. 1978. Discourse analysis and second language acquisition. In March (ed.), *Second Language Acquisition.* Rowley, Mass.: Newbury House Publishers.

Hawkins, J. 1980. On the theoretical significance of English/German syntactic contrasts. Paper presented at the International Seminar on Contrastive English/German Grammar, Stanford University.

Huebner, T. G. 1979. Order-of-acquisition vs. dynamic paradigm: a comparison of method in interlanguage research. *TESOL Quarterly* 13:1.

Hurtig, R. 1977. Toward a functional theory of discourse. In R. O. Freedle (ed.), *Discourse Production and Comprehension.* Norwood, N.J.: Ablex Publishing Corporation.

Kuhn, T. S. 1970. *The Structure of Scientific Revolutions.* Chicago: University of Chicago Press.

Lester, M., ed. 1970. *Readings in Applied Transformational Grammar.* New York: Holt, Rinehart & Winston.

Li, C. N., ed. 1976. *Subject and Topic.* New York: Academic Press.

Li, C. N. and S. A. Thompson. 1976. Subject and topic: a new typology of language. In C.Li (ed.), *Subject and Topic.* New York: Academic Press.

Munby, J. 1978. *Communicative Syllabus Design.* Cambridge: Cambridge University Press.

Newmark, L. 1970. How not to interfere in language learning. In M. Lester (ed.), *Readings in Applied Transformational Grammar.* New York: Holt, Rinehart & Winston.

Newmark, L. and D. Reibel. 1970. Necessity and sufficiency in language learning. In M. Lester (ed.), *Readings in Applied Transformational Grammar.* New York: Holt, Rinehart & Winston.

Quirk, R., S. Greenbaum, G. Leech, and J. Svartvik, eds. 1972. *A Grammar of Contemporary English.* London: Longman.

Rutherford, W. E. 1976. Second language teaching. In H. Brown and R. Wardhaugh (eds.), *A Survey of Applied Linguistics.* Ann Arbor: University of Michigan Press.

Rutherford, W.E. 1977. *Modern English* (2nd ed., Vol. 2). New York: Harcourt Brace Jovanovich.

Rutherford, W. E. 1978. Notional syllabuses, part 3. In C. Blatchford & J. Schachter (eds.), *On TESOL 1978.* Washington, D.C.: TESOL.

Rutherford, W. E. 1980. Aspects of pedagogical grammar. *Applied Linguistics* 1:1.

Samuelson, W. 1976. *English as a Second Language, Phase Three: Let's Write.* Reston, Va.: Reston Publishing Company.

Schachter, J. and W. E. Rutherford. 1979. Discourse function and language transfer. *Working Papers in Bilingualism* 19.

Schmidt, M. 1978. Coordinate structures and deletion in learner English. Master's thesis, University of Washington.

Seliger, H. 1979. On the nature and function of language rules in language teaching. *TESOL Quarterly* 13:3.

Selinker, L. 1972. Interlanguage. *International Review of Applied Linguistics* **10**:2.

Sharwood Smith, M. 1978. *Aspects of Future Reference in a Pedagogical Grammar of English*. Frankfurt: Peter Lang.

Smith, D.L. 1978. Mirror images in Japanese and English. *Language* **54**:1.

Thompson, S. A. 1978. Modern English from a typological point of view: some implications of the function of word order. *Linguistische Berichte* **54.**

Widdowson, H. G. 1978. Notional syllabuses, part 4. In C. Blatchford and J. Schachter (eds.), *On TESOL 1978*. Washington, D.C.: TESOL.

Activities for part three

1. As we have already noted, Bialystok's paper (part one) makes a strong case for recognizing a distinction between L2 linguistic knowledge and access to that knowledge. Sketch out a few kinds of consciousness-raising (CR) activities that might serve expressly to enhance the learner's ability to access his or her linguistic knowledge.

2. The Mackenzie paper favors a case-grammar approach to pedagogical grammar wherein, among other things, contrastive study is better able to "pinpoint how the different languages grammaticalize the same configuration of semantic structure." The Rutherford paper outlined a form of case-grammar-derived pedagogical activity in which the learner renders a bare-bones sequence of propositional content into well-formed written discourse (pp. 231–249). Use the Rutherford schema to contrast grammatically two languages of your choice along the lines suggested by Mackenzie; that is, conjure up some bit of bare propositional content, lay it out in rough schema for both languages, and then let the realization into grammatical well-formedness reveal the surface contrasts between the two.

3. Sharwood Smith makes a strong case in one of his papers for the infusion of psycholinguistic principles in the realization of pedagogical grammar—for example, the serious employment of visually revealing schemata. Can you devise some workable schemata that might serve to promote better understanding for the learner of either the verb valency principles or the adpositional characteristics that Mackenzie talks about?

4. The first of the two Sharwood Smith papers discusses and exemplifies some possible uses of an algorithmic approach to grammatical CR—for example, the distinction between English present form: simple and progressive. From what you know of grammar (and not necessarily English grammar), select another appropriate small area of grammatical focus and try to represent the facts in algorithmic form. In English, you might consider an aspect of the determiner system—namely, a/the/0.

5. Mackenzie talked about the desirability of the L2 learner's being his or her own researcher, so to speak, in discovering the facts of valency and case marking for the language the learner is trying to learn. Since conventional materials are deficient in these areas, Mackenzie suggests tutorial exercises to facilitate this kind of learning, though he does not actually provide examples of such exercises in his paper. What could an exercise of this kind look like? See if you can devise something conducive to the discovery of valency/adposition for a pair of verbs like *rob*/*steal*.

6. Draw up a lesson plan for a 45-minute class for intermediate students of, for example, English as a foreign language, and comment on the chosen teaching techniques in the light of one or more of the models discussed in part one and using the appropriate terminology.

7. Take a pair of languages in which different distinctions are made within one shared semantic area (see, e.g., 2(b) in the activities section for part two), analyze the differences, and devise an algorithm along the lines of the *mancu* example in the first Sharwood Smith paper in part three. Do this to demonstrate simply and explicitly to a speaker of one of the languages what was to be learned with regard to the other language.

8. Propose a way of testing the effectiveness of the different kinds of teaching techniques suggested in the papers in part three.

Name Index

Subject Index